Regressive Taxation and the Welfare State

Government size has attracted much scholarly attention. Political economists have considered large public expenditures a product of leftist rule and an expression of a stronger representation of labor interest. Although the size of the government has become the most important policy difference between the left and the right in postwar politics, the formation of the government's funding base has not been explored. Junko Kato finds that the differentiation of tax revenue structure is path-dependent upon the shift to regressive taxation. Since the 1980s, the institutionalization of effective revenue raising by regressive taxes during periods of high growth has ensured resistance to welfare state backlash during budget deficits and consolidated the diversification of state funding capacity among industrial democracies. The book challenges the conventional wisdom that progressive taxation goes hand in hand with large public expenditures in mature welfare states and qualifies the partisan-centered explanation that dominates the welfare state literature.

Junko Kato is Professor in Political Science at the University of Tokyo. She is the author of *The Problem of Bureaucratic Rationality* (1994).

Cambridge Studies in Comparative Politics

General Editor
Margaret Levi   *University of Washington, Seattle*

Assistant General Editor
Stephen Hanson   *University of Washington, Seattle*

Associate Editors
Robert H. Bates   *Harvard University*
Peter Hall   *Harvard University*
Peter Lange   *Duke University*
Helen Milner   *Columbia University*
Frances Rosenbluth   *Yale University*
Susan Stokes   *University of Chicago*
Sidney Tarrow   *Cornell University*

Continued on the page following the index.

Regressive Taxation and the Welfare State

PATH DEPENDENCE AND POLICY DIFFUSION

JUNKO KATO

University of Tokyo

CAMBRIDGE
UNIVERSITY PRESS

PUBLISHED BY THE PRESS SYNDICATE OF THE UNIVERSITY OF CAMBRIDGE
The Pitt Building, Trumpington Street, Cambridge, United Kingdom

CAMBRIDGE UNIVERSITY PRESS
The Edinburgh Building, Cambridge CB2 2RU, UK
40 West 20th Street, New York, NY 10011-4211, USA
477 Williamstown Road, Port Melbourne, VIC 3207, Australia
Ruiz de Alarcón 13, 28014 Madrid, Spain
Dock House, The Waterfront, Cape Town 8001, South Africa

http://www.cambridge.org

First published 2003

Printed in the United States of America

Typeface Janson Text Roman 10/13 pt.   *System* LATEX 2$_\varepsilon$ [TB]

A catalog record for this book is available from the British Library.

Library of Congress Cataloging in Publication Data
Kato, Junko, 1961–
Regressive taxation and the welfare state : path dependence and policy diffusion /
Junko Kato.
   p.   cm. – (Cambridge studies in comparative politics)
Includes bibliographical references and index.
ISBN 0-521-82452-4
1. Taxation. 2. Public welfare. 3. Expenditures, Public. I. Title. II. Series.
HJ2305.K28   2003
330.12′6 – dc21

2002035180

ISBN 0 521 82452 4 hardback

HJ
2305
·K28
2003

Contents

Preface

Twelve years have passed since the question of the financial foundation of contemporary welfare states first occurred to me while I was doing dissertation research on Japanese tax reform. In 1989, the consumption tax in Japan faced formidable opposition: in the public's mind, the new tax meant increasing already heavy taxes and damaging income equality. Despite its politicization, however, the total Japanese tax revenue as a proportion of the national economy has been lower than that of most other industrial democracies. Moreover, revenues from regressive taxes on consumption as well as a progressive income tax have financed high public expenditures in the Scandinavian countries, which have achieved the highest income equality among industrial democracies. I was amused by this discrepancy between the politicization of tax issues in Japan and the Japanese tax revenue structure compared with other countries. There seemed to be a completely different criterion from one country to another about "high" and "low" tax levels that was very likely related to how much revenue a country would raise from what kind of taxation. Politics matters in the public's tolerance for and its expectation of taxation. How does politics define the tax level and formulate the public's expectation about tax policies? To answer this question, I have compared the financial base of welfare states.

In the development of postwar tax policies, the introduction of general consumption taxes embodies a major shift – a revenue reliance shift from income to consumption. In this book, I review eight cases that illustrate the distinct timing of the shift from one country to another. The research began in the mid-1990s when the cross-national variation of welfare states was apparently preserved despite a welfare state backlash and globalization. More mature welfare states with a larger public sector appear to have resisted the welfare retrenchment more successfully than welfare states with a relatively modest size. Globalization and chronic budget debt have commonly influenced all welfare states but have not produced less convergence among them than expected. The book clarifies the path-dependent development of the state funding capacity that is compatible with but still distinct from the influence of the government's partisanship about the welfare state.

Without financial and institutional support, it would have been impossible to complete this book. Funding from the Abe Fellowship Program launched the research in North America and Europe in 1996 and 1997. A Matsushita International Foundation fellowship in 1998 financed the research on the development of tax and welfare policies in Australia and New Zealand. Writing and additional research on new developments were supported partly by a Suntory Foundation fellowship and a fellowship from the Ministry of Education of Japan. The Program on U.S.-Japan Relations, Center for International Affairs at Harvard University, provided an excellent environment from 1996 to 1997 to prepare for the field research in Europe and Oceania and to study the North American cases. In Europe, the European Institute of Japanese Studies of the Stockholm School of Economics, *Fondation Nationale des Sciences Politiques*, and London School of Economics extended superb institutional support for the research. The Research School of Social Sciences at the Australian National University also arranged a research visit in 1998, and the visiting program of the East-West Center in Hawaii hosted me during the most difficult process of revising the manuscript in summer 2000. Christina Davis, Kosuke Imai, Lee Jeong Man, Lim Sung Geun, Ritsuko Saotome, Edith Serotte, Okiyoshi Takeda, and Takako Torisu helped research each country's case. Yusaku Horiuchi provided superb expertise in assisting with the quantitative analysis. Chen-wei Lin, Terue Okada, Hikaru Hayashi, and Masahiro Kurosaki worked as research assistants at the University of Tokyo. Without their assistance, I could not have completed this project while teaching and working. Throughout the period, the Graduate Division of Advanced Social and International Studies and a broader academic community of the University of Tokyo provided an excellent academic environment.

Many policy makers of governments in the eight countries and international organizations granted me interviews. I am greatly indebted to these anonymous people. In addition to participants in seminars at the department of government at Harvard University (in 1988), the department of political science at Yale University (in 1998), the East-West Center (in 2000), and the University of Tokyo (in 2001), many political economists advised and influenced my research and writing. I would like to acknowledge especially Jim Alt, Robert Bates, Geoffrey Garrett, Jack Nagel, Oliver Oldman, Susan Pharr, Paul Pierson, Dani Rodrik, Frances Rosenbluth, Frank Schwartz, Sidney Tarrow, and Kathleen Thelen in the United States; Rune Åberg, Jonas Agell, Magnus Blomstrom, Nils Elvander, Åsa Gunnarsson, Nils Mattsson, Peter Melz, Leif Mutén, Stefan Svallfors, Torsten Svensson, and Björn Westberg in Sweden; Jean-Marie Bouissou, Eli Cohen, and Jean-Pierre Jallade in France; Ian Crawford, Patrick Dunleavy, Chris Giles, Jack Hayward, John Hills, Rudolf Klein, Cedric Sandford, and Albert Weal in the United Kingdom; Ellen Immergut in Germany; Brian Andrew, Chris Evans, Abe Greenbaum, and Deborah Mitchell in Australia; Jonathan Boston, Brian Easton, Palmer Matthew, and John Pebble in New Zealand; and Kenji Hirashima, Nobuhiro Hiwatari, Ikuo Kabashima, Ikuo Kume, Hiroshi Kurata, Masaru Mabuchi, Kazumitsu Nawata, Kaku Sechiyama, Toshimitsu Shinkawa, Naoki Takahashi, Kuniaki Tanabe, Keiichi Tsunekawa, and Yu Uchiyama in Japan. Francis Castles, Taro Miyamoto, Naoto Nonaka, Bruno Palier, Susan Rose-Ackerman, Bo Rothstein, and Hiroya Sugita read an earlier version of the draft, and Margaret Levi and Sven Steinmo the final draft. I greatly appreciate their advice and comments. I also wish to thank Lewis Bateman and Janis Bolster, editors at Cambridge University Press, for helpful advice, and anonymous referees for useful comments on the draft. Kay Mansfield carefully read and checked the draft at each stage of writing to completion. I appreciate her encouragement and friendship as well as excellent editing.

During the long process of research and writing, I came to enjoy finding new facts about the interaction of politics and economics in contemporary welfare states. I hope that you will share my excitement in exploring this curious phenomenon by reading this book.

Regressive Taxation and the Welfare State

PATH DEPENDENCE AND
POLICY DIFFUSION

1

Argument

PATH DEPENDENCY AND THE
DIFFUSION OF A REGRESSIVE
TAX

Economic stagnation and subsequent shortage of government revenue brought the welfare state under intensive censure in the 1980s. The welfare expenditures,[1] which had expanded smoothly during the postwar high-growth period, became a primary target of retrenchment. Despite this overall trend, however, a cross-national comparison of the welfare state defies a simplistic generalization. The golden-age expansion reinforced a demarcation between high-spending and low-spending countries, and moreover, since the 1980s, high-spending countries have proved much more immune to welfare retrenchment than low-spending countries have. As a result, neither rapid expansion during the early postwar period nor subsequent chronic budget deficits have caused a convergence of spending levels among welfare states (Figure 1.1). Tackling this puzzle head on, this study sheds new light on the funding base of the welfare state. Available financial sources serve to restore the public confidence in the welfare state that was severely challenged in the 1980s, whereas financial scarcity makes welfare state backlash inevitable. The divergent funding capacity of the welfare state is path-dependent upon the institutionalization of regressive taxes. The institutionalization of revenue raising from

---

[1] Generally, welfare spending or expenditure is used to mean a broader category than social security spending or expenditure and, thus, often includes the cost of health and sometimes education. Social security expenditure is usually related directly to social security programs. Such a distinction is, however, conventional. One may calculate either social security or welfare expenditures based on certain criteria, but there is no uniform definition of "expenditures" that are agreed upon and well applied across countries. Because the relative size of the welfare state across countries does not change significantly as a result of the definitions of welfare or social security expenditure, here these terms are used interchangeably. The quantitative analysis presented later uses a specifically defined "social security expenditure."

2

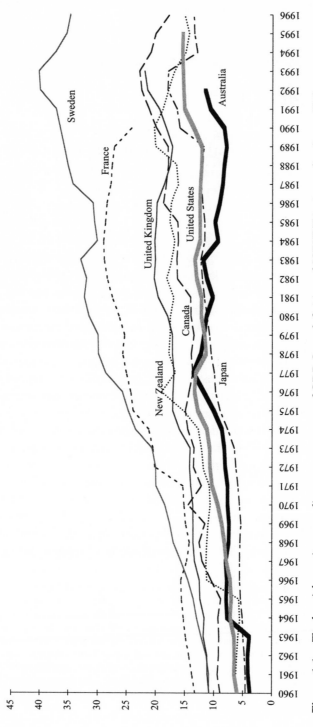

Figure 1.1. Total social security expenditure as percentage of GDP. See a definition of SSEXPT in Appendix. *Source:* ILO.

regressive taxes during a high-growth period has enabled the government to secure financial sources during times of low growth. In contrast, a government's attempt to institutionalize a regressive tax system during low growth is thwarted by public suspicion that a new burden would be exhausted to solve deficits without any welfare compensation. Tax politics ultimately explains the diversification of high-spending and low-spending countries.

How a welfare state is financed has attracted little attention aside from a small number of works on public finance (Steinmo 1993; Peters 1991) and those on the history of taxation that consider this contemporary problem (Webber and Wildavsky 1986; Levi 1988). A relative indifference to the funding base and the exclusive concern with taxation as a means for redistribution is closely related. More specifically, if one regards taxation as another measure for redistribution, one exclusive focus is a progressive income tax that applies discriminatory tax rates to redistribute income. The importance of the funding capacity of the welfare state is overshadowed by an overwhelming concern for redistribution through welfare programs and taxation. On the other hand, when one considers taxation important for financing the welfare state, the revenue-raising capacity of a regressive tax attracts new attention: a regressive tax, owing to its flat rate imposed on a uniform tax base, is more consistent with the financial needs of the government.

The Funding Base of the Welfare State and a Progressive Tax: A Cross-National Variation

The two oil shocks in the 1970s triggered the end of high growth. Economic consideration has since worked as a restraint on the welfare state, and the funding capacity of a government has come to influence welfare retrenchment. Increasing the visibility of the tax burden and avoiding easy revenue enhancements are more effective for welfare retrenchment in the long run than cutting benefits and welfare expenditures under deficit-ridden finance.[2]

---

[2] This point parallels that of Pierson (1994), who conceptually distinguishes two forms of welfare retrenchment based on a comparison between the United States and the United Kingdom in the 1980s. The "systemic retrenchment" that alters "the context for future spending decisions" is increasingly important for long-term change compared with "programmatic retrenchment," that is, cutting expenditures and lowering the level of provision in welfare programs.

The funding base of the welfare state, however, is hard to explore because of the complicated financial relationship between general revenue and expenditure. For example, a part of the loss of tax revenue can be attributed to tax exemptions and special tax measures (tax expenditures) that are considered another form of benefits if implemented for welfare purposes.[3] Alternatively, a financial flow from the social security system into the general tax revenue through taxes on social security benefits is now increasingly imposed or planned to be introduced in more industrial democracies. The social security budget surplus may also be used to contribute to decreasing the apparent deficits in the public sector and thus lowering the pressure on the government to increase taxes in general and/or cut public expenditures.[4] Similar to the current financial intricacy, historically, several contingencies and complicated interactions simultaneously caused the development of the welfare state and the construction of the tax state.[5]

Welfare state development went hand in hand with the development of the tax state owing to the increasing financial needs of the government for redistribution. Despite a recurrent debate about which principle is superior for redistribution,[6] the welfare state with higher income equality has tended to adopt universalism instead of targeting. This increases the importance of the government's funding capacity. Targeting, if it successfully selects beneficiaries based on income level (i.e., means-testing), achieves equality with less expenditure, whereas a universal principle inevitably requires high tax revenue for financing universal provision to all, based on criteria such as age, sickness, and disability regardless of income level (Table 1.1).[7] There is a "paradox of redistribution": "[t]he more we target

---

[3] On this problem, see Howard (1997). I will discuss this problem thoroughly in Chapter 4 in the section on the United States' case.

[4] A surplus within the social security system funded by contributions is included as a surplus in the government sector when the deficit is measured by the saving-investment gap of the general government in national account statistics.

[5] For example, during the interwar period of the Great Depression, policy makers recognized the failure of laissez-faire (Tanzi and Schuknecht 1995, 5), and big government was introduced at the same time as the surge of government-sponsored programs, including social security (Kelly and Ashford 1986). The postwar development of the welfare state was facilitated by the legacy of the state's capacity to raise revenue for urgent military expenditures during the two world wars (Peacock, Wiseman, and Veverka 1967; Klausen 1998).

[6] For example, see Skocpol (1991), Greenstein (1991), Rosenberry (1982), and Korpi (1980). Sen (1995) and Atkinson (1993) argue that, in reality, identifying beneficiaries and then implementing means-testing programs effectively are not easy.

[7] Of course, the distinction between universalism and targeting in practice is not as simple as discussed here. First, many countries combine the two different ideals in different ways

Table 1.1. *Universalism and targeting compared*

Principle	Coverage	Benefit
Universalism	Universal	Earnings-related or flat-rate
Targeting (means-tested)	Earnings-related	Flat-rate or earnings-related

benefits at the poor only and the more concerned we are with creating equality via equal public transfers to all, the less likely we are to reduce poverty and inequality" (Korpi and Palme 1998, 26). Among eleven countries compared by Korpi and Palme (1998), the Scandinavian countries plus France and Germany have larger expenditures with less targeting, and their level of income equality is higher than in the United States, Canada, Australia, and Switzerland, which have smaller expenditures with more targeting. This tendency qualifies the emphasis on the "qualitative" aspect of welfare provision at the expense of "quantitative" analysis focused on expenditures. As the critics of quantitative analysis argue, direct spending is not an exclusive means for redistribution, and more spending is not to be equated with more income equality in analyzing the effects of welfare programs. But, if more total spending tends to coexist with more income equality among the existing welfare states, one needs to examine how it has been financed. This also redirects attention to the role of taxation as a financing, in addition to redistributive, measure for the welfare state.

Progressive income taxation and a large social security program were an indisputable part of the welfare state in the 1950s and 1960s. During this process, the conventional view emerged wherein the contemporary welfare state was said to have expanded to raise revenue from progressive income taxation promoted by left-party governments. This view has implicitly and explicitly influenced the comparative perspective of the welfare state. For example, Esping-Andersen's (1990) "three-world"

and to different degrees. Second, in some countries, such as Sweden, many social insurance programs are occupation-based and tied to employment. Thus, a universal welfare state is the result of effective employment policy, that is, universal employment. Also, under the occupation-based system, the extension of universal coverage accompanies a new entitlement for those disadvantaged under the existing system that is more like targeting. Baldwin (1990, 113) distinguishes this as "vertical" rather than "horizontal" universalism.

classification – social democratic, conservative, and liberal welfare states[8] – focuses on the extent of labor's "decommodification"[9] – the states' protection of labor from market rule. The concept of decommodification relies on the experience of the Scandinavian social democratic welfare state, where the historic compromise between labor and capital first attempted to achieve distributive equality by introducing both social security programs and progressive taxation. In a "four-worlds" classification by Castles and Mitchell (1993, 103), tax progressivity and size of welfare expenditure are expected to be associated with the strength of the labor movement and government partisanship, respectively (Table 1.2),[10] and nonright hegemony, conservative, and liberal welfare states correspond roughly to the "three-world" characterization.[11] Direct attention to tax and welfare explains a new fourth category (the radical welfare state) of Australia, New Zealand, and the United Kingdom, which the "three-world" classification does not explain well,[12] but France, Canada, Austria, and Finland

---

[8] More specifically, the classifications are (1) social democratic welfare states, such as Denmark, Finland, the Netherlands, Norway, and Sweden, based on the principle of universalism with the highest scores in decommodification; (2) conservative welfare states, such as Austria, Belgium, France, Germany, and Italy, with a nonuniversalist, status-based, provision, exemplified by a generous pension scheme for state officials (etatism) or a larger number of occupationally distinct pension schemes (corporatism); and (3) liberal welfare states, including Australia, Canada, Japan, Switzerland, and the United States, inclined toward means-tested poor relief expenditures and strong private pensions or health insurance systems. For classification, see Table 3.3 in Esping-Andersen (1990, 74).

[9] A minimal definition of decommodification is that "citizens can freely, and without potential loss of job, income, or general welfare, opt out of work when they themselves consider it necessary" (Esping-Andersen 1990, 23). Empirically, it is measured by the quality of welfare provided through old-age pensions and sickness and unemployment cash benefits.

[10] As indicated in Table 1.2, the progressivity of a tax system is expected to be higher with a strong labor movement (high union density) and a welfare expenditure whose relative size is increased by nonright party governments. The progressivity of a tax system is measured by income and profit taxes as a percentage of GDP, and welfare expenditure is measured by household transfers as a percentage of GDP.

[11] Esping-Andersen's social democratic welfare state has a different label, nonright hegemony, here. To confirm the correspondence of the two classifications, compare the countries classified in footnote 8 with those in Table 1.2.

[12] Australia is classified as a liberal state, and New Zealand and the United Kingdom do not elicit specific characteristics in Esping-Andersen's classification. For example, Australia and the United Kingdom have low post-(income-)tax Gini coefficients of inequality, which are comparable to those of the social democratic welfare states of Sweden and Norway. New Zealand's post-(income-)tax Gini coefficient of inequality is much higher than those of the United Kingdom and Australia; in the three-worlds model by Esping-Andersen (1990), New Zealand is considered to have a low degree of decommodification, but in terms of social stratification, it appears as a medium socialist regime.

Table 1.2. *Political configurations and worlds of welfare*

		Nonright incumbency (household transfers as a percentage of GDP)			
		Low		*High*	
Trade union density (income and profits taxes as percentage of GDP)	*Low*	Canada (Radical) France (Conservative) Ireland Japan Switzerland US	**Liberal**	(West) Germany Italy Netherlands	**Conservative**
	High	Australia New Zealand UK	**Radical**	Austria (Conservative) Belgium Denmark Finland (Radical) Norway Sweden	**Nonright hegemony**

Sources: Constructed from Tables 3.3 and 3.7 from Castles and Mitchell (1993).
Notes: The classifications by financial terms are added in parentheses if they are different from the ones by political terms. For clarification, the names of the countries that are inconsistently classified are written in italics.

(in italics in Table 1.2) are inconsistently classified between the political and financial characteristics.

Wilensky's (1976) study is an exception to the existing emphasis on the progressive tax and leftist support for a welfare state and focuses rather on the contrast between "visible" and "invisible" taxes. Austria, Sweden, Belgium, the Netherlands, France, and West Germany achieved and were likely to maintain a high level of welfare provision owing not to a domestic corporatist arrangement but rather to the use of a less visible taxation such as indirect taxes on consumption. Conversely, Denmark, Finland, the United States, the United Kingdom, Switzerland, Canada, and Australia did not and were not expected to cope with the public intolerance of the tax burden caused by the extensive use of visible taxes on personal income, property (paid by households), net wealth, gifts, and inheritance. Although tentative and preliminary, Wilensky's analysis implies a close link between the welfare state and regressive taxation whose representative form is a general consumption tax, that is, an invisible tax. In contrast, a visible progressive income tax that is best for redistribution may not be an effective measure or a politically feasible solution for raising revenue. More important, as Wilensky predicted in the mid-1970s, except for a couple of cases, such as Denmark and Finland, the countries with invisible taxes have had a higher tax level and more universal welfare provision than the countries with visible taxes. In politics, when the gap between expected expenditure and necessary revenue is common knowledge, the weak revenue-raising power of the government more effectively constrains welfare expenditures. For the last decades of low growth, the diffusion of regressive (invisible) taxes has thus consolidated this diversification.

Cross-National Variation in Tax Revenue Structures

Between 1965 and 1980, the level of total tax revenue (as a percentage share of gross domestic product, GDP) and the composition of the tax revenue structure among eighteen Organisation for Economic Co-operation and Development (OECD) countries were different, although all countries increased their tax levels (Figure 1.2*a,b*). There were shifts in degree in a few countries relative to other countries; that is, some Scandinavian countries became higher-tax countries, and the United Kingdom reached a medium level. Each country's tax revenue structure and its relative size of total tax revenue were preserved; thus, the overall tendency was maintained in 1995 and 2000 (Figure 1.2*c,d*): high-tax countries have continued to increase their level with no sign of convergence with low-tax countries. A difference in relative composition of tax revenue that was already observed in the 1980s has thus only become explicit among countries.

The cross-national variation that emerged is more clearly summarized in Table 1.3, which cross-tabulates four clusters by Peters (1991) and six cases by Messere (1993). Peters's[13] "Anglo-American cluster" countries with a higher reliance on property, corporate, and personal income tax are in sharp contrast to the "Latin cluster" countries that rely heavily on indirect taxation including employers' social security contributions and general consumption taxes, such as the value-added tax, customs duties, and excises. "Broad-based taxation" is characterized by an almost equal use of all taxes that is close to the OECD average level of taxation. The "Scandinavian cluster" has a

---

[13] Peters (1991, 58–66) distinguishes four clusters by a cluster analysis explaining the variations in taxation among the twenty-two OECD members countries. Three countries – Iceland, Turkey, and Yugoslavia – are excluded for lack of data. Thus, in addition to the eighteen OECD countries analyzed here, Peters's analysis includes Greece, Luxembourg, Spain, and Portugal. He uses a composite measure of the percentage share in total revenue of eleven different taxes: personal income tax, corporate income tax, social security contributions, sales and value-added taxes, customs, excise and real estate taxes, and wealth, estate, and gift taxations.

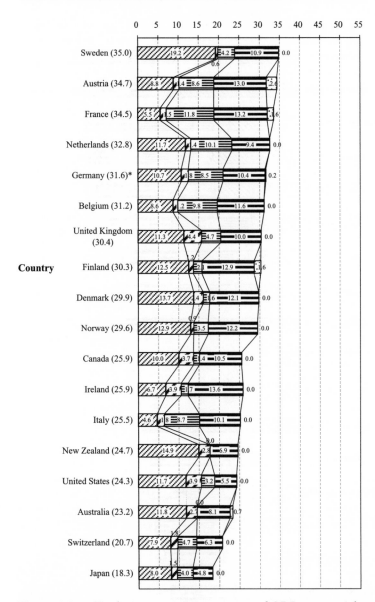

Figure 1.2a. Total tax revenue as percentage of GDP among eighteen OECD countries in 1965. Each tax revenue (as percentage of GDP) is shown on a bar. *Data for West Germany. *Source:* OECD 1997b.

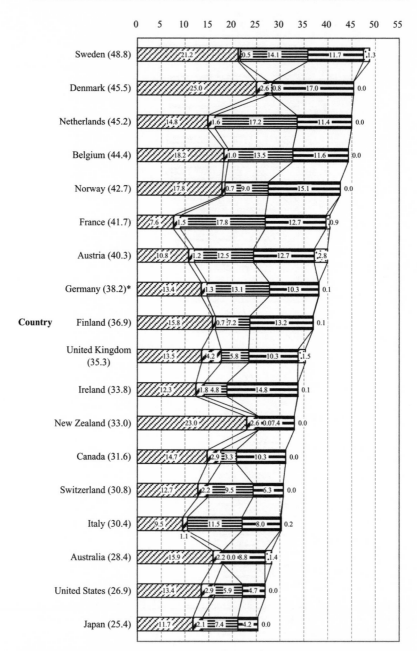

Figure 1.2b. Total tax revenue as percentage of GDP among eighteen OECD countries in 1980. Each tax revenue (as percentage of GDP) is shown on a bar. *Data for West Germany. *Source:* OECD 1997b.

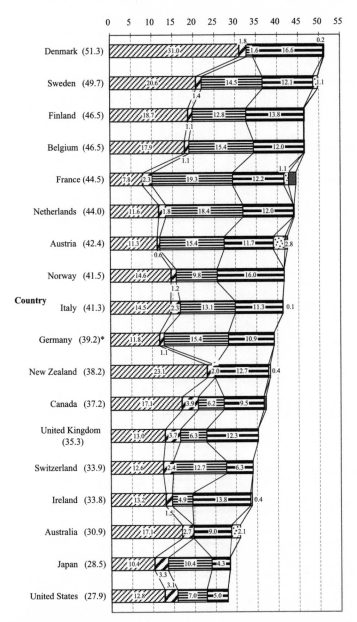

Figure 1.2c. Total tax revenue as percentage of GDP among eighteen OECD countries in 1995. Each tax revenue (as percentage of GDP) is shown on a bar. *Data for Unified Germany. *Source:* OECD 1997b.

11

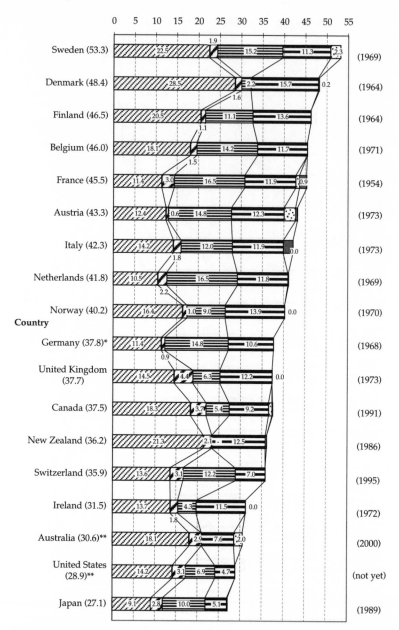

Figure 1.2d. Total tax revenue as percentage of GDP among eighteen OECD countries in 2000. Each tax revenue (as percentage of GDP) is shown on a bar. The year in parentheses is the year when the VAT was introduced. *Data for Unified Germany. **Tax revenue in 1999. *Source:* OECD 2001a.

Table 1.3. *Classification of tax revenue structure of OECD countries*

B. Guy Peters's Classification / K.C. Messere's Classification	Anglo-American Democracies and Their Friends	Scandinavian Countries	Broad-Based Taxation	Latin Cluster
Five non-European OECD countries plus Switzerland	U.S.A., Canada, Australia, Japan, New Zealand, and Switzerland			
Five southern European countries			Spain	France, Greece,[a] Italy, Portugal[a]
Five OECD countries with the highest total tax ratios		Denmark, Norway, Sweden	Belgium, Netherlands	
Two disparate European countries			Germany[b]	Ireland
A special case	United Kingdom			
Not classified		Finland	Austria, Luxembourg[a]	

[a] Not included in the quantitative analysis of this study.
[b] Referred to as "West Germany" in Peters; "unified Germany" in Messere.
Sources: Peters (1991, 60 - 66); Messere (1993, 95 - 102).

high tax levy – a higher reliance on personal income tax (combined with a lower reliance on corporate tax), a higher reliance on employers' (instead of employees') social security contributions, and the extensive use of a general consumption tax. As shown in Table 1.3, there are marginal differences between Peters and Messere: Messere strictly classifies slightly divergent cases such as the United Kingdom, Finland, and Germany but combines five high-tax countries, which Peters distinguishes by focusing on tax revenue composition.

Cross-national variation is, however, unexpected from the postwar history of tax policies among industrial democracies. First, the ideal of a comprehensive income taxation caused the diffusion and extensive use of a progressive tax during the early postwar period. This was the first major example of an academic idea that caused periodic shifts in tax policies in the same direction simultaneously across countries. Second, the worldwide tax reform trend in the 1980s thwarted this postwar ideal of progressive income taxation. Various problems with the progressive income tax became apparent after the 1970s, and the subsequent global policy shift reformulated the existing tax system. If the national tax revenue structure was diversified between 1965 and 1980 and the existing variation was only reinforced between 1980 and 2000, neither the ideal of a progressive income tax nor the reversal of that ideal in the 1980s led to the diffusion of similar tax revenue structures across countries.

To tackle this puzzle, the background and consequences of the global reform in the 1980s are clarified in terms of the reversal of the ideal of progressive income taxation.[14]

1. High inflation in the advanced democracies in the 1970s had pushed up nominal incomes, which had pushed many taxpayers (with substantially lower incomes) into higher tax brackets in a progressive tax system not indexed for inflation. Implementing special tax treatments and exemptions eroded the tax base and complicated the system. In addition, the governments could not efficiently raise revenue from income taxation that was sensitive to the global depression and stagflation after the mid-1970s. To cope with the increasing complexities and inefficiencies, since the 1980s, personal income tax rates, especially the top rates, have been reduced along with a compression of the number of brackets and a broadening of the base by repealing reliefs and exemptions in many countries (see Table 1.4).

2. A high corporate tax rate is likely to cause capital flight during the globalization of economic activities. This not only is harmful for a nation's economic competitiveness but also obstructs a government's attempt to secure revenue. Thus, a rate reduction and a broadening of the tax base were also advanced in corporate taxes.

3. The shift of revenue reliance from income to consumption is the last prominent feature of global reform because governments attempted to finance personal and corporate income tax cuts partly or fully by increasing other taxes. Aside from the exception of the "revenue neutral" reform during the U.S. Reagan administration, other countries tended to finance income tax cuts by shifting revenue reliance to a tax on consumption, especially the value-added tax (VAT) (Sandford 1993a, 14). This resulted in increasing revenue reliance on regressive levies – a flat-rate tax on consumption and social security contributions. Social security contributions[15] began

---

[14] For more detailed changes in the 1980s, see Pechman (1988), Boskin and McLure (1990), and Sandford (1993a; 1993b).

[15] Social security contributions earmarked for social security expenditures are technically distinguished from taxes but are classified as a part of the total tax revenue in statistics by OECD. This study follows the system of classification that is consistent with the argument

Table 1.4. *Variations in rate schedules of central government income tax,*
1986 and 1990

	Number of Brackets[a]		Top Rates		First Positive Rates	
	1986	1990	1986	1990	1986	1990
Australia	5*	4*	57	47	24	21
Austria	10	5	62	50	21	10
Belgium	12*	7*	72	55	24	25
Canada	10	3	34	29	6	17
Denmark	3	3	45	40	20	22
Finland	11	6*	51	43	6	9
France	12*	12*	65	57	5	5
Germany[b]			56	53	22	19
Ireland	3	3	58	53	35	30
Italy	9	7	62	50	12	10
Japan	15	5	70	50	10.5	10
Netherlands	9	3	72	60	16	13
New Zealand	6	2	57	33	17.5	24
Norway	8*	2*	40	20	3	10
Spain	34	16	66	56	8	25
Sweden[c]	10*	1*	50	20	4	20
Switzerland	6	6*	13	13	1	1
United Kingdom	6	2	60	40	29	25
United States	14	2	50	28	11	15

Notes: Where countries have substantial state and local government income taxes, the central government rate schedules will not reflect the full range of rates of tax on income of these countries.

[a]Excluding zero rate as a bracket. Those with a zero-rate bracket marked with (*).

[b]Number of brackets excluded because the tax schedule is based on a formula and does not have brackets.
[c]Refers to 1991.
Source: OECD 1993.

almost simultaneously with the increase in personal income taxation in the early decade and have continued to maintain their level until recently.

The shift summarized here is observed when revenue composition as a proportion of the total tax revenue is *averaged across eighteen OECD countries* over the last three decades (Figure 1.3). The unweighted average of

here. The regressivity of social security contributions could be alleviated by allowing exemptions or reductions for low-income earners, but their levies by a flat rate is principally regressive.

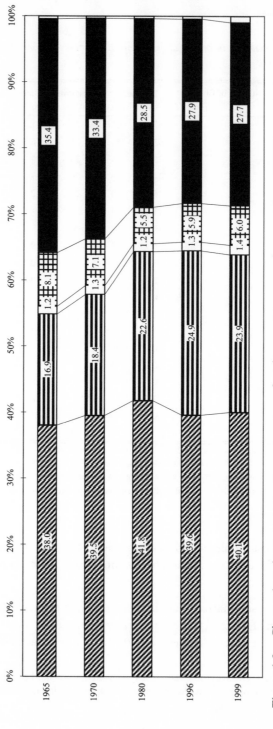

Figure 1.3. Changes in major revenue sources as percentage of total tax receipts averaged across eighteen OECD countries. *Source:* OECD 2001a.

revenue reliance on personal income tax grew until the mid-1970s and then stagnated. Although revenue reliance on a corporate income tax stagnated throughout the period, revenue reliance on social security contributions increased. The share of taxes on goods and services dropped and then leveled off to maintain a stable share since the 1980s: a general consumption tax has gradually increased a revenue share to substitute a part of the drastically declining share of other taxes (e.g., excise tax and duties).

However, a completely different picture emerges when each country's tax revenue structure and level of total tax revenue are compared. More appropriately, in the global tax reform across countries, a so-called "paradigm shift in the goals, instruments, and settings of tax policy has occurred with remarkable stability in levels and the distribution of tax burdens across capital, labor, and consumption" (Steinmo and Swank 1999, 23). The revised survey of tax changes among major OECD countries by Messere (1998) concurs with this point. High-tax countries continue to have the high total-tax level and tend to have a larger revenue reliance on regressive taxation (i.e., principally flat-rate taxation), especially taxes on goods and services and social security contributions. Because their reliance on progressive taxes on income and profits has been maintained (simply because their total tax burden is high), it is more accurate that high-tax countries have sought their additional or extra revenue from regressive taxation.[16] In contrast, low-tax countries have maintained the lower level of total tax revenue and lower revenue reliance on taxes on consumption. As a result, the tax revenue structure has maintained diversification in the level of total tax revenue as well as the revenue reliance on taxes on consumption.[17] Diversification in high-tax and low-tax countries results from distinct expectations of the role of government (expressed quantitatively). The correlation between tax level (total tax revenue as a proportion of GDP) and general government debt (as a proportion of GDP) of eighteen

[16] This is also consistent with Figure 1.3. In the unweighted averages of tax composition across countries, the increasing revenue reliance on a general consumption tax has coexisted with a reliance on a progressive income tax, the revenue reliance on which stagnated and was then maintained.

[17] The only exception is Denmark, which relies heavily on taxes on income and profits, but this is explained by that country's special method of financing its social security system directly through general tax revenue. (If simplified, the income tax in Denmark includes a role in budget finance that corresponds exactly to that of social security contributions in other countries.)

OECD countries in 2000 is statistically insignificant (−0.1028).[18] The result refutes the possibility that the low-tax countries postpone the imposition of the tax burden until a future generation and that high-tax countries impose it on the current generation.

Policy Diffusion as a Case of Path Dependency

This section will first introduce the framework of policy diffusion analysis and then explain how a revenue reliance shift to a regressive tax has occurred more intensively and frequently in larger welfare states.

Path-Dependent and -Independent Arguments

How to finance a contemporary welfare state varies from one country to another. Will these variations become even more distinct, will their paths cross eventually, or will cross-national variation be preserved despite a certain degree of convergence? These questions concern path-dependent and -independent arguments in comparative political studies. The path-dependent argument is regarded as a methodological strategy to cope with a small-N problem (i.e., too many variables to be controlled with a small number of available cases to analyze using a historical sequence). The variation in the factors from one case to another in history confirms a causal relationship. First, extending a search into history increases the number of cases for relevant comparison; second, dividing the paths at a critical juncture leads to both comparable (similar) and contrasting (different) cases; and finally, variables are regarded as a set if a pattern of changes is theorized based on chronological order.[19] In this regard, the same logic in comparative approaches in general has applied to the path-dependent explanation.

The path-dependent explanation is most extensively used by historical institutionalists (Thelen 1999; Pierson 2000). Historical contingencies

---

[18] All data are from OECD. General government debt is general government gross financial liabilities as a percentage of nominal GDP. No significant correlation with general government net financial liabilities is observed (−0.1346). Debt data are found on the OECD home page (http://www.oecd.org/EN/statistics/0,,EN-statistics-20-nodirectorate-no-1-no-20-no-no-2,FF.html).

[19] This strategy corresponds to three solutions for a small-N problem: (1) increase the number of cases; (2) employ contrasting cases instead of comparable cases, that is, use a completely different systems design instead of a similar systems design; and (3) reduce the number of variables using a strong theory (Collier 1991).

and accidental factors are integrated as institutional dynamics and are presumed to contribute to diverging paths that lead to similar or different consequences, which, again, are empirically shown as institutional similarities and differences. Institutional analysis comprehends a variety of factors with consistency and integrity in an encompassing assumption about specific institutions[20] and theorizes that a current variation (what happened) is an inevitable consequence of the path that each country or society has followed.[21] A good example of studies that take advantage of the strength of this approach is Steinmo's (1993) study of tax politics.[22] He explains the variety in Swedish, British, and American tax systems in terms of the evolutions and changes in political institutions since early in the twentieth century.[23] He compares the timing and manner of institutional formation and change, which influence subsequent processes and policy outcomes and ultimately produce cross-national variation. For example, the Swedish political institutions have explained persuasively and neatly their tax policy-making and tax revenue structure. The Swedish case here is also a "crucial case" (Eckstein 1975). Sweden, a typical example of a mature welfare state, relies on regressive taxation in addition to a progressive income tax that has been regarded as the most auspicious way to finance the welfare state. The strong institutional focus, however, does not aim to confirm or refute the conventional assumption about the relationship between progressive taxation and the welfare state in general. More specifically, it is left to another study whether regressive financing is peculiar to the Swedish social democratic institutions or is more generally observed in large welfare states (i.e., independently of political institutions).

How has the regressive tax been adopted and diffused across countries, and why have some countries and not others used it extensively?

---

[20] In this approach, an institution may be regarded as a variable with many facets that may otherwise be treated as different independent variables (Geddes 1992; Thelen 2003). Assuming multiple causal relationships in qualitative comparative analysis (QCA) using Boolean algebra is also a modified form of the same approach (Ragin 1987; 1994, 312).

[21] For example, Thelen (1999) justifies the institutional focus as follows. "It is too contingent in that the initial choice (call it a 'critical juncture') is seen as rather open and capable of being 'tipped' by small events or chance circumstances, whereas in politics this kind of blank slate is a rarity, to say the least" (Thelen 1999, 385).

[22] Although Steinmo claims that his argument is based on historical new institutionalism (Thelen and Steinmo 1992), his study uses the idea in the same way that Thelen (2003) does without mentioning path dependence specifically.

[23] This strategy can also be extended to explore political and economic institutions, which are likely to increase the total tax burden (Steinmo and Tolbert 1998).

In contrast to institutional analysis, using this emphasis on policy diffusion, the study borrows an idea used in economics to analyze technological diffusion.[24] Although they are distinct phenomena, technological diffusion is comparable to the diffusion of a policy, especially its mechanism and the reasons for the diffusion. Political scientists have already studied policy diffusion in general, but the prominent existing literature (Hall 1989; Goldstein and Keohane 1993) has rarely analyzed it as a result of path dependence. An important subject of the study of path dependence[25] in economics, aside from institutional changes in economic performance (North 1990), is the mechanism of diffusion of technology.

In economics, technological diffusion is of special interest because it causes "inefficiency" that is not expected from a neoclassical model. In other words, irremediable "errors" (such as suboptimal outcomes or inefficiencies from the standpoint of neoclassical economics) are caused by "sensitive dependence on initial conditions," and efficient results are "locked-in by historical events."[26] In this historical lock-in, an inferior technology is diffused at the expense of a superior one. Differing from the dynamics of the adoption of technologies with constant and diminishing returns, technological diffusion with increasing returns causes an historical lock-in under specific conditions (Arthur 1989).[27] In this strong form of path dependence,

---

[24] Pierson (2000) disputes the utility of the approach by Liebowitz and Margolis (1995) on which this study is based because of "little relevance to the development of institutions" (Pierson 2000, 257). Although the two positions appear diametrically opposed, Pierson's position is theoretically consistent with that of the present study. This study focuses on policy diffusion instead of institutional change and thus finds the idea of technological diffusion relevant to the political analysis, whereas Pierson refutes the utility of the same idea owing to a lack of interest in institutional evolutions, which are his primary subject of analysis.

[25] In economics, the term "path dependence" is used more frequently, whereas the term "path dependency" is often used in political science. I regard both as corresponding ideas in different disciplines and treat them as such in this study.

[26] These terms were first used by Arthur (1994); they are also used by Liebowitz and Margolis (1995).

[27] Under increasing returns, the technologies that are dominant at the initial stage or at a certain point in time are more advantageous than others. As a result, the diffusion process becomes self-enforcing for the existing technologies and makes a sharp contrast with constant or diminishing returns on which conventional economic theory builds. With constant and diminishing returns, the process is "*predictable* if the small degree of uncertainty built in 'averages away' so that the observer has enough information to predetermine market shares accurately in the long-run." It is also "*path-efficient* if at all times equal development (equal adoption) of the technology that is behind in adoption would not have paid

which is also called the "third degree" of path dependence, *information and knowledge concerning technologies are available but not diffused*; thus, the outcome remains inefficient and irremediable (Liebowitz and Margolis 1995, 207). A real (third degree of) path dependence, however, rarely occurs.[28] Many "exogenous" factors such as communications, property rights, and market institutions contribute to alleviating the influence of initial endowment or previous situations and retrieve a path from a (third degree of) path-dependent result. When one observes the same (efficient) outcome, many contingent factors (to which formal models pay no attention) may contribute to avoiding a lock-in – a divergent and unexpected inefficient outcome. Historical contingencies are important even when inefficient results are *not* dominant.

With several qualifications, the economic idea of path dependency is applied to policy diffusion. First, and differing from the economic assumption of a universal market across borders, a cross-national distinction is relevant in a comparative political study. Of special interest here is the process by which historical contingencies that differ from one country to another cause the diffusion. Second, a policy shift is not distinctively characterized as an "efficient" or "inefficient" outcome as defined by the technological diffusion. A policy can be examined for its consistency in achieving a specific aim, but here there is no uniform definition of "efficiency" as in economics. Thus, different kinds of policies are not necessarily exclusive competing alternatives, and the cross-national variation is often found in different degrees and extents of implementation of different kinds of policies. Historical contingency accompanying the policy diffusion disputes the omnipotence of information and knowledge in two different ways. First, policy diffusion, regardless of consciousness or correct understanding of the effect brought by it, will bring the same consequences. Alternatively, the countries may fail to use or incompletely implement a policy even if the desirable effect of the policies has been common knowledge. These implications correspond

off better" (Arthur 1989, 1118–19). With constant and diminishing returns, the allocation process is thus *"ergodic* (not path-dependent) if different sequences of historical events lead to the same market outcome with probability one" (Arthur 1989, 118). On the contrary, the important properties of the increasing returns are *nonpredictability* and *potential inefficiency*: technological adoption is influenced and magnified by chance events and, thus, is path-dependent.

28 According to Liebowitz and Margolis, the preceding restricted conditions are hard to hold in a frequently cited case of path dependence, like the one of videotaping formats (i.e., a choice between VHS and Beta).

to technological diffusion;[29] the political implications of policy diffusion are clarified in the next section.

Comparing Different Paths

The Framework of the Explanation   Why has the early shift of revenue reliance from income to consumption led to the expansion of the welfare state? Going beyond simple causality, the spending pressure that arises from the expansion of the welfare state and the revenue-raising power of the tax state have a complicated relationship. To clarify, I present five propositions about the state of public finance and tax policies among industrial democracies and state their political implications.

> *Proposition 1 (on the spending pressure of social security expenditures)*: In contemporary welfare states, social security expenditure is a common source of most important spending pressure.
>
> *Political implication of Proposition 1*: Maintaining or cutting social security expenditure is one of the most politicized financial issues among welfare states.
>
> *Proposition 2 (on government funding capacity and financial crisis)*: During a chronic budget deficit, the government's capacity to raise revenue serves to sustain the level of public expenditures.
>
> *Political implication of Proposition 2*: An effective revenue-raising measure makes it more politically feasible to maintain the level of expenditures during a budget deficit.
>
> *Proposition 3 (on tax reform)*: The introduction of a new tax requires more administrative costs and time to ensure the public's understanding than increasing the rate of the existing tax.
>
> *Political implication of Proposition 3*: Strong political opposition is more likely to be organized against a new tax than the reform of an existing tax.
>
> *Proposition 4 (on a regressive tax as a policy alternative)*: Facing the difficulty of raising enough revenue from the progressive income tax, a regressive tax on consumption has become an important alternative.

---

[29] The first case corresponds to the technological diffusion influenced by historical contingencies; the second one corresponds to a historical lock-in of technological diffusion as a result of the third degree of path dependence.

Political implication of Proposition 4: Policy makers who aim to finance a shortage of revenue, if they are rational, try to increase revenue reliance on a regressive tax.

Proposition 5 (on the tax effect on income redistribution): The shift to a revenue reliance on a regressive tax does not automatically result in less income equality.

Political implication of Proposition 5: Whether the regressivity of taxation can be offset depends on the politics that influence the government's effort to promote income equality using a social security system.

Several supplementary statements are necessary to understand the preceding propositions in the context of this study. Social security expenditures have caused the biggest spending pressure in contemporary democracies and thus are more likely to be the target of spending cuts when there is a budget deficit (Proposition 1). The state's capacity to raise general revenue inevitably affects how and to what extent its social security system can resist the fiscal retrenchment and welfare state backlash that have occurred since the 1980s (Proposition 2). It follows that a government that does not have an effective revenue-raising measure tries to introduce one, but this incurs greater costs than the incremental rate increase (Proposition 3). The electorate suspects the government will impose a new tax without repaying it with public expenditures and services, and thus the opposition is inevitably strong against the introduction of a revenue-raising measure. This distinction between the imposition of a new tax and an incremental increase in the existing tax illuminates the importance of the timing of the introduction of the new tax policy. A regressive tax serves to enhance revenue effectively during a financial crisis in the public sector (Proposition 4). The extensive use of the regressive tax does not necessarily contradict income equality (Proposition 5). For example, the universal and egalitarian provision of benefits under proportional taxation can redistribute income in the Swedish case (Rothstein 1998, 147–9) and thus, here, proportional (regressive) taxation is regarded as an effective measure to finance the welfare state. The imposition of higher regressive taxes has an affinity with the idea that governments rely more on redistribution for income equality through expenditures to offset the regressivity of the tax.

These five propositions imply different tax revenue structures across countries and governments' subsequent adjustments in social security and taxation. The difference from one country to another corresponds to the path that each welfare state has followed. I first distinguish two major paths by presenting the following hypothesis.

Hypothesis: The welfare state that institutionalized a powerful revenue-raising capacity early on is more likely to continue to expand or maintain social security expenditures to resist the fiscal crises that have occurred since the 1980s. In the same vein, late institutionalization tends to lead to less spending and welfare retrenchment.

"Early" means well before the postwar high growth was ended by the worldwide recession in the early 1970s, and "late" means since the mid-1980s when a welfare state backlash was expected in all the industrial countries. Before the early 1970s, the revenue-raising power of a regressive tax had not yet been common knowledge, and budget deficits had not yet become salient. The problem in applying this hypothesis to actual cases lies in identifying this "timing." A common and unmistakable indicator is needed to identify and compare the timing of the institutionalization of revenue-raising capacity, while a progressive income tax and a regressive consumption tax coexisted in postwar tax systems for many years. In the postwar development of tax policies, the most superior type of general consumption tax, the value-added tax, is the most important measure to shift revenue reliance from a progressive (income) tax to a regressive (flat-rate) tax in common with industrial democracies.[30]

The VAT was unknown until the late 1960s when several European countries introduced it simultaneously. Since the mid-1970s, facing chronic budget deficits, policy makers recognized the need to secure revenue from and shift revenue reliance to something other than a progressive income tax. The conversion to the VAT from other general consumption taxes during the last two or three decades[31] (Table 1.5) has served to raise revenue more effectively, and VAT rates have increased rapidly to the current high level in the OECD countries (Table 1.6). The implementation of the VAT characterizes well the variation in each country's current tax revenue structure that has significantly increased since the late 1960s when the VAT began to

---

[30] Social security contributions, the other regressive levy, have increased the revenue share at the same time as the general consumption tax in most high-tax-burden countries.

[31] A simple classification of the tax on consumption distinguishes a broadly based tax on general consumption from taxes on specific commodities and services. There are multistage and single-stage taxes on different types of general consumption. Single-stage taxes include the retail sales tax and the wholesale sales tax. Multistage taxes are the VAT, which does not accumulate amounts from one stage to another (a subtraction type), and the cascade or turnover tax, which accumulates tax amounts (an accumulation type).

Table 1.5. *General consumption tax systems in 1967 and 1995*

Countries	2 January 1967	2 January 1995	Year VAT Introduced
Australia	W	W	2000
Austria	C	VAT	1973
Belgium	C	VAT	1971
Canada	$M^a + R^b$	$VAT^a + R^b$	1991
Denmark	W	VAT	1967
Finland	VAT^c	VAT	1964
France	VAT^d	VAT	1954
Germany	C	VAT	1968
Greece	M	VAT	1987
Iceland	R	VAT	1990
Ireland	W + R	VAT	1972
Italy	C	VAT	1973
Japan	None	VAT	1989
Luxembourg	C	VAT	1970
Netherlands	C	VAT	1969
New Zealand	W	VAT	1986
Norway	R	VAT	1970
Portugal	W	VAT	1986
Spain	C	VAT	1986
Sweden	R^e	VAT	1969
Switzerland	R^e	R^e	1995
Turkey	None	VAT	1985
United Kingdom	W	VAT	1973
United States	R^f	R^f	No VAT

	Number of Countries[g]	Number of Countries[h]	
Single-stage			
M Manufacture	2	0	
W Wholesale	6	1	
R Retail	7	3	
Multistage			
C Cascade	7	0	
VAT	2	21	
No general consumption tax	2	0	
Total	26	25	

[a]At federal level only.

[b]At provincial level only.

[c]Partial only. Full VAT in 1976.

[d]Partial only. Full VAT in 1968.

[e]W in certain cases.

[f]At state and local level only.

[g]Canada and Ireland counted twice.

[h]Canada counted twice.

Source: OECD 1993, 77. Slightly updated.

Table 1.6. *Current rates (%) of VAT in the OECD countries*

Country	Reduced Rate	Standard Rate
Australia[a]	–	10
Austria[b]	10, 12	20
Belgium	0, 6, 12	21
Canada[c]	0	7/15
Czech Republic	5	22
Denmark		25
Finland	8, 17	22
France[d]	2.2, 5.5	20.6
Germany	7	16
Greece[e]	4, 8	18
Hungary	0, 12	25
Iceland[f]	14	24.5
Ireland	0, 3.3, 10, 12.5	21
Italy	4, 10	20
Japan		5
South Korea		10
Luxembourg	3, 6, 12	15
Mexico	0, 10	15
Netherlands[g]	6	17.5
New Zealand[h]		12.5
Norway	0	23
Portugal[i]	5, 12	22
Spain	4, 7	16
Sweden	0, 6, 12	25
Switzerland[j]	2.3/3.5	7.5
Turkey[k]	1, 8	17
United Kingdom[l]	0, 5	17.5

Note: Rates as at 1 January 2000 if there is no specification.
[a] Rate as at 1 July 2000.

[b] 16% applies in the Austrian tax enclaves Mittelberg and Jungholz.

[c] 15% harmonized sales tax (HST) applies in those provinces that have harmonized their provincial retails sales tax with the federal GST (the 15% HST is composed of a provincial componenet of 8% and a federal component of 7%).
[d] Standard rate is 19.6% as of 1 April 2000.

[e] Tax rates are reduced by 30% in some remote areas.

[f] Standard rate is 20% as of 1 January 2001.

[g] Standard rate is 19% as of 1 January 2001.

[h] For long-term stay in a commercial dwelling, GST at standard rate is levied on 60% of the value of the supply.

[i] The rates applicable in the Autonomous Regions of Madeira and the Azores are respectively 4%, 8%, and 12%.

[j] 2.4% / 3.6% and 7.6% as of 1 January 2001.

[k] There are also higher rates of 23/40%.

[l] The standard rate is applied to a reduced value on imports of certain works of art, antiques, and collectors' items, resulting in an effective rate of 2.5%.

Source: OECD 2001c.

be implemented (see, for example, Sandford 1993b, 3; Boskin and McLure 1990). As a flat-rate regressive tax on a broad base, the VAT, when implemented, has a strong revenue-raising power that the income tax lacks. The broad tax base on consumption, which does not fluctuate as much as income during economic ups and downs, guarantees large amounts of revenue even with a slight increase in a flat tax rate. The tax base has not been narrowed as much as the income tax by political pressure: taxing the added value at each transaction stage makes tax exemptions technically more difficult than otherwise. Moreover, the VAT is likely to increase tax compliance in general because, in all transaction activities, tax-filing units (i.e., firms) must report their transactions to the tax authority.[32] Considering the VAT's revenue-raising capacity, its adoption and the intensity of its implementation serve as good indicators of a state's capacity and intent to raise revenue, especially in industrial democracies.

The introduction of the VAT during the early period symbolized the smooth institutionalization of revenue-raising measure that came to have a critical influence. The public, with no experience with budget deficits, had no way to oppose the new tax, while the VAT's revenue-raising capacity was unknown to all but a small number of policy makers. With an effective revenue machine, however, governments since the 1980s have tended to resist expenditure cuts that would sacrifice income redistribution and equality; the public has supported this structure (political implications of Propositions 3 and 4). A diametrically different consequence is observed in cases of the late introduction of the VAT in which a budget deficit tends to arouse public suspicion about increasing tax only to solve deficits. Strong opposition to revenue enhancement forces the government to cut expenditures and retrench the welfare state. These divergences are consistent with the cross-national variation in tax revenue. Figure 1.2(d) shows that as a proportion of total tax revenue to GDP is higher, the year of introduction of the VAT is earlier. A government that has institutionalized a regressive tax promotes income equality by a larger welfare provision (Proposition 5).

---

[32] This effect of mutual watching between tax units combined with the potential government capacity to find inaccuracies may be extended to income taxation. It is unrealistic that a government can point out each inaccuracy in a tax filing even with all the available information and mutual watching between traders: there are a large number of tax-filing units and complexities of transaction compared with a limited number of tax officials. However, the possibility that the government may find tax evasion increases tax compliance even if the possibility is low. This is now conventional wisdom among tax specialists and policy makers.

Here, the available revenue-raising measure not only distinguishes the government's financing strategy but also causes the diversification between high- and low-tax countries. In this regard, although its revenue is not earmarked for welfare expenditures, the different timing of the VAT illuminates the extent of changes in the government financial strategy that determine the subsequent ease for the government's extraction of revenue. Consequently, the different timing of policy diffusion had an irreversible influence on subsequent policy choices, and thus made the paths of policy changes divergent across countries. These consequences parallel those expected from technological diffusion.

From left to right, Figure 1.4 shows each country's simplified tax revenue structure and level of social security expenditures in the order of the year the VAT was introduced in each country (the year of introduction is written above each country's name). The high-tax countries with more reliance on taxes on goods and services were more likely to introduce the VAT earlier – before 1970. The borderline cases are the ones that introduced the VAT in the early 1970s when the oil shock ended the postwar high-growth period and the revenue-raising power of the VAT became common knowledge. The U.K. case in Chapter 3 specifies the impact of the VAT's introduction on the borderline case. Among the countries that introduced the VAT since the 1980s, Canada and Switzerland have had higher tax and spending than expected. Switzerland had long had the retailers' sales tax and replaced it with the VAT in 1995. The Canadian case will be explained in detail in Chapter 4 together with the New Zealand anomaly of relatively high revenue reliance on taxes on goods and services. Despite these exceptions, however, the timing of the VAT's introduction is a good indicator of tax revenue structures across countries.

Variation among Industrial Democracies and the Distinctive Path of Developing Countries This study employs eight countries as cases among the industrial democracies – Australia, Canada, France, Japan, New Zealand, Sweden, the United Kingdom, and the United States – that are spread out across different types of tax revenue structures (Table 1.3) as well as different types of welfare states (Table 1.2). They are classified into the two different paths taken by the politics behind the revenue reliance shift to a regressive tax. These paths illuminate distinct approaches to revenue extraction that influence the funding base of the welfare state.

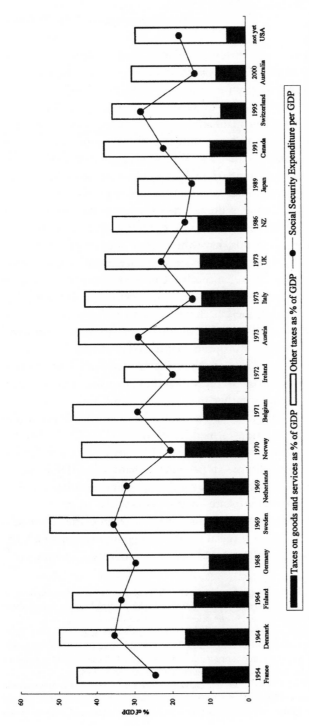

Figure 1.4. Levels of social security expenditures, total tax burden, and taxes on goods and services (as percentage of GDP) of OECD countries. See a definition of SSEXPT in Appendix. The data for social security expenditures are for 1990 for France, 1996 Denmark, 1996 for Finland, 1996 for Germany, 1996 for Sweden, 1993 for Netherlands, 1992 for Norway, 1995 for Belgium, 1996 for Ireland, 1996 for Austria, 1993 for Italy, 1993 for the United Kingdom, 1996 for New Zealand, 1996 for Japan, 1996 for Canada, 1995 for Switzerland, 1991 for Australia, 1995 for the United States. The tax data are for 1999. *Source:* OECD 2000; ILO, Cost of Social Security 1990–96 (http://www.ilo.org/public/english/protection/socsec/publ/css/cssindex.htm).

Group 1: Countries in which early VAT introduction epitomizes a revenue reliance shift well before *the governments experienced chronic budget deficits* Most of the western European countries apparently belong in this category. They had a certain form of general consumption tax before the adoption of the VAT became mandatory to enter the EC (European Community). An early revenue reliance shift is obviously expected from the western European countries that had already used another general consumption tax, transformed it into the VAT upon entrance into the EC, and enjoyed high welfare provisions supported by strong political representation of labor interests. If one examines the variation in Europe, however, this conventional explanation does not hold. Only two small countries,[33] Denmark and the Netherlands, have these three properties. Even these countries fail to follow expectations if they are examined in detail. Denmark has large revenue reliance on income taxation and has experienced the most extensive tax revolts (i.e., a resistance to high-tax burden) in western Europe.[34] Also, the Dutch welfare state is known for its rapid expansion in the 1960s, which is often distinguished from the incremental growth in the other western European countries (Cox 1992).

This study uses France, Sweden, and the United Kingdom as cases. Although they are categorized in the same group, they are important representatives of the variation rather than the unity in Europe. France is a typical example of the European countries that had a long history of a general consumption tax and transformed it into the VAT in 1968 when the VAT was adopted as a mandatory requirement by the EC. France also has high social security expenditure – its percentage share to its GDP is second highest after the Scandinavian welfare states. But, it has never been considered a typical European welfare state – neither as a social democratic welfare state nor a conservative one with strong Christian Democratic presence in party politcs. France has high social security expenditures despite a long-term conservative rule until 1981 and has a low progressive income tax.[35]

---

[33] Belgium may also be included here if one ignores its large share of income taxation to total tax revenue. The percentage of revenue from the VAT to the GDP in Belgium is well above the OECD average but below that of the other European countries.

[34] In Denmark, in addition, representation of agrarian interests was stronger than labor interests, and labor unions were more decentralized than in neighboring countries. As a result, the Danish welfare state was much more modest than the Swedish one, that is, it involved a weaker central planning and supply side policy (Esping-Andersen 1985).

[35] Castles and Mitchell (1993, 119, see especially Proposition 6) explain the inconsistent classification between a political (liberal welfare state) and financial (conservative welfare state) configuration (Table 1.2) as a result of political competition between Catholicism and

The French Socialists entered office very late – in 1981 – and France's tax system, which relies heavily on social security contributions and the VAT, is considered regressive. In this regard, the French case contrasts clearly with the Swedish case in which the leftist party government intentionally institutionalized and implemented a regressive form of taxation to finance increasing social security expenditures.

Sweden is a typical Scandinavian welfare state characterized by the strength of organized labor and the Social Democratic Party. Its total tax strikes a high level, and the revenue from a general consumption tax is as important as the income tax for financing big government. It has a long history of a general consumption tax introduced during the war, abolished after the war, and then restored in 1959. The Swedish policy makers were fully conscious of the VAT's revenue-raising power, about which French counterparts had no knowledge. The tax was converted to the VAT in 1969 and, thus, the adoption of the VAT was decided independently of Sweden's recent entrance into the EU (European Union) by policy makers who recognized its revenue-raising power. Despite these different processes and reasons for the VAT's introduction, its early introduction caused both governments to change strategies and finance high expenditures with a regressive tax. It also contributed to the resistance to public expenditure cuts. The comparison between Sweden and France demonstrates that the very early institutionalization of the VAT, regardless of policy makers' original intentions, led to the same result in two countries with a distinct tradition of government partisanship.

The United Kingdom is a hybrid case when compared with France and Sweden. The United Kingdom had once been known as a welfare state comparable with Sweden and was on the border in terms of early and late introducers. The United Kingdom's entrance into the EC was a major reason to adopt the VAT in 1973. The VAT is far from extensively used compared with Sweden and France because of their lower rates and larger exemptions. In accordance with the United Kingdom's lower revenue reliance on regressive taxation, its level of total tax is low; it has fallen from above average in the 1960s to below average in the 1990s among eighteen OECD

socialism. In this regard, the French case may be explained more persuasively by Castles's conception of the Catholic family of nations in which Catholic reformism contributed to the achievement of a high level of welfare provision through Catholic population and/or Christian Democratic presence in party politics (Castles 1994). Although it is the major religion in France, Catholicism never developed a unitary political movement with a dominant influence (van Kersbergen 1995, 36–8).

countries. However, the revenue reliance shift from income to consumption has had an important (though more limited than in Sweden and France) impact. For example, the VAT has become an important source of revenue to finance an income tax cut, especially since the 1980s when the country experienced the welfare state backlash during the neoconservative rule.

In all these countries, the revenue reliance on social security contributions and a general consumption tax appears closely related; there is a contrast between the high levels of total taxation in Sweden and France and the modest one in the United Kingdom. This is not a coincidence because the diffusion of the VAT symbolizes the revenue reliance shift and the increasing reliance on regressive taxation of which social security contributions are an important part. Their interactions will be more persuasively shown in the three countries' cases in Chapter 2.

Group 2: Countries in which a revenue reliance shift was attempted by the VAT's introduction after they had experienced deficit finances In this group, New Zealand, Japan, Canada, and Australia have introduced the VAT since the mid-1980s, when they already had chronic budget deficits, and the United States has not yet introduced it. This group consists of non-European countries that have neither a big public sector nor large social security expenditures. When the VAT was introduced in New Zealand, Japan, Canada, and Australia, because of the experience of other countries, especially in Europe, it was already regarded as a powerful means to increase revenue and a regressive form of taxation. The Japanese and Canadian governments encountered strong public opposition to the VAT's introduction; however, New Zealand, which introduced a VAT as high as 10 percent, observed no opposition. It achieved a revenue reliance shift to the tax on consumption and succeeded in reducing public spending and budget deficits. In Australia, the proposals to introduce the VAT were thwarted twice in the mid-1980s and again in the early 1990s. The introduction of the VAT in 2000 was not easy but occurred with less opposition than in Japan and Canada.

The apparent distinctions among those countries can be attributed to how the VAT was proposed to cope with potential opposition. New Zealand, which introduced the VAT earliest in 1986, proposed it to replace a deficient turnover tax. More important, the VAT was part of a tax reform upheld by extensive deregulation of the nation throughout the 1980s. The tax system was simplified, the tax base was broadened, and marginal tax rates decreased sharply. Interestingly, in New Zealand, the revenue from the VAT is rapidly increasing, but government expenditures remain effectively repressed. This consequence is in sharp contrast to the European experience. In addition, the reform of the social security system in the early 1990s has transformed universal entitlement programs into means-tested ones. Here, increasing the reliance on regressive taxation does not serve to expand the welfare state, again, unlike the European cases.

The consequences of the introduction of the VAT in Japan and Canada are distinct from those of their predecessors in Europe and also different from that in New Zealand. The chronic budget deficits in the public sector and the reshuffling of the public financial system were the reasons for the introduction of the VAT in both countries. As a result, the VAT was proposed as a means of revenue enhancement and fiscal solvency, that is, for a tax increase. In Japan, the government proposed the VAT three times after 1979 and finally introduced it in 1989. But then the 3 percent tax became one of the important reasons for the governing Liberal Democratic Party's massive loss in the following national election.

In Canada, the VAT's introduction in 1991 intensified public antipathy toward the incumbent Progressive Conservatives, which eventually caused the demise of their rule. In both Japan and Canada, the VAT is expected to become an increasingly important revenue source in the future. But the tax rates are still modest (i.e., as low as 5 and 7 percent, respectively, as of 2001). At the turn of the century, the Canadian government solved a budget deficit by a spending cut, whereas the Japanese still suffered a looming deficit with stagnated tax revenue during a prolonged recession. In other words, the attempted revenue reliance shift to consumption did not result in revenue enhancement in the two countries. This consequence is an interesting reminder that high tax progressivity classifies Canada as a radical welfare state according to Castles and Mitchell (1992, 1993) despite an unexpectedly weak union (see Table 1.2), and Japan achieves high income equality despite the long-term predominance of the conservative Liberal Democratic Party (see Chapter 4). The modest sizes of their welfare states at the turn of the century imply that countries with high progressivity and income equality without the government's high funding capacity are more vulnerable to welfare backlash since the 1980s.

We have not seen the consequence of the recent introduction of the VAT in Australia, but, again, it is expected to be somewhere between the Canadian and the Japanese cases and its neighbor, New Zealand. In Australia, the tax rate and the revenue-raising power of the VAT are higher than in Canada and Japan and lower than in New Zealand. In the United States, the scholarly debate about the VAT has been active, but the proposal has never been politicized. The United States relies heavily on income taxation, and the social security system is generally regarded as much weaker than that in its European counterparts.

Group 3: Newly industrializing countries   In addition to the eight industrial democracies, this study deals with a general tendency among newly industrializing countries. Here, an interesting comparison will be presented between Korea and Japan with Taiwan as a secondary case. The existing advanced industrial democracies have changed their major revenue source from a simple indirect tax, such as a tariff, to income taxation and then shifted to a general consumption tax such as the VAT. However, the availability of information about more advanced tax systems has permitted some newly industrializing countries (NICs) and developing countries to adopt the VAT at a much earlier stage of industrialization and democratization than the existing industrial democracies. The governments of industrial late-comers have known the possibility of rapid expansion of the public sector and been aware of a variety of means to raise revenue by learning from the experience of their predecessors. In this regard, their path toward developing modern taxation and institutionalizing the social security system appears different from that of existing industrial democracies. This difference may well be derived from the available policy information that parallels the case of technological diffusion and will illuminate the ultimate cause for the path dependence among industrial democracies. The point will be further clarified after these cases are introduced in Chapter 4.

Quantitative Evidence: Qualifying the Effects of Globalization and Government Partisanship

A cross-national comparison thus far presents the possibility that the tax state and the welfare state have a reciprocal relationship in which one strengthens or weakens the other. At the same time, however, it is possible to argue that their relationship is spurious in the sense that some other factor intervenes to influence both the tax state and the welfare state in the same direction and makes the relationship appear to exist. Government partisanship and economic globalization, which are closely related in influencing the tax state and the welfare state, are plausible candidates for such an intervening factor. It is also plausible that association of extensive use of a general consumption tax and a large welfare state can be attributed to the geographical location of the countries in question. This section will consider these possibilities in order.

Government Partisanship, Globalization, and the Welfare State

Despite the use of different data and different assumptions, quantitative studies of the postwar expansion of the welfare state draw a surprisingly similar conclusion that welfare spending is increased by the frequent and durable dominance of a leftist party in the government (Castles 1998; Crepaz 1998; Hicks and Misra 1993; Hicks, Swank, and Ambuhl 1989; Huber, Ragin, and Stephens 1993; Pampel and Williamson 1988).[36] The foundations of welfare programs in many countries had been institutionalized prior to the period that has been analyzed.[37] Although some quantitative studies on the welfare effort before the Second World War such as Hage, Gargan, and Hanneman (1989) and Schneider (1982)[38] provide a variety of implications about the contemporary state of welfare, they neither contradict nor challenge the preceding conclusion that the postwar development of the welfare state has been influenced by the length and extent of leftist rule.

The effect of globalization was once considered linked with the leftist support for the welfare state. In the Scandinavian welfare states in the 1960s and 1970s, a high industrial concentration in an openness of economy, via high unionization, led to the dominance of a leftist government and the institutionalization of collective bargaining that ultimately caused the expansion of the public economy (Cameron 1978). Small European states with highly open economies, such as the Scandinairan countries, Austria, and Switzerland, have also had large public sectors by adopting a strategy of "domestic compensation" during international liberalization in the

---

[36] They often distinguish different categories of welfare spendings. For example, Pampel and Williamson (1988) show that means-tested spending is mostly dominated by class-related variables such as a high unionization rate and that total welfare spending (composed mainly of social insurance benefits) is largely determined by the share of the aged in the total population. In the recent study of twenty-one OECD countries by Castles (1998), leftist incumbency is not necessarily associated with high specific expenditures on social security transfer, health, and education; however, it is positively associated with high total expenditure.

[37] For elaboration of this point, see Amenta (1993, 757).

[38] The quantitative analyses during the prewar period have incomplete data and many other uncontrolled factors, such as the influence of rapidly increasing military expenditures in some countries. In this regard, the evolution of the welfare state may be examined better by historical and descriptive works, for example, Kohler, Zacher, and Partington (1982) and Ashford (1986). There are also periodic observations of social policy development from the interwar period to recently (Vaisanten 1992) and studies of the social security program from the late nineteenth century to the postwar period (Collier and Messick 1975; Abbott and DeViney 1992).

1950s and 1960s and then institutionalizing extensive social expenditures for investment and subsidies as well as income transfers (Katzenstein 1985).[39]

Since the 1980s, however, welfare states have experienced constraints on spending due to chronic revenue shortfalls or the exhaustion of funds. Intensifying economic competition as a result of globalization has made it difficult for governments to impose heavy taxes to finance a welfare state at will. A focal point of controversy in the existing literature is whether a government can maintain the tax revenues and welfare expenditures that are required by maintaining current social policies and programs in the face of international economic competition during globalization. A government that ceases to impose heavy taxes on personal and corporate income, fearing capital flight, faces difficulties in maintaining progressivity of taxation. In the recent surveys of the tax systems of the OECD countries (Owens 1997; Tanzi 1996), revenues from personal and corporate income taxes have generally declined except in a small number of countries. This is a consequence of tax competition defined as "harmful tax practices," which consist of tax "avoidance and evasion" from one country, "spillover effects" of domestic tax regimes, and the resulting "misallocation of resources" (Owens 1997, 2054–5). If we simplify the overall picture of tax competition, these three symptoms are related. Because of the globalization of the economy, it is easier for individuals and capital to cross borders to "evade" and "avoid" heavy taxes on economic activities. Facing the problem of such tax migration, governments have tended to adopt tax systems that favor mobile economic activities and footloose capital (spillover effects). As a result, indirect taxation has been devised to discourage cross-border shopping. Personal income taxation takes into consideration labor mobility, and capital taxation is preferable for competitive industries. The tax regimes that try to prevent tax migrations are likely to misallocate resources.[40] The problem of tax competition is, therefore, closely related to the problem of losing progressivity in taxation. Progressive taxes on personal and corporate income exacerbate tax migration because savings and investment incomes easily cross borders, and both competitive human and financial capital are mobile. To prevent tax migration, the income tax rate structure should be

---

[39] Their view is also consistent with the concept of "embedded liberalism" in international relations (Ruggie 1983).

[40] For a detailed discussion of harmful tax competition and globalization, see OECD (1998b) and Tanzi (1995).

less progressive, and less mobile economic activities such as consumption should be taxed more heavily.

Increasing difficulty in raising revenue intensifies the policy trade-off of a welfare state (i.e., a trilemma of fiscal discipline, earnings equality, and employment growth) (Iversen and Wren 1998). The social democratic welfare state pursues equality and employment at the expense of budgetary restraint, whereas the neoliberal welfare state maintains fiscal discipline and high employment at the expense of earning equality, and the Christian democratic welfare state achieves fiscal discipline and earning equality by sacrificing employment. Here, economic globalization is considered a challenge for the welfare state[41] that compensates domestic social groups, which have been exposed directly to the mercy of external economic changes. But the literature studying the cases of the social democratic countries rejected the sweeping effect of globalization. Small countries in northern Europe – Denmark, Finland, Norway, and Sweden – have been traditionally dependent on trade but have slowly removed constraints on cross-border capital flows and preserved their left-labor strength and accompanying policies (i.e., high public spending, generous welfare provision, and progressivity in taxation) during globalization (Garrett 1998).[42] In this regard, the existing literature in political science agrees on the limited impact of globalization despite different focuses and emphasis in empirical analysis (Huber and Stephens 1998; Stephens, Huber, and Ray 1999; Iversen and Cusack 2000; Iversen, Potusson, and Soskice 2000; Pierson 2001; Swank 2000, 2002; Steinmo 1997a; 1997b).[43]

---

[41] Together with the effect of globalization, Iversen and Wren (1998) emphasize the effect of the expansion of the service economy.

[42] Taking global tax policy changes such as corporate income tax cuts and the simplification of the income tax system into consideration, Garrett (1999) argues that the effect of a corporate tax rate cut has been weakened by the repeal of special tax measures to promote investment incentives. This point is confirmed by Ganghof's (2000) analysis that denies a convergence effect of globalization over corporate taxation.

[43] For example, Stephens, Huber, and Ray (1999) generally have reservations about the extent of welfare retrenchment despite the rapid globalization of the economy. Swank (2000) especially questions the intensity of welfare retrenchment in Sweden, Finland, Denmark, and Norway. Swank (2002) also argues the limited systematic effect of globalization on welfare states and finds the adverse effect of international capital mobility on welfare policies only with high (more than 10 percent of) budget deficits. Huber and Stephens (1998) attribute the Nordic countries' (Austria, Norway, Finland, and Sweden) economic difficulties to their governments' mistakes in macroeconomic policies instead of their social democratic corporatism. Iversen and Cusack (2000) refute the statistical relationship between globalization and labor-market risks; instead, they argue that increasing uncertainty and dislocation in the labor market caused by deindustrialization contribute to welfare state

Contrary to the explanation of globalization's impact put forth by political scientists, economists first consider the impact of globalization more qualified (Tanzi and Schuknecht 1995); second, even when its impact is focused, they analyze it independently from the impact of government partisanship. Here, open economies that are more vulnerable to external shocks tend to have a large public sector that serves to cope with the shocks. A link between a large public sector and the openness of the economy is identified without considering the leftist government as an intervening variable (Alesina and Wacziarg 1998; Rodrik 1996).[44] This view leads to a different conclusion about the effect of globalization, especially since the 1990s. For example, the openness of the economy stagnates the growth of social spending and government consumption as proportions of the GDP if a variation of external risk (i.e., the volatility of terms of trade) is controlled in the analysis of fourteen OECD countries from 1966 to 1991 (Rodrik 1997, 60–4).[45] This result indicates the concentration of taxation on labor because governments are expected to shy away from taxing capital for fear of capital flight.[46]

Despite the apparent differences, these two views have two important parallels. First, globalization makes it difficult for governments to raise

expansion. Iversen et al. (2000) observe the changes in wage bargaining and economic coordination. They have reservations about economic performance and the pursuance of labor interest in the 1990s that still distinguishes the Scandinavian social democratic countries from other industrial democracies. Pierson (2001) qualifies the effects of globalization on welfare states whereas Steinmo (1997a; 1997b) refutes the effect of globalization on tax revenue.

[44] Differing from Rodrik (1996), Alesina and Wacziarg (1998) use the country size measured by population as an important mediator to link economic openness and government size. Their reasoning is as follows. First, a country with a large population can decrease its per capita expenditure to provide partially or completely nonrival public goods. Thus, it tends to have a smaller government compared with its population size. In a country with a smaller population, this mechanism works in the opposite direction. The implicit assumption here is that all populations share the cost of public-goods provision. Second, because the scale of the economy influences productivity, smaller countries cannot afford to be closed, but larger countries can. In the same vein, globalization encourages ethnic and cultural minorities to split and form (or to remain in) a small country; globalization allows a country to have a market beyond its political borders.

[45] Rodrik also explains the close association between government expansion and external risk in over 100 countries by the social protection against external risk – in rich countries, through social security and welfare expenditures, and in poor countries, through government consumption (Rodrik 1997, 57–60).

[46] Alesina and Perotti (1997) provide a similar argument and present the possibility that increasing labor taxation to finance pension and unemployment benefits will eventually increase wage pressure by labor unions, pushing up labor costs and hurting competition.

revenue from the existing tax system. Globalization makes the provision of welfare protection for labor difficult. But this observation leaves the possibility that specific countries preserve more generous welfare provisions than other countries that have been more directly exposed to globalization. Economists are negative about this possibility, whereas political scientists argue that the social democratic countries are embodying it. They differ in whether the response to globalization differs from one country to another. The second and more important parallel is the increasing regressivity of taxes across countries. Although the burden of social insurance programs is shifting from capital income to labor income, the social democratic corporatist countries increasingly rely on regressive taxes on consumption. This is unexpected from the assumption that leftist governments pursue income equality through a progressive form of taxation. Garrett (1998, 154–5) explains that the regressivity of taxation is mitigated by exemptions in the social democratic countries.[47] However, when the government redistributes its revenue through a social security system, revenue raising by regressive taxes does not necessarily contradict the pursuance of income equality. The problem of regressivity can be solved outside the tax system (i.e., through social security programs), instead of solving it marginally inside the tax system by applying exemptions. Here, we can find a possible link between globalization and the diffusion of regressive taxation that is used as an effective financial measure by a large welfare state.

While supporting the persistent cross-national variation in taxation and welfare discussed in the existing literature, this study grapples with the assumption behind the argument. The existing literature implicitly assumed the association between tax progressivity, large government size, and leftist partisanship of the government in the partisanship-centered explanation (Garrett 1998; Boix 1998; Iversen 1999; Hicks 1999; Huber and Stephens 2001). For example, the Social Democrats' alliance with agrarian

---

[47] Garrett argues that the regressivity is mitigated by tax exemptions and reductions of taxes on basic goods such as foods and clothes, but the social democratic countries do not necessarily allow more tax exemptions and reductions as exemplified by the Swedish VAT case in Chapter 2. They have fewer exemptions than other countries (OECD 1997a, Chapters 1 and 2; Tables 3.6, 3.7, and 3.8 in OECD 2001b), and their VAT rates, even lower and reduced rates, tend to be higher than in other countries (Table 1.5). The effective VAT rate (VAT revenue divided by the potential VAT base, i.e., consumption minus VAT) is lower than the standard rate in these countries (Figure 5 in OECD 2001a, 31), and thus the VAT rate (expressed by the standard rate) appears much higher than it actually is. But even considering this factor, the VAT is generally more extensively imposed in the high-tax-rate countries.

and Catholic parties together with neocorporatist organization was imperative for welfare state formation in the 1930s and 1940s and was followed by the Social Democrats' alliance with the Liberals in the mid-twentieth-century consolidation (Hicks 1999). Social democratic ideology also serves to link economic institutions (including union organization and patterns of wage bargaining) with the economic strategy of a government (including monetary and fiscal policies) (Iversen 1999). For the last two decades of slow growth, the social democratic government has simultaneously pursued economic growth and income equality by promoting both labor and capital productivity by public intervention, whereas the conservative government has delegated more to market mechanisms to avoid market distortions (Boix 1998).

As exemplified among the existing industrial democracies, the pursuance of income equality eventually leads to universalism, which accompanies a larger public sector with a strong funding capacity. The pursuance of state funding power ushers in an increasing reliance on regressive taxes that is effective in raising revenue and thus resisting welfare retrenchment during deficit-ridden government finance. In this respect, the study's focus on state funding capacity qualifies the partisan-centered explanation of the welfare state but fortifies its argument about the persistent and consistent pursuance of income equality under leftist rule. Leftist governments are ready to adopt any appropriate policy measures rather than being unconditionally dedicated to the principle of the progressivity of taxation. At the same time, however, a government long dominated by conservatives, if it has institutionalized strong funding power via regressive taxes, responds to welfare retrenchment in the same way that a long-term, leftist-prone government does. In this context, although it embraces the importance of partisan politics, this study does not necessarily regard strong funding capacity as the monopolization of a leftist government.[48] During financial difficulties, a government with a strong funding base, regardless of its partisanship and the original intentions of policy makers, has resisted welfare retrenchment. This study explores the ultimate cause of the

---

[48] Bradley et al. (2001) show results of statistical analyses that are consistent with this point. That is, larger taxes and transfers are associated with further reduction in inequality regardless of government partisanship. However, the social democratic government also shows a strong association with further reduction in equality even controlling for the effect of the (large) size of taxes and transfers. In contrast, the Christian democratic government has a positive association with the size of taxes and transfers but a negative one with the reduction in inequality.

resistance to welfare retrenchment in the funding capacity of the welfare state.

A Common Tradition of Taxation and the Welfare State in Europe

If a larger revenue reliance on regressive taxes has occurred coincidentally among specific countries that have a long tradition of welfare, the association among them is spurious, that is, without any causal relationship. This is more challenging than either the globalization thesis or the partisanship-centered explanation and is plausibly applied to western European countries that were the oldest welfare states in which the VAT has been adopted as a result of the mandate of the integration of the European market.[49] The VAT as a technically superior form of taxation may be an obvious choice to facilitate the market integration under its mandatory adoption by the European Union (EU, formerly European Community or EC). In this regard, the implementation of the VAT has been regarded as a purely economic phenomenon independent of the influence of domestic politics in each country.

Was the diffusion of the VAT a coincidence accompanied by European integration? The long history of a single-stage general consumption tax (i.e., the retail and wholesale sales tax) certainly encouraged the members to make the VAT (the most superior form of a broad-based tax on consumption as described later) a common tax system. A detailed investigation of the so-called EU effect for the European cases is found in Chapter 2, but a quick look at Figure 1.2 will at least question this simple reasoning for the VAT's diffusion. The EU member countries rely more on revenue from taxes on goods and services (and again the VAT is the most effective such tax) than nonmember countries; however, among the EU members, revenue reliance on taxes on goods and services is significantly varied. In other words, the mandatory adoption of the VAT has had influence in quite different degrees from one country to another.

During economic globalization, the simplicity and neutrality of the VAT become even more advantageous than the income tax owing to easier coordination across borders (Musgrave 1997, 466). Simplicity refers to the least complexity in implementing and administering a tax system. A tax system is more neutral if it is less distorting of free-market decisions. The VAT is simple and neutral because it has a limited number of tax-filing units (i.e.,

---

[49] For this process, see Aaron (1981; 1982).

firms in different stages of transactions) and spreads the total tax burden over consumers at the final stages.[50] The technical superiority, however, is not an exclusive reason for the VAT diffusion. First, satisfying one principle always interferes with another principle in the same tax system: its flat (regressive) rate goes against the equity principle,[51] which is the strength of the comprehensive income tax. Second, even its strength in simplicity and neutrality is easily lost by compromising measures in practice. The VAT systems across the world have used tax exemptions on specific commodities and special tax treatments for small-scale firms or lower and/or zero tax rates on basic commodities (e.g., foods and clothes) and services that hurt the tax's neutrality and simplicity while incompletely eliminating the regressivity.

Consequently, the diffusion of the VAT is not necessarily explained by the contingent effects of European integration or its superiority as a form of taxation. The diffusion seeks a political explanation that has resulted in the coexistence of a high level of total taxation and revenue reliance on regressive taxation with the expansion of the welfare state.

Quantitative Analysis

The quantitative analysis here will confirm the relationship between the level of social security expenditure and the tax revenue structure (i.e., government reliance on a regressive general consumption tax), while considering other political and economic factors such as partisanship and globalization on the welfare state. Even when controlling for all other

---

[50] The tax on a previous transaction stage is transferred to the current stage, and the tax on the current exchange (including the tax on the previous stage) is then transferred to the next stage. The tax is transferred by addition to the exchange price. The tax burden is borne by consumers at the final stage of transaction (the destination principle).

[51] The principle of equity provides a "fair" tax burden on specific economic actors, persons, families, and corporations, based on certain criteria such as ability to pay or benefits obtained from the public service provided by tax revenue. The comprehensive income tax is superior in terms of equity but, in implementation, is weak in simplicity (due to discriminatory measures such as progressive rates) and neutrality (due to tax evasion that influences economic decisions). No country has ever institutionalized a comprehensive income tax in an ideal way because of increasing tax loopholes and tax exemptions. In practice, this compromise has a problem corresponding to that of the VAT, which will be described later. An income tax in practice incompletely applies its strength – a principle of equity – while further hurting simplicity and neutrality. On the contrary, as described later, the VAT in practice increases simplicity and neutrality while solving a problem of regressivity (less equity).

relevant factors, this analysis demonstrates a strong association between increases in social security expenditure and a revenue reliance shift to a general consumption tax. This analysis was performed across eighteen OECD countries from the mid-1960s, the heyday of the welfare state, to around 1990 when the possible bankruptcy of the welfare state had become common knowledge.

Model and Data   To analyze pooled time-series and cross-sectional data such as are found in the eighteen OECD countries from 1965 to 1992, one must use panel regression models (i.e., a fixed effect model and a random effect – two error components – model). The basic structure of the fixed effect model is

$$Y_{it} = \beta_0 + \beta_1 X_{1it} + \cdots + \beta_j X_{jit} + \cdots + \beta_k X_{kit} + \gamma_t \zeta_t + \gamma_i \eta_i + \varepsilon_{it},$$

$$i = 1, 2, \ldots, N$$

$$t = 1, 2, \ldots, T$$

There are k independent variables. ζ_t is a year dummy assigned 1 for the year t. η_i is a country dummy assigned 1 for ith country. ε_{it} is an error term.

The basic structure of the random effect model is

$$Y_{it} = \beta_0 + \beta_1 X_{1it} + \cdots + \beta_j X_{jit} + \cdots + \beta_k X_{kit} + \gamma_t \zeta_t + u_{it}$$

$$u_{it} = \eta_i + \varepsilon_{it}{}^{52}$$

$$i = 1, 2, \ldots, N$$

$$t = 1, 2, \ldots, T$$

As is often the case in political economic analyses, this analysis includes important independent variables that have the same values for the same country, i, regardless of year, t, such as dummy variables that indicate the form of political institutions specific to the country or geopolitical situation or status of that country. This contradicts the assumption of the fixed effect model. Thus, here, the data will be analyzed only by the random effect model. Whereas one analysis is the random effect model as indicated

---

[52] Both $\{\eta_i\}$ and $\{\varepsilon_{it}\}$ are independent and identically distributed (i.i.d.) random variables with mean 0 and variance, $\sigma_\eta^2, \sigma_\varepsilon^2$ respectively. $\{\eta_i\}$ and $\{\varepsilon_{it}\}$ are independent. In the random effect model, $E(\eta_i|X_{it}) = 0$ and $E(\eta_i^2|X_{it}) = \sigma_\eta^2$ is assumed. In both models, obviously $E(\varepsilon_{it}|X_{it}) = 0$ is assumed. For details about the technical aspects of the analysis, see Hsiao (1986).

previously, the other includes a trend term, $t + t^2$,[53] instead of the year dummy.

The focus of this analysis is the relationship between social security expenditure and the extent of tax revenue reliance on regressive taxation (a general consumption tax here). The inclusion of variables relating to social security expenditure and tax revenue in the same equation presents a problem of simultaneity. This analysis uses the instrumental variable method to cope with this problem. In the first-stage regression, the level of social security expenditure is estimated. In the second-stage regression, which estimates the level of revenue reliance on the general consumption tax, this fitted value is included as an independent variable.

Detailed information about all variables is included in the Appendix.[54] Variables are defined as follows. GCTAXP is a dependent variable in the second-stage regression and measures taxes on general consumption as a percentage of GDP.[55] SSEXPT measures total social security benefit expenditures as a percentage of GDP and is a dependent variable in the first stage of regression.

Four instrumental variables include two variables relating to the tax revenue structure. SSCONTOT measures total social security contributions as a percentage of GDP,[56] and CITAXP measures taxes on corporate income as a percentage of GDP. Two variables relate to globalization, that is, OPEN, which expresses openness of the economy by the total volume of trade as a percentage of GDP, and CONCEN, which expresses the extent of dependence on exports and thus vulnerability to external risk.

---

[53] The trend term, $t + t^2$, is based on the approximation of the shape of the plot variables to be analyzed from the year $1, \ldots, i, \ldots$ to n.

[54] The missing values are specified by linear interpolation.

[55] The quantitative analysis uses the revenue from a general consumption tax. The other kind of general consumption tax in the earlier period was replaced by the VAT in almost all the countries during the period of the analysis. Revenue from the general consumption tax is a good predictor for the later growth of revenue reliance on the VAT that was ultimately introduced.

[56] The data used for SSCONTOT are calculated from the total amount of social security receipts, which include taxes and receipts other than social security contributions. They are used to include New Zealand and Australia in the analysis. These two countries do not have social security contributions that correspond to those in other countries. If the value of the variable is 0 throughout the period, these two important cases are excluded from the analysis. An analysis using social security contributions as data and excluding these two countries does not produce a divergent result. Thus, the use of social security receipts here is a relevant approximation of the level of social security contributions and is justified as a means to include New Zealand and Australia in the analysis.

DEFICITP, government deficit or surplus as a percentage of GDP, is a political economic variable, and POP65P, total aged population (65 years and over) as a percentage of total population, is a socioeconomic variable.

There are four political variables. PARTY is a dummy variable for left party leadership in a party government. This variable is scaled from 1 to 5; the more leftist a government is, the closer the value is assigned to 5. ALTGOV expresses the frequency of alteration of governments by the number of governments formed for the previous three years. FEDDUM is a dummy variable for the federal system; EUDUM is a dummy variable for EU member countries.[57] UNEMPL (unemployment rate), GROWTH (economic growth rate), and CPI (consumer price index, all items) are macro-economic indicators that express the overall perfomance of each country's economy.

In the first-stage regression, the dependent variable, SSEXPT, is regressed by all independent variables, and the regression gives the fitted value that predicts the level of social security expenditure, SSEXPT-pred. In the second-stage regression, among the independent variables used in the first-stage regression, four independent variables – two relating to tax revenue structure (SSCONTOT and CITAXP) and two expressing the extent of globalization of economy (OPEN and CONCEN) – are dropped (instrumental variables). In the second stage, the dependent variable, GCTAXP, is regressed by the remaining independent variables and the fitted value obtained in the first stage (SSEXPT-pred).

Results and Interpretation   Tables 1.7 and 1.8 summarize the results of the first- and second-stage regressions, respectively, whereas Table 1.9 shows the simple correlation between the main variables, and Table 1.10 summarizes the descriptive statistics of all variables. In both Tables 1.7 and 1.8, the results of two random effect models with a trend term (Models 1 and 2) and of two random effect models with the year dummy variable (Models 3 and 4) are shown.[58] The values of R-squares in Models 1 and 2 are almost the same as those in Models 3 and 4 in both stages. This

---

[57]   The value of FEDDUM for each country is the same across the period of this analysis, that is, from 1965 to 1989. The value of EUDUM of several countries across the period has changed. But, the two dummy variables have a consistent relationship; for example, almost all the countries with federalism are non-EU member countries throughout the period.

[58]   Because several dummy variables were included, the random effect models are employed, but the trial results using the fixed effect models did not produce divergent results from the ones presented here.

Table 1.7. *Random effect estimations of social security expenditure as percentage of GDP (first-stage regressions)*

Independent Variables	Model 1 COEF.	Model 1 STD. ERR.	Model 2 COEF.	Model 2 STD. ERR.	Model 3 COEF.	Model 3 STD. ERR.	Model 4 COEF.	Model 4 STD. ERR.
SSCONTOT	0.943	0.012 ***	0.929	0.012 ***	0.943	0.012 ***	0.896	0.012 ***
CITAXP	0.124	0.040 ***	0.079	0.034 **	0.121	0.041 ***	0.031	0.037
CONCEN	-1.907	1.074 *			-2.583	1.117 **		
OPEN			0.008	0.004 **			0.007	0.003 **
DEFICITP	-0.015	0.012	-0.006	0.012	-0.001	0.013	0.000	0.014
POP65P	0.074	0.048	0.137	0.045 ***	0.046	0.050	0.208	0.037 ***
PARTY	0.035	0.022	0.037	0.022 *	0.035	0.022	0.055	0.025 **
ALTGOV	0.033	0.030	0.043	0.030	0.050	0.031	0.087	0.034 **
FEDDUM	0.070	0.476	0.251	0.326	0.046	0.572	0.336	0.189 *
UNEMPL	0.059	0.018 ***	0.058	0.018 ***	0.042	0.019 **	0.074	0.020 ***
GROWTH	-0.002	0.012	-0.007	0.012	-0.001	0.014	-0.015	0.016
CPI	0.004	0.004	0.004	0.004	0.001	0.004	-0.006	0.004
EUDUM	-0.099	0.157	0.059	0.151	-0.078	0.163	0.440	0.149 ***
TREND (T)	0.006	0.019	-0.009	0.020				
TREND2 (T2)	-0.001	0.001 **	-0.001	0.001 *				
Y65					0.329	0.477	-0.047	0.714
Y66					0.359	0.470	0.006	0.708
Y67					0.378	0.462	0.033	0.701
Y68					0.324	0.455	-0.020	0.695
Y69					0.293	0.451	-0.005	0.693
Y70					0.217	0.446	-0.117	0.691
Y71					0.217	0.438	-0.130	0.684
Y72					0.217	0.428	-0.110	0.675
Y73					0.008	0.421	-0.379	0.674
Y74					0.073	0.408	-0.353	0.667
Y75					0.464	0.387	0.077	0.641
Y76					0.474	0.368	0.136	0.626
Y77					0.471	0.356	0.132	0.616
Y78					0.531	0.344	0.191	0.605
Y79					0.249	0.333	-0.076	0.599
Y80					0.272	0.339	-0.098	0.604
Y81					0.337	0.324	-0.032	0.590
Y82					0.438	0.312	0.089	0.574
Y83					0.216	0.302	-0.115	0.561
Y84					0.389	0.298	0.058	0.561
Y85					0.353	0.293	0.041	0.559
Y86					0.379	0.290	0.124	0.555
Y87					0.121	0.286	-0.087	0.554
Y88					0.126	0.284	-0.027	0.555
Y89					-0.002	0.283	-0.183	0.557
Y90					-0.028	0.290	-0.162	0.562
Y91					-0.355	0.292	-0.482	0.557
Y92							-0.096	0.574
CONSTANT	-1.602	0.607 ***	-2.724	0.563 ***	-1.370	0.958	-2.809	0.963 ***
sigma_eta	0.924		0.593		1.125		0.272	
sigma_epsilon	0.571		0.570		0.572		0.570	
RHO	0.723		0.520		0.795		0.185	
R^2 (WITHIN)	0.984		0.983		0.983		0.983	
R^2(BETWEEN)	0.953		0.974		0.955		0.963	
R^2(OVERALL)	0.966		0.978		0.966		0.972	

Notes: *** 1% significant level; ** 5% significant level; * 10% significant level (two-tailed). Number of observations = 482 (Model 1, Model 3), = 484 (Model 2, Model 4). Number of categories (countries) = 18.

Table 1.8. *Random effect estimations of general consumption tax revenue as percentage of GDP (second-stage regressions)*

Independent Variables	Model 1 COEF.	STD. ERR.	Model 2 COEF.	STD. ERR.	Model 3 COEF.	STD. ERR.	Model 4 COEF.	STD. ERR.
SS EXPT-PRED	0.067	0.016 ***	0.066	0.015 ***	0.076	0.016 ***	0.078	0.016 ***
DEFICITP	0.079	0.014 ***	0.078	0.014 ***	0.051	0.015 ***	0.052	0.015 ***
POP65P	0.029	0.061	0.029	0.061	0.059	0.061	0.048	0.061
PARTY	-0.056	0.026 **	-0.057	0.026 **	-0.054	0.027 **	-0.056	0.027 **
ALTGOV	0.036	0.036	0.036	0.036	0.033	0.037	0.031	0.037
FEDDUM	-1.329	1.137	-1.336	1.128	-1.252	1.250	-1.270	1.240
UNEMPL	0.008	0.022	0.009	0.022	0.015	0.024	0.011	0.023
GROWTH	0.026	0.015 *	0.026	0.015 *	0.021	0.016	0.022	0.016
CPI	0.036	0.005 ***	0.036	0.005 ***	0.043	0.005 ***	0.044	0.005 ***
EUDUM	1.823	0.192 ***	1.816	0.191 ***	1.913	0.197 ***	1.887	0.196 ***
TREND (T)	-0.013	0.024	-0.012	0.023				
TREND2 (T2)	-0.002	0.001 ***	-0.002	0.001 ***				
Y65					2.234	0.577 ***	2.800	0.794 ***
Y66					2.279	0.567 ***	2.844	0.785 ***
Y67					2.350	0.558 ***	2.917	0.775 ***
Y68					2.443	0.549 ***	3.010	0.767 ***
Y69					2.504	0.544 ***	3.068	0.762 ***
Y70					2.639	0.537 ***	3.204	0.758 ***
Y71					2.770	0.527 ***	3.336	0.748 ***
Y72					2.627	0.515 ***	3.194	0.736 ***
Y73					2.191	0.507 ***	2.761	0.731 ***
Y74					2.036	0.491 ***	2.607	0.718 ***
Y75					1.717	0.465 ***	2.292	0.689 ***
Y76					1.512	0.442 ***	2.083	0.669 ***
Y77					1.508	0.427 ***	2.078	0.656 ***
Y78					1.538	0.412 ***	2.109	0.644 ***
Y79					1.322	0.400 ***	1.890	0.636 ***
Y80					1.456	0.407 ***	2.028	0.638 ***
Y81					1.272	0.389 ***	1.845	0.622 ***
Y82					1.032	0.374 ***	1.607	0.606 ***
Y83					0.914	0.362 **	1.488	0.593 **
Y84					0.890	0.357 **	1.460	0.591 **
Y85					0.753	0.351 **	1.320	0.586 **
Y86					0.707	0.346 **	1.272	0.583 **
Y87					0.695	0.343 **	1.259	0.582 **
Y88					0.574	0.341 *	1.134	0.582 *
Y89					0.403	0.340	0.961	0.582 *
Y90					0.422	0.348	0.978	0.588 *
Y91					0.284	0.350	0.843	0.582
Y92							0.564	0.596
CONSTANT	2.070	0.937 **	2.077	0.928 **	-1.114	1.306	-1.583	1.439
sigma_eta	2.263		2.245		2.499		2.479	
sigma_epsilon	0.698		0.698		0.689		0.689	
RHO	0.913		0.912		0.929		0.928	
R^2 (WITHIN)	0.671		0.672		0.642		0.643	
R^2 (BETWEEN)	0.329		0.336		0.321		0.328	
R^2 (OVERALL)	0.387		0.392		0.374		0.380	

Notes: *** 1% significant level; ** 5% significant level; * 10% significant level (two-tailed). Number of observations = 482 (Model 1, Model 3), = 484 (Model 2, Model 4). Number of categories (countries) = 18.

Table 1.9. *Simple correlation between main variables*

Correlation matrix

	GCTAXP	SS EXPT	SSCONTOT
GCTAXP	1.000		
SS EXPT	0.728	1.000	
SSCONTOT	0.675	0.980	1.000

Variance-covariance matrix

	GCTAXP	SS EXPT	SSCONTOT
GCTAXP	7.559		
SS EXPT	13.870	48.078	
SSCONTOT	13.272	48.582	51.168

Note: Number of observations = 540.

Table 1.10. *Descriptive statistics*

	Mean	Std. Dev.		
		Overall	Between	Within
Endogenous variables				
GCTAXP	5.428	2.749	2.546	1.193
SS EXPT	18.500	6.934	5.274	4.665
Instrumental variables				
SSCONTOT	19.779	7.153	5.484	4.766
CITAXP	2.608	1.207	0.897	0.833
CONCEN	0.143	0.068	0.061	0.034
OPEN	58.911	27.939	27.196	8.987
Exogenous variables				
DEFICITP	-3.136	3.600	2.356	2.777
POP65P	12.439	2.425	2.093	1.316
PARTY	2.359	1.505	0.811	1.281
ALTGOV	2.709	1.111	0.686	0.888
FEDDUM	0.333	0.472	0.485	0.000
UNEMPL	5.174	3.963	2.595	3.055
GROWTH	3.020	2.608	0.789	2.492
CPI	64.717	30.812	8.386	29.712
EUDUM	0.400	0.490	0.469	0.181

means that Models 3 and 4 have the same explanatory power as Models 1 and 2, which include more independent variables.

Of the two instrumental variables that measure the extent of globalization, the coefficients of CONCEN are statistically significant with negative signs, and those of OPEN have statistically significant coefficients but with positive signs (Table 1.7). These results seem to confirm that the extent of a country's openness should be distinguished from the volatility of that country's trade (Rodrik 1997, 57–60). The way in which globalization affects a country varies depending on the aspect of globalization that influences the country. The relationship between globalization and welfare will not be explored in detail here, but a complicated and subtle relationship is implied, and this disputes a simple generalization such that globalization uniformly would work against the welfare state in the same way as in the existing literature.

The two instrumental variables expressing tax revenue structure, SSCONTOT, have statistically significant coefficients and positive signs. From Models 1 through 3, the coefficients of CITAXP are statistically significant with positive signs. This means that, as Garrett (1999) argues, the corporate tax burden increases as public expenditures such as social security expenditure increase, but it also refutes a simplified picture that fear of capital flight makes a government shy away from taxing corporations during globalization.

In the second-stage regression (Table 1.8), the SSEXPT-pred variable obtained from the first stage of regression has statistically significant and positive coefficients in all models. All coefficients are significant at the 1 percent level. Thus the results indicate a very strong association between the level of social security expenditure and the extent to which the state relies on general consumption tax. Among the other independent variables, DEFICITP, PARTY, GROWTH (only in Models 1 and 2), CPI, and EUDUM have statistically significant coefficients. The GROWTH and CPI coefficients have positive signs. These results show that the reliance on a general consumption tax increases as the society becomes more affluent and the inflation rate increases, respectively. The DEFICITP coefficients with positive signs also reflect more political interaction between the affluence of the society and the tax revenue structure. An increasing deficit requires a government to have a stable and strong revenue machine such as a general consumption tax. POP65P and UNEMPL coefficients are not statistically significant, and thus their relationship with a revenue reliance shift from an income tax to a general consumption tax has not been confirmed. EUDUM coefficients have positive signs and are statistically significant at the 1 percent level. Thus, the mandatory adoption of the VAT among member countries had a significant influence on their tax revenue structures. This result also confirms that the strong association between

GCTAXP and SSEXPT-pred is not a result of the mandated adoption of the VAT among EU member countries, most of which are mature welfare states.

The political variable, PARTY, has a statistically significant and negative coefficient sign in each model. Because a more leftist government was assigned a larger value (i.e., closer to 5), the results indicate that a leftist government is likely to be less dependent on a general consumption tax to raise revenue. Alternatively, the following simple causal link does not hold: a leftist government spends more for social security, and the revenue needs for social security make the leftist government more reliant on a general consumption tax. This result at least leaves the possibility that a general consumption tax may be an effective revenue source for a government to finance an increasing social security expenditure *independently of its partisan composition.*[59]

Conclusion   The results of the quantitative analysis here are consistent with several important points in the argument. First, globalization influences the level of social security expenditure, but that influence is complicated as the recent literature argues. The result hinges on what one means by "globalization," and it is, at least, necessary to distinguish the extent of openness and volatility to external change (risk) of each country's economy. In addition, the relationship between the extent of globalization and the level of social security expenditure is neither simple nor direct. Although the relationship between globalization and the welfare state is not the focus of the analysis here, the results reject a simple causal relationship between economic globalization and domestic political institutions.

Second, the analysis confirms a strong association between a higher social security expenditure and a greater revenue reliance on a general consumption tax. The revenue from social security contributions and general consumption taxes has been important to maintain a level of tax revenue across the OECD countries for the last decades. A higher revenue reliance on regressive taxes is associated with a high level of social security expenditure controlling for the effect of globalization. This straightforward relationship

---

[59] Because left partisanship and high social security expenditures coexist in many EU member countries, the negative coefficient of PARTY at the 5 percent significant level may not fully confirm that the leftist government is less dependent on a general consumption tax to raise revenue.

contrasts sharply with the complicated relationship between globalization and the welfare state.

Third and most important, the association between social security expenditure and a revenue reliance on regressive taxation is statistically significant even if controlling for other political and economic factors. The tax revenue structure is a predictor of high social security spending that is independent of government partisanship. For example, countries with a high level of spending are more likely to have a higher revenue reliance on regressive taxes. But, a leftist government that has higher spending is not necessarily reliant upon regressive taxes. This complicated relationship will be explained in more detail in the case studies. The quantitative analysis at least concludes that domestic political institutions are far from an exclusive determinant for a tax revenue structure. This leaves the possibility that a contingent factor, such as the timing of policy diffusions, is a better predictor of a tax revenue structure.

Conclusion

The quantitative analysis confirms only the statistically significant association of specific variables. How the analysis is modeled here might lead to an interpretation that a country that has a large public sector and social security expenditure tends to extract more revenue from all kinds of taxes including the general consumption tax.[60] The case studies of several OECD countries in the following chapters will dispute this and explain the complicated causal relationship. Increasing regressive tax revenue does not necessarily finance social security expenditures directly, but a revenue shift to regressive taxes makes it politically easier to maintain a large public sector. Among existing welfare states, a large public sector leads to more income equality through redistribution. More important, a large government funding capacity has cultivated a political condition to resist the welfare backlash since the 1980s. The argument explicates a *political*, rather than *financial*, relationship between a revenue reliance on regressive taxes and the size of the welfare state.

---

[60] For example, consider standardization (i.e., by dividing by GDP) of the three variables – social security expenditure, social security contributions, and a general consumption tax revenue. This is appropriate considering that all OECD countries have incurred increased tax burdens over the last two or three decades and sought tax measures to finance them; however, it also supports the obvious result described previously. A simple correlation matrix of these major variables (Table 1.9) shows a high correlation between them, and this possibility cannot be rejected.

The cases will demonstrate that the timing of the introduction of a regressive revenue machine is a critical indicator for the subsequent maintenance of the welfare state, especially the resistance to welfare retrenchment. Further augmentation of progressivity in a tax system is no longer regarded as an imperative; for example, a new flat-rate social security tax other than social security contributions has recently begun to be used (i.e., in France).

Chapter 2 explains the European cases of Sweden, the United Kingdom, and France, focusing on their differences. Chapter 3 introduces two pairs of comparisons in North America and Oceania. In Chapter 4, the Japanese case is introduced, and the mechanism of policy diffusion is further explored, examining the cases of newly developing countries. Chapter 5 summarizes the findings of Chapters 2 through 4.

2

European Variation

SWEDEN, THE UNITED
KINGDOM, AND FRANCE

This chapter will present the cases of three western European countries to illuminate the cross-national variation in tax and welfare policies. Following a summary of the limited impact of the common market integration and the persistent cross-national variation, each country's case will demonstrate that the variation resulted from the distinct paths of the formation of state funding capacity and the timing of the institutionalization of regressive taxes.

Variation in Welfare and Taxation

The Limited Impact of Common Market Integration

Europe is not unified. Policy coordination always faces obstacles from domestic political constraints from common market member countries. For example, coordinating the level of entitlements and benefit provisions in each country was far more than a technical problem that involved harmonization of the existing programs across borders. Among new or recent common market member countries outside Western Europe, as the adoption of the Social Charter[1] in 1989 symbolizes, integration caused an increase in the level of welfare provision. For the Western European countries, however, the problem was the size of the welfare state, which had already become enormous. As monetary integration became more of a reality, the fiscal policy requirement became more explicitly politicized: the Western European countries were required to finance social security spending under the Maastricht limit on budget deficits. In this regard,

[1] This charter was adopted at that time by all member countries except the United Kingdom.

integration was likely to tie government hands to manage the public sector and finance the welfare state so as to repress both budget deficits and public spending; cross-national variation persists in welfare provision among Western European countries.

Coordinating a tax system in an integrated market is as difficult as, but more explicit than, coordinating a welfare policy. In the common market of the EU, tax competition over cross-border corporate activities and financial flows (such as interests, savings, and dividends) is more salient than universally observed during economic globalization. Without coordination, the same corporate profits may be redundantly taxed in different member countries, that is, where a company is incorporated, where profits occur in production or sales, and where shareholders of the company live and earn dividends. Conversely, cross-border corporate activities may result in capital flight from high- to low-tax countries or in tax evasion unless there are effective means for governments to comprehend them.

The harmonization of consumption taxes is also necessary to avoid cross-border shopping, leading to damages to domestic consumption and, ultimately, revenue loss. This coordination is technically easier than direct taxes on business due to the integration of other indirect consumption taxes into the VAT. When the Treaty of Rome advocated harmonization (Article 99) in 1957, only France incompletely implemented the VAT, which was to become the model among the then EEC member countries. In the mid-1990s, the adoption of the VAT was taken for granted among the fifteen EU member countries. To facilitate the introduction, in 1970, when the First Council Directive set the date for the introduction of the VAT, five out of seven member countries at that time introduced it. In 1987, the European Commission required the members to have only two rates, a standard rate between 14 and 20 percent and a reduced rate between 4 and 9 percent. The Council Directives in December 1991 and October 1992 decided on a standard rate of no less than 15 percent and a minimum rate of no less than 5 percent.[2] The narrow band of VAT rates, however, does not necessarily constrain the nation's revenue-raising capacity[3] nor facilitate the rates of

---

[2] In some cases, rates lower than 5 percent including zero rates are allowed.

[3] Constraining the VAT rate is often expected to lead to the declining financial capacity of the state. An example of this view is Leibfried and Pierson (1995, 72): "[i]n theory, governments that find that their VAT revenues have been lowered will be free to increase other taxes, but this may be no simple task. Because indirect taxes are politically easier to sustain than direct levies, the new rules may create growing constraints on member-state budgets, with clear implications from national social policies."

the countries on a single harmonized rate. Rather, "[t]he choice of this rate would naturally be contentious; the rates currently levied by member states presumably reflect social and political preferences" (Smith 1997, 17). In some countries, the VAT is not politically feasible compared with a direct levy, and the mandatory imposition of the VAT may raise more revenue by increasing the rates to the lower limit of the band and abolishing tax exemptions for coordination. In contrast, the countries that raise large revenues from the VAT have already reached their own tolerable upper tax rate limit that is politically and economically sustainable (as explained in the cases of Sweden and France). If the link between the tax and the welfare state is not simplified by tax coordination in Europe, how are they related and how do they interact?

The Politics Behind Cross-National Variation in Taxation and Welfare

During the last three decades, the differences in tax revenue structures among the Western European countries have become apparent, and the cases here are no exceptions. Sweden raises its large revenue from taxes on income and profits, goods, and services (including the VAT), and employers' social security contributions. France relies heavily on taxes on goods and services (including the VAT) and both employers' and employees' social security contributions. The United Kingdom is a hybrid case and raises revenue from personal and, to a lesser extent, corporate income taxes with a relatively high share from property taxes, a smaller share from social security contributions, and an increasing reliance on taxes on goods and services. Sweden has consistently maintained the highest tax level. Although the United Kingdom moved from above to below the average among the eighteen OECD countries, for the last decades, France has maintained a level that is nearly as high as the standard of the northern European countries (Figure 1.2). This level in France is comparable to that in Belgium and the Netherlands, but, considering that these two countries have smaller economies and are prone to the influence of the neighboring Scandinavian countries, France's high tax level stands out.

The VAT as a major regressive tax not only characterizes the tax revenue structure but also appears to correlate with the level of total taxation. Although the mandatory adoption of the VAT has not led to a convergence of different partisan dynamics from one country to another, there is no simple generalization to explain the cross-national variation. For example,

Sweden and France have different political reasons for extensive use of the VAT. The Swedish case is a clear example of social democratic confidence in its revenue-producing power: its regressivity, which the left does not like, is offset by redistribution through the social security system. The French statist tradition prevented the revenue-producing power of the VAT from becoming the locus of partisan conflict under the conservative hegemony of the Gaullists. Whereas the conservatives supported its neutrality on market allocations and the simplicity of its tax system, the left often advocated the promotion of progressivity in income taxation, but the regressivity of the VAT had not been politicized until its rate reached a very high level – close to 20 percent.

In the United Kingdom, the VAT was introduced because of the country's entry into the EEC and increased its revenue incidentally without an explicit political decision. The introduction of the VAT in 1973 was supported by the Conservative Party, which put a priority on entry into the EEC. Since then, the revenue from the VAT has financed an income tax cut and enhanced revenue, but the VAT revenue remains about half of the entire revenue from taxes on goods and services.

The left-right cleavage does not fully explain the tax revenue structure nor the development of the welfare state. Baldwin (1990) challenges the social interpretation of the welfare state that focuses on labor interest under social democratic rule. He argues that the tax-financed, flat-rate, egalitarian benefits like those in Sweden and the United Kingdom developed *after the war as a result of the strong influence of middle-class interests*. Conversely, the weakness of the left party does not explain why the countries on the Continent failed to establish universal and egalitarian entitlements. Sweden had established the foundation of a universal welfare state in the late nineteenth century without a strong labor movement or left party. During the postwar period, Sweden adopted a tax-financed, flat-rate, egalitarian approach and then introduced superannuation provided to salaried workers in general. These measures were consistent with middle-class interests. In contrast, the United Kingdom fell short of the Scandinavian standard of high welfare: both the Labourites and the Conservatives appeared to take "redistribution" more seriously in the sense that the means-tested measures adopted during the postwar period were restricted to the poorest wage earners. France had once been ahead of Sweden and the United Kingdom in developing social security, exemplified by a national pension fund and accident insurance in the mid-nineteenth century. But, since then, the strong French state withdrew from financing social security: the government never added a substantial amount of general tax revenue or subsidies to finance the social security fund paid (as social security contributions) and managed by social partners, that is, employers and employees. It was not until the 1970s that France fully adopted some universal measures during a period of conservative hegemony supported by middle-class interests and opposition from the left.

Baldwin's argument should not be stretched to deny entirely the influence of the left party and labor interests. But the need to compromise with middle-class interests is worth serious attention. Obviously, the easiest way for the government to compromise with the middle-income earners who were a majority social group was to provide enough benefits to make them support the proposed burdens for welfare provision.[4] The logic behind this political support will be explored in detail in Chapter 5. But the implication from the European cases parallels the finding in the existing comparative analysis that the advantage of universalism exceeds targeting in the promotion of income equality in a mature welfare state (see Chapter 1). The universal entitlement of benefits is supposed to provide benefits to all of those covered regardless of their economic prowess and results in a large expenditure. The need to respond to middle-class interests thus explains the unexpected coexistence of larger social security expenditures and larger revenue reliance on regressive taxes among the Western European countries. In Sweden, the middle-income group, which neither pays nor gets the most, provides critical support for redistribution when opposition and support tend to divide between high-income groups that get less than they pay and low-income groups that get more than they pay (Rothstein 1998, 153). Representation of middle-class interests cultivates the conditions under which the combination of proportional taxation and a universal welfare provision is supported by society.

If a government has long-term prospects for expanding public expenditures, it needs to secure a financial source for doing so. For the last two decades, the governments of industrial democracies have suffered chronic deficits, and financial management has become an even more critical issue. This is why the timing of the introduction of a strong revenue machine is critical in determining the state's revenue-raising capacity. Sweden is a typical

---

[4] Although it is hard to define the middle class as a relevant concept in different societies, here they are the middle-income earners who constitute a majority if the population is distributed normally in terms of income level. Thus, their support for a universal welfare state depends on the risks and uncertainty they face (Baldwin 1990, 14–18).

case of early introduction of the VAT (i.e., well before the experience of chronic budget deficits).

Sweden: A Mature Welfare State with Regressive Taxation

The Politics of a Mature Welfare State: Redistribution and Taxation

High Taxation and the Welfare State: An Institutional Perspective
Sweden is the epitome of a big welfare state. The corporatist arrangement under Social Democratic dominance long supported wage bargaining and consensus making in social and economic policies between state, business, and labor. Tax policy was not an exception to this.[5] The tax policy characteristics, at least until the 1980s, correspond to the corporatist arrangement, that is, the accommodation of both business and labor interests. The business interests are represented in a lower corporate tax: the tax rate is relatively high, but the tax base is narrowed by special measures and exemptions that serve to increase the incentives for firms to invest and expand further.[6] The steeply progressive individual income tax structure embodies the labor demand for a direct transfer from the rich to the poor together with redistribution through the social security system. That is, "[t]he high levels of taxation in Sweden mirror a highly developed welfare state with substantial public redistributions in cash and in kind" (Hansson and Stuart 1990, 130).

The tax revenue structure in Sweden relies heavily on progressive income taxation on the one hand and regressive taxes including the VAT and social security contributions on the other. The foundation for progressive income taxation was the result of radical tax reforms in 1947 and 1948, which the Social Democrats decided to implement under the strong leftward pressure exerted by the overt electoral popularity of the Communists. In the 1950s and 1960s, when the Social Democratic rule was stable and the Swedish corporatist decision making was at its peak, notable changes occurred in the field of indirect taxation. The national sales tax that had been abolished in 1948 was reintroduced in 1959 and then converted into the VAT in 1969.

---

[5] A variety of literature explores the Swedish model with different focuses on party politics and specific economic policies. For example, see Shonfield (1965); Esping-Andersen (1985); Przeworski (1985); Pontusson (1992); Rothstein (1998).

[6] This is pointed out by political scientists such as Steinmo (1988) and Pontusson (1992, 69–70). A tax specialist finds this system problematic in terms of neutrality (Ljungh 1988, 203–4).

The constitutional reform in the late 1960s abolished the Upper Chamber of the Riksdag, where the Swedish Social Democratic Party (hereafter SAP) had had a majority, and ushered in the SAP's loss of power in 1976 for the first time in forty-four years.[7] Because the Social Democrats had always held a majority in the abolished upper house but rarely in the lower house, their rule was specifically weakened. In addition, all the parties, including the previously intact SAP, became more sensitive to the interests of unorganized constituencies, whereas the strong interest organizations of labor and business continued to be powerful.[8] The obvious outcome was increased spending to curry the favor of both organized interest and unorganized constituencies. In this regard, Sweden was destined to be a high-tax country in the 1970s and 1980s, although its tax level (as a percentage of GDP) in the mid-1950s was almost the same as the OECD average (Norman and McLure 1997, 122).

This heavy tax is closely related to Sweden's reliance on regressive taxation, which was often overshadowed by its comprehensive income tax system. Figure 2.1 shows that the percentage share to the GDP of taxes on goods and services has increased and then maintained in the same way as the one of taxes on income and profits while the share of social security contributions has increased significantly especially since the 1980s. This peculiar tax revenue structure of the most advanced welfare state had been in place before the rapid expansion of the public sector became apparent. To explore this, first, the process of the reintroduction of the sales tax and its conversion to the VAT will be reviewed.

Reintroduction of the Sales Tax and Conversion to the VAT: A Foundation for High Taxes and the Welfare State   The major concern about the tax policy among industrial democracies in the 1950s and 1960s was its impact on economic growth to facilitate postwar recovery and industrialization. In the report of a tax conference held in the Brookings Institution in 1963, the introductory chapter cited the divergent average rate of growth in real gross national product (GNP) from the highest (9.5 percent in Japan) to the lowest (3.3 percent in the United States) (Keith 1966, 1). Sweden was placed between the rapidly growing Japan, Germany, and Italy and the

---

[7] Immergut (2000) explains the Social Democrats' apparently irrational support of the constitutional change by citing the necessity to cope with the pressure from the communists and to revise their coalition strategy.

[8] Here I concur with Steinmo (1993, 131) that the constitutional reform had a greater impact on tax and spending policies than the alterations in party government.

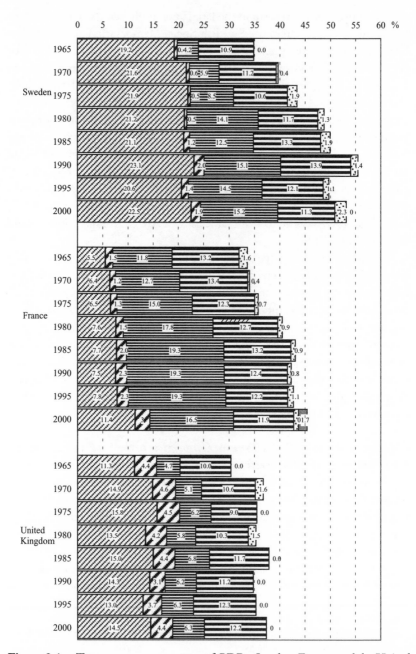

Figure 2.1. Tax revenue as percentage of GDP – Sweden, France, and the United Kingdom 1965–2000. *Source:* OECD 1997b.

slower growing United Kingdom, Canada, and United States. Its high tax burden was not considered problematic.[9] But, policy makers in Sweden recognized the latent problem of heavy taxation, and the reintroduction of the sales tax in 1959 was a response to the increasing revenue need.

In 1947, radical tax reform was enacted under Finance Minister Ernst Wigforss. This reform enhanced the progressivity of the income tax system; that is, it imposed a heavier tax on those in higher income tax brackets and added a second death tax and estate tax to the existing tax on inheritance. More important, the Social Democratic government repealed the uniform 5 percent rate of the sales tax that had been used for wartime fiscal management. At the end of the 1950s, Norr, Duffy, and Sterner (1959, 141) wrote, "Sweden is the only country in western Europe to have introduced a general sales tax in the past decades and then to have abandoned it." The abolition contributed to a sharp drop in revenue from indirect taxes in the 1950s. Indirect taxes – sales and excise taxes, customs and duties, and so on – which had accounted for about 70 percent of the tax revenue at the national level prior to World War I, had fallen to about 40 percent in 1954. That was the lowest ratio in Western Europe (Norr et al. 1959, 141).

The reintroduction of the sales tax in 1959 in Sweden was totally unexpected. At first, no political parties supported the reintroduction of the sales tax. The Social Democratic government had repealed it because of its regressivity; thus, the left, including the Social Democrats and the Communists, obviously opposed its reintroduction. The right opposed it for quite a different reason: they were concerned that the revenue expected from it would increase public spending instead of reducing the income tax. Despite the opposition from the politicians, the experts continued to support the reintroduction of the sales tax. Even within the Swedish Confederation of Unions (LO), economists had proposed its reintroduction immediately after its abolition in 1948.[10] Experts and economists persuaded the Social Democratic policy makers, including Finance Minister Gunnar Sträng, to consider shifting revenue reliance to an indirect tax as a politically feasible

---

[9] Scholars emphasized the variety of favorable measures for economic growth such as the free depreciation of machinery and equipment in corporate taxation (Mutén and Faxén 1966). Mutén, one of the authors of the chapter on Sweden in that volume, wrote twenty-five years later, "[t]he system that I and other Swedish experts were bragging about [in the 1960s] is now on the verge of being scrapped" (Mutén 1988, 216).

[10] For example, Gösta Rehn supported it because the indirect tax on consumption would control inflation more effectively and result in maintaining a substantially high level of wages, which was in the interest of workers (Rehn 1952, 50–1).

choice that would not alienate middle-class voters and capitalists by heavier taxes on income.[11]

Some public financial economists regarded the reintroduction of the sales tax as a tradeoff between direct taxation (i.e., an income tax) and indirect taxation (i.e., a general consumption tax) and paid special attention to its effect on income distribution, incentives, and stabilization policy.[12] However, the most important impact was on the revenue need. The reintroduction of the sales tax served to reduce government borrowing that had had a crowding-out effect on investments in industrial and housing sectors in the 1950s (Nabseth 1966, 390). The reintroduced sales tax not only initiated a shift from direct to indirect taxation but also contributed to the expansion of the public sector (Elvander 1972). It ultimately reflected the government's preference for raising more revenue from a general consumption tax rather than the expansion of either the income tax or the existing excise tax.[13] The sales tax was considered a means to raise more revenue without distortion, although, in retrospect, the expectation about the budgetary situation of the government at that time was still overtly optimistic.

In the campaign of the parliamentary election in September 1960, the sales tax reintroduced at the beginning of that year had become politicized along with the social security issue. Although the Social Democratic government defended the sales tax to balance the budget and finance social welfare expenditures, the Conservative Party proposed to cut the social welfare expenditures to abolish the sales tax. In an opinion survey on this cleavage, although voters for other parties (i.e., conservative, liberal, and center parties) did not change or decrease their support, the SAP voters increased support for the sales tax from 39 percent to 66 percent after the election campaign (Särlvik 1967, 167, 178–9). The Social Democratic government had campaigned for support for the sales tax to finance social security programs, and the voters, especially those with strong partisan and welfare orientation, responded to the party appeal. More important, those who were exposed to the election campaign were more likely to have a favorable opinion about the sales tax regardless of the strength of their partisanship in terms of party identification and welfare policy orientation.

---

[11] For example, see Steinmo (1993, 127). In my interview with tax specialists in Sweden (September 1997), they concurred with the influence of tax experts at that time.

[12] For example, see Hansen (1958, 260–78).

[13] For example, see Norr (1961, 175).

The idea to finance a welfare state with a regressive consumption tax was first put forth by experts, then adopted by the Social Democratic policy makers, and finally diffused among voters.

The sales tax, which became effective at 4 percent in January 1960 with virtually no exemptions (not even foods or capital goods), raised revenue rapidly from 9.1 percent of the national-level total revenue for the first year to 20.5 percent in 1967–8 when the rate went up to 10 percent.[14] After this revenue had continued to skyrocket for eight years, it was obvious that the conversion to the VAT in 1969 would lead to a much larger revenue yield than was expected to partially replace that gained from an income tax.

Labor had been reluctant about the reintroduction of the sales tax but became a supporter of the VAT, which was a more powerful revenue machine. In 1969, for example, a joint committee of the SAP and LO headed by Alva Myrdal recommended that the governing SAP increase the indirect tax in the future and couple it with a lighter burden in the middle-income tax rate brackets.[15] Swedish society became the "affluent society," which Galbraith believed could afford to pay its increasing social welfare expenditures with the additional revenue from the wider use of a tax on increasing consumption.[16] The marginal tax rates on earned income up to about 100,000 Kronor (about $20,000) in 1968 were the world's highest. With the increasing revenue need, an almost fifty-year-old tradition of heavy reliance on direct (income) taxation had shifted to taxes on consumption.

The experts clearly recognized the problem of the regressivity of the VAT, whose effect would be larger as reliance on its revenue-generating ability increased, but from the beginning they believed strongly that it could be solved *outside* the VAT system.

The burden of indirect taxes on lower-income recipients can be made up in part by adjustments in the income tax, and in still larger part through the social security

---

[14] Ministry of Finance (in Sweden), *The Swedish Budget 1969–70*, 41.

[15] Myrdal et al. (1969, 37, 39).

[16] This situation is vividly illustrated as follows: "Given the level of direct taxation, Sweden's powerful labor and cooperative movements came to the same conclusion as government, business and academic opinion – if rising public expenditures require significant amounts of additional tax revenue (and they do), an increase in income tax rates was not the appropriate way to raise that additional revenue. . . . The only new source available was an indirect tax of broad application" (Norr and Hornhammar 1970, 385). Norr and Hornhammar (1970, 379) cite Galbraith (1958, 1st ed., 315; 1969, 2nd ed., revised, 271–84).

and welfare systems. . . . *To the Swedes, the problem of the lower-income groups is more a problem of social and welfare policy than of tax policy.* (Norr and Hornhammar 1970, 386–87, italics added)[17]

The idea to raise revenue from regressive taxation and then redistribute it extensively has since enjoyed strong support among the Swedish tax experts (Åberg 1989; Korpi and Palme 1998).[18] The subsequent development of the VAT in Sweden demonstrates how this idea dominated the tax change. The VAT was introduced in 1969 at 10 percent, which was close to the minimum rate applied or contemplated in other European countries. Also, in 1970, 4.1 percent of the VAT revenue to the GDP was below the OECD Europe average of 4.9 percent. But, in 1990, after twenty years, the VAT standard rate became 25 percent and the proportion of its revenue to the GDP rose to 8.3 percent – well above the average of OECD Europe of 7.3 percent.

Universal Welfare, Middle-Class Interests, and Taxation Sweden's adoption of the VAT in 1969, considering that it had not yet participated in the EC, would have been impossible without the reintroduction of the sales tax a decade before. The reintroduction of the sales tax and the policy orientation to raise more revenue from a general consumption tax had occurred long before the EC initiative to introduce the VAT. In this respect, the influence of the EC should not be exaggerated. The conversion of the sales tax to the VAT accompanies another important tax policy change in the late 1960s – an employers' payroll tax on all wage outlays of 1 percent. This was implemented to make up for the loss of the corporate tax

---

[17] An idea similar to the one cited here by Norr and Hornhammar can be found in *Nytt Skattesystem*, Statens Offentliga Utredningar (Swedish government publications, hereafter SOU) (1964, 25, 82–3).

[18] Several expert commissions led policy debates from the time of the proposal to reintroduce the sales tax to its conversion to the VAT. In 1951, an expert committee indicated the difficulty of raising more revenue from direct taxes and suggested that new social circumstances might allow the adoption of a tax on general consumption (*Den Statliga Direkta Beskattningen*, SOU 1951, 15). In 1957, the expert committee investigated the amounts that alternative forms of single-stage consumption taxes at retail and wholesale stages would raise (*Den Statliga Indirekta Beskattningen*, SOU 1957, 13). In 1964, the committee recommended the introduction of the multistage VAT instead of a single-stage (retail) sales tax (*Nytt Skattesystem*, SOU 1964, 25). In 1967, the committee studied the form of the VAT to be introduced (Betänkande angående indirekta skatter och socialförsäkringsavgifter (del. I: Mervärdeskatt), Stencil Fi 1967, 10).

revenue from the introduction of the VAT.[19] Since then, contemporary Swedish taxation has been characterized by a large revenue reliance on employers' social security contributions (i.e., payroll taxes earmarked for social security expenditures).[20] In other words, the reliance on regressive taxation (i.e., the VAT and social security contributions) in the contemporary Swedish tax system had its origin in the tax reform of the late 1960s.

The governing Social Democrats had been forced to cope with middle-class interests until the 1970s by extending welfare benefits and coverage to emerging groups of the middle class (Svensson 1994). Universal coverage included farmers in the Pension Reforms in 1913 and led to the introduction of earnings-related benefits – the Supplementary Pension Reform in the 1950s – which symbolized the "middle-class welfare state." Such universal and earnings-related benefits required large expeditures, and the state needed to furnish strong revenue production power. In this respect, both tax and welfare reform orientations during the earlier period were connected to the Social Democratic governing strategy.

Chronic Deficits and Tax Policy Changes Since the 1980s

The reign of the bourgeois coalition of the Liberal Party (*Folkpartiet*), Center Party (*Centerpartiet*), and Conservative Party (*Moderata Samlingspartiet*) from 1976 to 1982 did not bring many policy changes. Rather it continued the high level of spending inherited from the Social Democrats more inefficiently. The result was a large budget deficit – 9.5 percent of the GDP in 1982 when the SAP came back into office. The high marginal tax rate had been recognized for a decade. A public weary of high income taxes caused both the parties in office and in opposition to agree to cut the high marginal tax rates at the beginning of the 1980s ("wonderful night"). This ushered in tax reform in 1982. According to Hansson and Stuart (1990, 132), "the total taxation of marginal earned income averaged across the population, including marginal personal income, payroll, and indirect taxes and the tax-like effect of income-indexed transfers,

[19] While the consumption of capital goods was taxed in the single-stage retail sales tax system, capital goods were tax exempted in the VAT system. For more details about this change and problems related to it, see Norr and Hornhammar (1970, 392, 417).

[20] In the OECD classification, a tax levied as a proportion of payroll or the number of employees is a payroll tax, but the taxes on payroll, if earmarked for social security expenditures, are classified as social security contributions. This study follows the OECD classifications; payroll taxes earmarked for social security expenditures are called social security contributions although they are called payroll taxes in some countries.

reached a peak of 73.2 percent in 1982." The reform also rectified the measures that favored deficit-financed consumption and investment. The tax reform decided in 1982 fell far short of solving the problems associated with high taxation, bracket creep, lower working incentives, inefficient allocation of resources to tax-favored economic activities, inflation, and so on. The Social Democrats continued to make an effort to reduce the budget deficit to 5.7 percent in 1985. The economy, fortunately, recovered quickly. In the late 1980s, the budget deficit was eliminated by increasing revenue during a period of booming economy. Since the mid-1980s, however, there has been a need for structural reform of public finance. This was the background that led to major tax reform in the early 1990s.

The major achievements of the 1991 tax reform (decided in 1990) under the ruling Social Democrats with the cooperation of the Liberals was a radical cut in marginal tax rates that, at the same time, simplified the tax schedule and broadened the tax base. The progressive income tax structure was slashed to one rate, 20 percent, whose threshold income would be above that of a majority of Swedes. The maximum tax rate, combined with the 31 percent average local tax rate, increased to 51 percent,[21] which was much lower than the maximum rate of about 80 percent applied at the peak. As a result, the rate structure was simplified to two brackets, that is, 51 percent and 31 percent, at the national and local levels. Abandoning the principle of global income taxation went hand in hand with simplifying the tax on earned income and led to separate tax schedules for earned income and capital income. The new tax rate on capital income was set at 30 percent, and the statutory tax rate on corporate income was cut from 57 percent to 30 percent. The revenue loss from this cut was supplemented by base broadening, that is, the elimination of a variety of special tax treatments including the investment funds system since 1938 (reformed in 1955), which allowed corporations to avoid taxation on profits that had been set aside for future investments.[22] The reform of the VAT fell short of the initial ambition to apply the uniform 23 percent rate to all transactions. But the standard rate was raised to 25 percent. The base broadening of the VAT was achieved by imposing the tax completely on service activities (excluding the public sector and finance) and smaller tax exemptions, and the limited

---

[21] It was temporarily increased to 55 percent owing to budget deficits after 1992.

[22] The investment funds system was considered a countercyclical macroeconomic policy and a labor market policy based on the Swedish corporatist arrangement. The clearest presentation of this view is found in Pontusson (1992).

application of lower rates contributed to making taxation more neutral over economic activities. It was different from the ad hoc one-by-one measures that had been used before.

With the major changes detailed earlier, the tax revenue reliance shifted substantially from personal earned income to capital income and the VAT. The revenue loss resulting from the personal income tax cut was expected to be 6 to 7 percent in proportion to the GDP – a drastically high level compared with the 1 to 2 percent projected in the U.S. Reagan tax reform in 1986. About 40 percent of the loss was to be financed by capital income taxation; 30 percent, by the VAT; and 15 percent, by base broadening of the personal income tax (Agell, Englund, and Södersten 1996, 645). Even after the 1991 reform, the personal income tax is still one of the highest among the OECD countries, but a declining trend is clear. For example, in 1990 (i.e., before the reform), the personal income tax as a percentage of GDP was 21.4 percent, and, in 1995, five years after the reform, it was 17.5 percent. This drastic revenue reliance shift did not lead directly to worsening income distribution. More specifically, although it is hard to know the long-term effects of the reform, "the effects of lowering marginal tax rates . . . , taking into account differences in household size, are counteracted by an increased equalization effect from *children's allowances and housing allowances*" (Agell et al. 1998, 188).[23]

Base broadening and a statutory tax cut had been major aims of tax reform in other countries preceding the Swedish reform – most notably the U.S. reform in 1986, which determined the trend of the global tax reform, and the Danish reform in 1987, which first introduced a separate tax on capital income labeled the "dual Nordic income tax system."[24] However, the Swedish reform was even more radical than these reforms, which had

---

[23] Agell et al. (1996) also mention the possibility that incomes before taxes have become less equal and argue that "[t]he increased wage dispersion appears to be the continuation of a trend that has been going on since the middle of the 1980s, for which TR91 (i.e., the 1991 tax reform) can hardly have had any decisive importance" (Agell et al. 1998, 189). There is another view in which the weaker effect of redistribution through income tax has been a cause for increases in income inequity in Sweden since the 1980s compared with other Nordic countries such as Finland (Gustafsson et al. 1999).

[24] Some technical analysis shows that the dual income tax may not be counter to the principle of comprehensive taxation. Sørensen (1994, 76) summarizes his analysis as follows: "While dual income taxation clearly violates the principles of the conventional personal income tax, we argued that it might in fact be more in line with the philosophy of a true Haig-Simons comprehensive income tax, given the practical impossibility of including changes in human capital in the tax base, and given the difficulties of undertaking systematic inflation adjustment of taxable nominal capital income."

been considered sweeping and thorough in the mid-1980s. It was called "the reform of the century" and regarded as the most thorough reform in an industrial democracy during the postwar period.

Tax reform was sold to the public and interest groups with the promise not to change tax equality and income distribution. In a press conference about the proposals for a tax commission on capital incomes on October 15, 1986, Minister of Finance Kjell-Olof Feldt presented the idea of comprehensive income tax reform, which no one had expected.[25] Followed by his initiative, tax expert commissions were appointed in June 1987.[26] Reflecting the broad range of tax reform, three commissions were appointed; a committee for the reform of individual taxation (RINK), a committee on indirect taxation (KIS), and a committee on business taxation (URF). Fifteen to twenty lawyers and economists including those from the Ministry of Finance worked as the secretariats while asking for assistance from university professors in fiscal law and economics.[27] The most politically sensitive parts of the tax reform – the tax rate and the financing tax cut – were decided and discussed within a small circle of assistants to Feldt and Vice-Minister of Finance Erik Åsbrink.[28]

The reform plan was presented to Prime Minister Ingvar Carlsson in October 1988 immediately after the September election. Well before the presentation of the proposals from all the commissions in June 1989,[29] Feldt succeeded in obtaining support from the labor unions.[30] Beginning

---

[25] In terms of this decision, Salsbäck, who was a secretary-general in the tax department of the Ministry of Finance, writes: "When discussing the content of the press release with Mr. Feldt, I showed him a text stating that work on a comprehensive capital income tax reform was about to start. Mr. Feldt thought it over for maybe five seconds and said: 'No it's too limited, it should cover income tax in general'" (Salsbäck 1993, 201). Also, see Steinmo (1993, 188–9).

[26] It took more than eight months after the press conference to make a consensus within the governing party.

[27] Usually, in addition to party politicians and experts from inside and outside the Ministry of Finance, representatives of major interest groups including business and labor were included on tax commissions. But this time the commissions on direct and indirect taxation did not include the representatives of interest groups.

[28] He also chaired the committees on individual and business taxation. The former Director-General of the tax department chaired the committee on indirect taxation.

[29] The tax commission reports include: *Reformerad Inkomstbeskattning*, SOU 1989: 33, Vols. I–IV; *Reformerad Företagsbeskattning*, SOU 1989: 34, Vols. I–II; *Reformerad Mervärdesskatt*, SOU 1989: 35, Vols. I–II.

[30] In a press conference in the previous November, Feldt and a trade union leader, Stig Malm, had criticized the existing tax system and advocated the need for reform (Salsbäck 1993, 204).

in January 1989, Feldt and his party had concentrated on obtaining support from the Liberals, headed by Westerberg, and finally received it.[31] In February 1990, Feldt resigned because of a political crisis triggered by the government's attempt to prevent the devaluation of the Swedish krona and exacerbated by the announcement of the application for EC membership. Åsbrink became his successor so the tax reform remained intact. Following the schedule presented earlier, which had been considered unrealistic, the tax reform was to become effective in January 1991 – seven months before the general election in September that year – to avoid making tax reform an electoral issue. In the 1991 general election, however, the Social Democrats were replaced by a bourgeois coalition.

Around the beginning of 1992, economic recession, the result of an overheating economy in the late 1980s, became apparent. The reform was intended to make up the revenue loss caused by the income tax cut with the VAT, which had yielded excessively large revenues in the late 1980s owing to overconsumption. This intended effect of reform worked against the economic conditions at that time by discouraging consumption. It is next to impossible to estimate the independent influence of tax reform on the recession in a macroeconomic time series. But, the tax reform appeared to contribute at least to the worsening budget deficit, which had grown as high as 11 percent of the GDP. Agell et al. (1996) consider the 1991 tax reform a secondary factor in deepening the severe macroeconomic crisis but, according to them, "[i]n the best of all possible worlds, TR91 [i.e., the 1991 tax reform] would have been implemented in the middle of the 1980s" (Agell et al. 1998, 160). At least the timing of the reform was not good.[32]

Taxation and the Welfare State in the 1990s

The 1991 Reform: Affirmation of the Swedish Model   Progressive income tax had continued to increase since the 1960s. Rapidly increasing taxes

---

[31] The approval of the LO and the Liberals was given with the condition that the reform would not shift the tax from the rich to the poor – the tax rate cut should be compensated by a variety of personal allowances and special tax measures.

[32] For example, Andersson and Mutén (1994, 1160) write: "When the over-consumption became obvious and asset prices started falling, the excessive borrowing resulted in credit losses. At the same time, a long overdue tax reform had been put in place, making borrowing considerably less favorable, and thus exacerbating the adjustment in the financial sector by rightly increasing the incentives to work and save."

from the 1970s until the early 1990s established an image of the Swedish welfare state that relied heavily on progressive income taxation. However, this is obviously due to a high inflation rate that drastically increased the income tax in a steeply progressive rate structure. It was not until the late 1970s that the high taxation had become a subject of public debate. In the 1970s, the skyrocketing inflation rates reached unexpected double-digit levels after the oil shock. Even the most egalitarian policy makers in the 1960s neither expected nor wanted such a high level of income taxation as the Swedes had as a result of the bracket creep caused by inflation.[33] Therefore, the 1991 tax reform was not a reversal of the existing policies but was instead considered the extension of a precedent-setting tax.

At the beginning of this section, four characteristics of the postwar Swedish tax system were specified: the high progressive taxation on earned income, the relatively light corporate taxation involving a variety of special tax measures, the extensive use of the VAT, and the heavy reliance on social security contributions. The 1991 reform has significantly modified and qualified the first two characteristics but preserved and even strengthened the last two. The concern about the high income tax was a prime motivator for the 1991 tax reform, and revenue reliance has shifted more to social security contributions and the VAT. Already in the 1960s, long before that reform, however, the tax experts had recognized the need to shift revenue reliance from a progressive income tax to regressive taxes.

The Political and Technocratic Nature of Tax Policy Making   Tax policy making in Sweden is highly technocratic and, at the same time, political in the sense that the technocratic device often contributes to making a high tax level politically acceptable to the public. The most notable example is keeping the proportional and regressive taxes – the VAT and social security contributions – less visible than the income tax. Thus, the heavy VAT burden has been the subject of public concern less often than the heavy income tax. The Swedish VAT (*moms, mervärdesskatt*) has long been included in pricing. This price inclusiveness practice is stipulated in the Price Information Law for Consumer Protection and Value Added Tax Law.[34] This

---

[33] I acknowledge Jonas Agell and Nils Elvander for calling my attention to this point.

[34] The Price Information Law for Consumer Protection (paragraph 5) states that the price must include the VAT, and the VAT Law (chapter 11, paragraph 5, no. 2) states that the tax amount for each rate of the VAT should be stated (with some small exceptions). I thank Björn Westberg for his infomation about legal matters.

inclusion of the VAT in the listed price is considered part of the right of consumers to know the all-inclusive competitive price. That is, every item to be claimed to consumers must be included in a listed price when consumers decide to purchase goods or services. The net price, excluding the VAT, is thus prohibited from being presented when consumers decide to purchase an item. Because the net payment, excluding the tax, is rarely shown on a receipt, when they pay, consumers do not consider the VAT an extra payment added to the value of the purchased goods or services.[35] The Swedish practice had been independently determined before the same price inclusiveness practice was facilitated by the EU coordination of the VAT among member countries.[36]

Public finance textbooks often stipulate that an indirect levy such as a general consumption tax is invisible. If put more precisely, it may be invisible according to policy devices, but it is not always invisible to consumers. For example, the VAT becomes invisible only in a price-inclusive practice. The politics matter here. In countries that have introduced the VAT since the 1980s when government budget deficits became public knowledge, including of the VAT in a listed price was not a politically feasible proposal. For example, in Japan (in one of the cases introduced in Chapter 5), the public suspected that the increasing VAT would be less recognized if the tax were included in prices. Facing strong opposition, the government had no way to propose price inclusiveness.

The high burden of the employers' social security contributions, as high as 32.92 percent of total wage and salary outlays in 1997, is kept even more invisible than the VAT. Employees' payment strips or salary receipts never list employers' social security contributions in Sweden, while in France, where the employers' burden is also high, this is clearly shown to employees. In Sweden, therefore, although the employers consider social security contributions to be employment costs and payments to employees, employees do not consider employers' social security contributions to be part of their salaries. More important, when the Swedish taxpayers (excluding employers) complain about their "high" tax, these contributions are not included, although they constitute a high percentage of their salaries and are important tax revenue. The invisiblity of employers' social security

---

[35] How much is paid for the VAT is clearly and separately shown on the receipt as is the total payment. This practice informs the consumers of the tax amount (as the law demands) but, does not inform the net value of goods or services after subtracting the tax amount from the listed price.

[36] I thank Peter Melz for calling my attention to this point.

contributions is both a highly political measure and a technocratic device for hiding the tax burden.[37]

The effective use of a technocratic device may be fortified by the high degree of reliance on an expert committee in Swedish tax policy making or, more generally, a reliance on tax experts inside and outside the government dating back to the 1930s (Norr, Duffy, and Sterner 1959, 53, 74). The appointment of and investigation by a Royal Commission (i.e., an expert tax committee) were started in 1949 by the Social Democratic government, and these procedures have continued to the present. The expert committee is appointed upon the request of the Riksdag or the government's initiative before major tax legislations. Aside from the Riksdag members and government officials, its members broadly include private tax experts and representatives of industrial or labor groups, and its investigation is intense and substantial. Lawyers or law specialists are generally influential inside the government and frequently occupy important positions such as secretaries of ministries (i.e., top-ranking bureaucrats and secretaries of government committees).[38] Tax expert committees also have been dominated by law specialists; committee chairs have usually been lawyers. An administrative and tax court in each province (Län) have high status in deciding tax cases,

---

[37] The conservative government in the early 1990s decided to show the amounts of employers' social security contributions on salary receipts, but the SAP reversed this decision upon its return to power. I thank Nils Mattsson for pointing out the importance of this fact. The burden has been hidden for two different but interrelated reasons. Decreasing public antipathy toward the high tax is an obvious reason, but, in addition, a high flat-rate levy on wage income has been hard to politicize because such an imposition inevitably results in the transfer or redistribution from promising to declining industrial sectors. Here, the conflicting sectoral interests threaten the national unity of labor as well as capital interests, and both labor and business elites want to keep secret that they have compromised over the imposition of a flat-rate levy. This "hidden" nature of social security contributions may be changing from the 1990s to 2000s because the pension reform in 1998 decided to divide the burden in half between employers and employees while wages are increased by additionally increased burden on employees. In other words, the employers' net payment to employees is the same but becomes visible as an addition to wages replacing parts of social security contributions. I thank Taro Miyamoto for pointing out the importance of this fact.

[38] I thank Åsa Gunnarson for pointing out this characteristic of Swedish tax policy making. Government committees as well as ministries have important roles in Swedish policy making. For example, Melz writes: "Sweden has a tradition of extensive preparation of legislation by work in Government Commissions. A Commission could either be Parliamentary (members on the commission are M.P.s) or an expert commission. Commission Reports (*Statens Offentliga Utredningar*, SOU) are circulated for comments to organizations, courts, universities etc. Based on these comments, the Government presents a bill (proposition) to the Parliament (Riksdagen) . . . Amendments in the Parliament are rare" (Melz 1997, 102).

and four regional courts and the administrative supreme court are at the top of the system.

Since the 1991 tax reform, however, the influence of tax lawyers has declined as the influence of economists has increased. The tax department of the MOF has traditionally been dominated by lawyers,[39] but now one out of ten bureaucrats is an economist, and the MOF is now increasingly employing those with Ph.D.s in economics.[40] The shifting emphasis from law expertise to economics reflects the changing socioeconomic conditions surrounding the tax policies. In the late 1960s, when the VAT was introduced, high economic growth accompanied natural growth of revenue annually. In the early 1990s, when the revenue reliance shifted from income to consumption in addition to revenue shortage and budget deficit, the globalization of the economy became a major problem. The revenue-raising considerations in the 1990s had to be made under the severe fiscal constraints and complexities of global economic activities. This change led to the larger role for economists in the 1991 reform and has since consolidated their active participation in tax policy making.[41]

Economic Changes: Public Support and the Future of the Welfare State

The Foundation of Public Support The economic downturn in the early 1990s has had a far greater influence on the Swedish welfare state than a mere obstacle to tax reform. This economic crisis is not only regarded as the collapse of the Social Democrats' "Third Road (between Keynsian reflation and Thatcherite austerity policies)" (Stephens 1996) but also considered to have put an end to the "Swedish model" in which economic management and generous welfare provision were closely related to good socioeconomic performance. In addition to the political arrangement, the Swedish model has boasted of specific fits between the welfare state and the economy. They are low unemployment based on an active labor market

---

[39] The judges being trained or working in the court system often enter the Ministry of Finance (MOF) in the middle of their careers, and a majority of judges on the supreme administrative court have previously worked in the MOF.

[40] Interviews with an MOF bureaucrat in Stockholm and an economist in Uppsala (September 1997).

[41] In the early 1980s, some politically appointed economists, especially Social Democratic economists, participated in tax policy making. Their participation was temporary, but the economists who have become involved in tax policy making since the late 1980s have tended to remain in the MOF for a long time.

policy and centralized wage bargaining; stable growth helped by international competitiveness; higher income equality achieved by a large social security expenditure and universal employment; fiscal discipline achieved by a relatively efficient public sector and high taxation.[42] In the early 1990s, however, Sweden plunged into a crisis such as it had never experienced – huge budget deficits, higher unemployment than had been seen since the 1930s, and the continued drop in the GDP growth rate, which fell to below 0.5 percent between 1990 and 1993. The economic crisis inevitably crowded the future of the Swedish welfare state.[43]

Despite this, Sweden experienced a negligible decline in all categories in social expenditures in the 1990s (Eitrheim and Kuhnle 2000). In contrast with other Nordic countries, owing to the severe impact of recession from 1990 to 1991, the returned Social Democratic government implemented cutbacks, which may indicate its qualified support for universalism exemplified by the pension reform in 1998.[44] But the institutionalized universal welfare state will not be threatened in the near future.[45] The early timing of the institutionalization of the strong revenue machine (i.e., well before the chronic budget deficit) has certainly contributed to the amicable relationship between the government and people. The Swedish tax has increased to a much higher level than in other OECD countries from its average level in 1960, but there has been no tax revolt. A consensus has been reached about the tax level imposed on the public to finance the public sector. For example, public opinion became even more supportive of the current tax level in reference to the benefits level.[46] In Sweden, the combination of an effective tax revenue structure and high expenditures has not been a

---

[42] For example, see Freeman (1995), Cousins (1999, 24), Therborn (1989), Clayton and Pontusson (1998).

[43] For example, see Freeman, Topel, and Swedenborg (1997). Hansen et al. (1993) extend this transformation to all the Scandinavian countries, not particularly to Sweden.

[44] This reform was implemented in 2001, placing a new restriction on the universal basic payments that were to be replaced by employment-based pensions and thus resulting in no or fewer payments.

[45] Kuhnle (2000) details this point.

[46] In this regard, Hadenius (1986, 23) shows an extremely interesting contrast between the surveys conducted in 1968 and 1981–2. The negative view of high marginal taxes increased from 70 percent (exceeding the positive view by 51 percent) to 84 percent (exceeding the positive view by 72 percent) from 1968 to 1981–2, whereas the view that the burden was reasonable in reference to one's own benefits increased 32 percent (surpassed by the negative view by 11 percent) to 62 percent (exceeding the negative view by 25 percent) during the same period. During this period, the total tax burden increased by 10 percent in terms of the GDP share.

project merely in the minds of experts and Social Democrat politicians; it has deeply rooted public support. Compared with people in the United States and United Kingdom, the people in Sweden are more likely to consider taxation and redistribution policies as being integrated and, as a result, are more satisfied with the distribution of taxes (Edlund 1999, 126–8). This becomes apparent in the referendum that decided the Swedish entry into the European Union: maintaining a high welfare provision was one of the important reasons to determine the votes both for and against the entry with a close margin (Aylott 1999, 62–70, 85–8).[47]

High public support for the welfare state in Sweden is clear in a sequence of Svallfors' analyses of the data from the International Social Survey Program (ISSP). In Sweden and Norway, public support for the state's intervention in redistribution and egalitarian income distribution is highest among eight industrial democracies (Svallfors 1999).[48] The public support for the welfare state (even financing expensive programs by taxation) in Sweden has remained generally high and stable since the 1980s to the 1990s (Svallfors 1995; 1997b). It is even independent of trust for political institutions and government and a sense of political efficacy and is attributed to the Swedes' firmly established belief in the welfare state (Svallfors 1997a). The high welfare provision that they have enjoyed is regarded as more stable than public trust and efficacy, and, thus, the Swedes do not easily lose confidence in their welfare state as they experience the loss of political trust and a decline in political efficacy.

Is it possible that middle-class support for the Swedish welfare state will end during an economic crisis that threatens the high income replacement levels and high quality of welfare provision? In the 1990s, low- and middle-level nonmanual workers became supportive of the welfare state just as the (manual) workers did, although high-level nonmanual workers and elite groups have come to be critical of it (Svallfors 1999). In Sweden, therefore,

---

[47] Aylott bases his analysis on Elvander's (1994) distinction of two types of "welfare nationalism," an "isolationist" variant, which argues for maintaining a high welfare standard separately from the EU (and thus opposes the entry), and a "missionary" type, which argues for offering a welfare state model to the EU (and thus supports the entry) (Aylott 1999, 67–70).

[48] These eight countries correspond to four regime types listed by Esping-Andersen (1990) and Castles and Mitchell (1993) (see Chapter 1) as follows: social democratic (Sweden/Norway), conservative (Germany/Austria), liberal (United States/Canada), and radical (Australia/New Zealand). Another interesting finding by Svallfors (1997b) is that the pattern of formation of social groups and classes is the same from one country to another. In other words, the high public support in common in the social democratic countries is not a result of the formation of similar or corresponding social groups and classes.

a large segment of middle-class workers still supports the welfare state. This tendency at least distinguishes the Swedish bastion of social democratic power from other European countries such as the United Kingdom where the middle class has supported the debacle of the universal welfare state.

How has the 1991 tax reform affected this high and stable public support for the welfare state? Despite extensive efforts to broaden the base, the drastic income tax cuts could have divided the rich and the poor into winners and losers, respectively. What was going on in the public's mind during this major tax policy change? A survey study of public opinion (Edlund 1999) illuminates the very uneasy and ambiguous impact of the 1991 tax reform on the public, especially among traditional Social Democrat supporters. In September 1992, just a year after the election, only 12 percent of respondents answered that the tax reform had influenced their votes (2 percent responded "influenced significantly" and 10 percent, "to some extent"), whereas 79 percent answered "not at all."[49] When the respondents are broken down, male, professional, and higher-income earners were more supportive of the reform than the traditional supporters of the Social Democrats, and workers and low-income earners tended to answer "don't know" and reserved judgment.

In this regard, the 1991 tax reform has not produced a clear political cleavage nor explained the SAP's defeat in the following election. However, the reservation of judgment by the party's core supporters may mean, as Edlund emphasizes, that the tax reform has been politicized as a "cutting marginal tax rates" reform. The government wanted to sell the tax reform as a complete package that would cut income tax rates but, at the same time, broaden the tax base and enhance redistribution through special tax measures such as child allowances. Instead, the worst image for the Social Democrats was created when the marginal income tax cut became the most emphasized in the politicization of the reform. The traditional supporters of the SAP were uncertain about how they could evaluate this reform, whereas the rich, who believed that they benefited from it, did not switch their support to the party.

Postscript for the Turn of the Century Facing the turn of the century, the Swedish government enjoyed a budget surplus supported by economic

---

[49] In the same vein, 20 percent answered that the tax reform had influenced their current political sympathies (4 percent "significantly" and 16 percent "to some extent"), whereas 80 percent answered "not at all."

growth in recovering from the 12 percent GDP deficit in 1993 during the recession. In 1998, Sweden showed the strongest fiscal balance among the participant countries of the European Monetary Union. Since the early 1990s, the government has pushed both a tax increase and expenditure cut. The most effective revenue sources – the VAT and social security contributions – seem to have reached the limit of their burden recently. The 25 percent VAT standard rate is too high for the Swedish government to push up even without the upper limit set by the EU. The immediate reduction of the rate on foods that had been increased in the 1990s was a political response to the public outcry against high taxes. Thus, the Swedish government has searched for a new tax base as it has been doing continuously for the last decades. The most likely candidate for the next tax base seems to be in real estate, which is very unexpected considering the highly techonocratic and complicated system of Swedish taxation. The government has also increased the energy consumption tax, which was inevitable because of the country's severe climate in the winter: this imposition has maintained the level of revenue from excise taxes (Figure 2.2). The revenue from taxes on real estate has also increased since the 1980s from a negligible level, whereas the revenue from the wealth tax has remained stable (Figure 2.3). They are immobile and invisible revenue sources and thus effective revenue-raising measures.[50]

It remains to be seen to what extent Sweden has returned to these most preliminary forms of taxation, but there is no sign that a high tax level revenue reliance on regresssive taxes will be retrieved in the near future. Even with the search for a new tax frontier, they are imperative components of the Swedish taxation that finances a large welfare state.

The United Kingdom: The Ambiguous Impact of Neoconservative Rule

The United Kingdom is a liberal welfare state but is different from its North American counterparts – the United States and Canada. It had once been a forerunner of welfare states in the 1950s. However, "a quarter century of 'Butskellite' agreement between Conservative and Labor parties was seen to yield in 1979 to the radically anti-consensus policies of Thatcherism" and then to "the policy stance of Blair's New Labor on 'welfare to work'"

---

[50] I acknowledge Jonas Agell for calling my attention to an increase in these taxes and giving useful information about them.

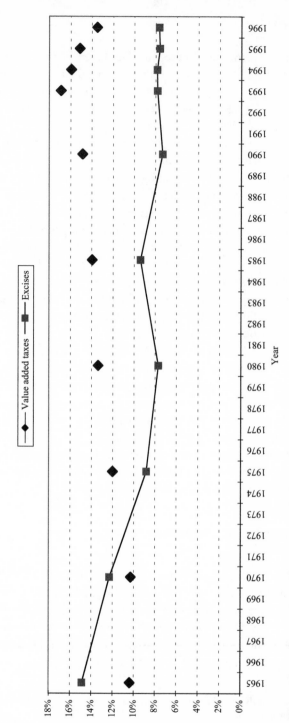

Figure 2.2. Proportions of taxes on general consumption (sales tax in 1965, VAT after 1965) and excises to total tax revenue in Sweden. *Source:* OECD 1997b.

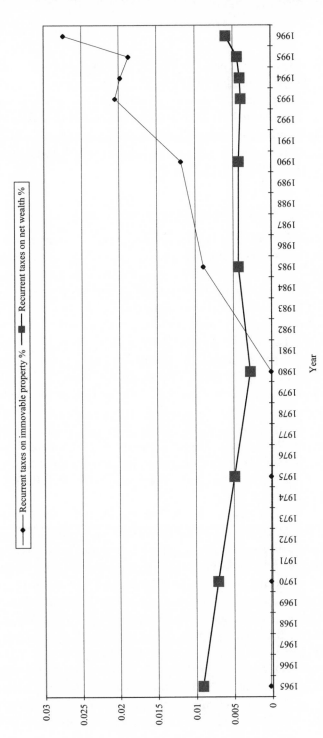

Figure 2.3. Proportion of taxes on real estate and of wealth tax to total revenue in Sweden. In OECD statistics, real estate tax is classified as 4100 and wealth tax is classified as 4200. *Source:* OECD 1997b.

(Pierson 1998, 155, 158). Tax policy in the United Kingdom has also been influenced by the many ups and downs in partisan politics that are comparable to those in welfare. The problem of state funding capacity has not been resolved. Although neither left nor right dominated in making the decision, the influence of an external factor such as integration under the EU prevailed; the revenue enhancement provided by the introduction of the VAT is a good example of such a factor.

Politics Matters: The Inherent Instability of British Taxation

Tax Politics British Style   During the postwar period, the United Kingdom has rarely experienced a radical change or an overhaul of the existing tax system, but it has had an accumulation of piecemeal changes that have involved frequent introductions, abolitions, and modifications of new taxes. As shown in Figure 2.1 the basic structure of tax revenue composition has been stable with minor ups and downs in revenue composition that have occurred frequently. Especially from the 1960s to 1979, the tax system experienced frequent changes during the alternation of power between the Conservative and the Labour Parties. The exception is Thatcher's neoconservative revolution in the 1980s, in which tax policies were regarded as important means for economic restructuring. This process culminated in the unpopular poll tax in 1990 (in Scotland, in 1989), which resulted in the ousting of Thatcher by her own party. In the 1990s, the relative stability of tax policy was observed (except for the replacement of the poll tax by the council tax) under John Major for seven years until 1997, when the office went to the Labour Party.

This lack of radical changes in the tax system dates back to the prewar era. In the interwar years during the Great Depression, the United Kingdom did not institutionalize an "historic compromise" between capital and labor as Sweden did. On the other hand, throughout the 1930s, despite the Conservative majority gained in the 1931 elections, the progressivity of income taxation that had been established in 1909 by the People's Budget under Lloyd George was sustained. This progressivity and increasing coverage of income taxation continued with the short interruption of a wartime economy until 1979, when Thatcher's first budget attempted to reduce the top rate drastically (Dilnot and Kay 1990, 152–3). As a result, "[t]he whole of the revenue . . . in the 1980s could have been obtained by taxes more than a half century old if British government had done absolutely nothing . . . in the years since 1948" (Rose and Karran 1986, 125). In other words, the changes had brought about a substantial transformation in the tax revenue structure.[51]

Frequent changes without a consistent orientation have not necessarily been caused by the alternation of power between the two ideologically distinct parties because neither Conservatives nor Labourites maintain explicit ideological orientation in tax policy making,[52] nor do the administrative departments concerned with tax policy making – Treasury, Inland Revenue, and Customs and Excise. Although the Treasury is a powerful organization in charge of macroeconomic policy and spending,[53] and the tax policy making appears centralized in the Chancellor of the Exchequer, Customs and Excise and Inland Revenue are still independent of the Treasury and have their own direct relationships with the Chancellor. They rarely take the initiative for tax proposals, and the details of tax policy are decided within parliament. As a result, in the longer term, in any part of the policy-making circle, particular objectives have not been sought, and a tax policy has been used for short-term demand management. The repeated basic story line is: "New governments enter office with a massive reform agenda, but they are soon buffeted by economic reality and ultimately retreat from the full implementation of their agenda" (Steinmo 1993, 146).

Because of the subtle mix of apparent instability and substantial stability, tax politics is, therefore, often characterized by terms such as "administrative adaptation" (Hood 1985) or "political inertia." "[N]on-decision-making is preferred to decision-making" and "doing nothing and relying upon existing taxes is preferable" to "taking responsibility for introducing new tax measures" (Rose and Karran 1986, 5). The VAT stands as an exception to the ad hoc tendency, but why?

A Radical Policy Change with Few Political Costs   The introduction of the VAT in the United Kingdom surprisingly lacks political drama. Major

---

[51] Most major policy changes since 1964 were repealed or modified (Sandford 1988; 1993a, 33). For example, the capital gains tax (CGT) introduced in 1965 has been extensively modified; a classic type of the corporate tax (CT) in the same year was replaced by an imputation system of the CT in 1973; the selective employment tax (SET) was repealed; and the capital transfer tax (CTT) in 1974–75 was renamed the inheritance tax after modifications in 1986.

[52] The only difference lies in the Conservatives' relative strength in staff service in tax policy making and Labour's more cautious approach to new taxation resulting from a weaker intraparty research department (Robinson and Sandford 1983, 82).

[53] For a more detailed study of the Treasury, see Chapman (1997) and Thain and Wright (1995).

characteristics of the introduction of the VAT are summarized in several points.

The introduction was based on external political consideration. The VAT was considered primarily in relation to other European countries in the European Economic Community (EEC). The VAT was brought to the political agenda by members of the Conservative Party who desired entry into the EEC. The VAT had originally attracted policy makers' attention because of the possible connection between the tax and member countries' trade success, especially because the United Kingdom had been rejected from joining the EEC. Once entry into the EEC had been put on the agenda, the introduction of the VAT itself appeared inevitable. "[T]he question asked of Customs and Excise was not so much 'whether?' as 'how?' – more particularly, in those early days after the election, 'how soon?'" (Johnstone 1975, 13).[54]

The introduction of the VAT was not based on long-term planning for a tax system, especially within the bureaucracy. The introduction of the VAT was included in the Conservative manifesto for the 1970 general election, and, after the Conservative Party took office, the bureaucrats were consulted. There is no indication that they actively coped with the politicians' initiative to introduce the VAT. In the 1963 budget statement, Reginald Maudling, the Chancellor of the Exchequer of the Conservative government at that time, first mentioned the VAT. The VAT was considered officially as a future policy option in the report of the Richardson Committee in 1963–4 by Maudling, but the report concluded negatively regarding the VAT, referring to the superiority of the existing purchase tax.[55] The Customs and Excise Department, later in charge of administering the VAT, had provided the secretariat of the Committee and was consulted by the National Economic Development Office to issue its reports. But, the experience of these earlier years had not aroused interest in the VAT in the Department.[56] The

---

[54] Hood (1985) classifies the introduction of the VAT as a typical result of "external disturbance" among the tax structure developments beteween 1939 and 1982. Prest (1980, 17–18) also concurs with Johnstone that the VAT introduction in the United Kingdom was considered in terms of participation in the EEC.

[55] Command 2300, 1964, *Report of the Committee on Turnover Tax* (London: Her Majesty's Stationery Office).

[56] The Intelligence Branch of the Department, later renamed the Departmental Planning Unit, engaged in the early examination of the VAT in terms of tax theory and the experience of other countries. The unit was isolated in the Department: it was "relatively unconcerned with the nuts and bolts of tax collection" of other parts of the Department and other parts

role of experts outside the government was also limited, although the economists had been exploring the possibility of introducing the VAT since the 1960s.[57] The long-term planning, even if it had existed among tax specialists outside the government, had no opportunity to gain life in the policy-making process.

The introduction of the VAT involved very few political costs. The United Kingdom had not had a general consumption tax with a broad base: the VAT replaced a purchase tax dating back to 1940 and a selective employment tax introduced in 1963, but both of the existing taxes were far from a general consumption tax. Despite a high 10 percent standard rate from the time of its introduction, however, the VAT was accepted as smoothly as in most Western European countries, which had had a long history of a general consumption tax. The government announced the introduction of the VAT in a Green Paper on Budget in March 1971. It then postponed the legislation of the VAT, which had been planned as a separate bill before the end of 1971, until the ordinary finance bill in the spring of 1972. The early announcement and the delay of legislation should imply a longer interval during which the public might have organized opposition to the VAT. However, political opposition to the tax increase did not occur.

The introduction of the VAT was not the result of policy concerns of revenue departments, that is, securing revenue for increasing public expenditures. The revenue departments themselves were strikingly indifferent to the revenue-raising power of the VAT. The only concern was business' uneasiness. Treasury took care of that by implementing the special tax treatment for exemptions.[58] Nor did the politicians intend to secure the revenue. From the mid-1960s to mid-1970s when the VAT was planned, proposed, and implemented, the two predominant concerns were "the need to encourage economic growth (and consequently boost tax revenues) and the desire for

---

of the Department "were not, in general, required to be intimately in touch with what the Unit was doing about the VAT" (Johnstone 1975, 12).

[57] For example, "G. S. A. Wheatcroft (a professor emeritus of the University of London) was appointed by the Chancellor of the Exchequer as honorary adviser to Customs and Excise on technical VAT problems. He was the medium by which preparatory work on VAT undertaken by the Conservative Tax Policy Group was fed into the civil service machine" (Robinson and Sandford 1983, 96). Johnstone (1975, 15) concurs with Robinson and Sandford's assessment of his role as limited.

[58] The administration split into two large divisions: one to take care of political consideration, that is, VAT liability (VL), and the other concerned with implementation and revenue, VAT machinery (VM).

greater equity in the tax structure" instead of "the need for new revenue" (Robinson and Sandford 1983, 218).[59]

The weak link between revenue and expenditure led to the preservation of expenditures financed by the VAT expected. For example, despite Thatcher's extensive effort to retrench the welfare state in the first half of the 1980s (more precisely from 1979 to 1985), the VAT revenue doubled.[60] I will come back to this point after reviewing tax policy changes from the 1980s to the early 1990s.

Chronic Deficits and Tax Policy Changes Since the 1980s

The tax reform in the 1980s started substantially in 1979 when the first budget by the Thatcher administration was made by Chancellor of the Exchequer Geoffrey Howe. After Howe was replaced by Nigel Lawson in June 1983, this period ended with the resignation of Lawson in October 1989 during the political turmoil caused by the poll tax. Major tax policy changes during the period are spread out in several fields. First of all, in income tax, the basic rate was reduced from 33 percent to 30 percent and then to 25 percent, and the top rate was reduced from 83 percent to 60 percent and then to 40 percent. As a result, all but one of nine higher rates in 1978–9 were abolished, leaving a two-rate system consisting of a 25 percent basic rate and 40 percent higher (or top) rate. Investment income surcharges were reduced by trebling the threshold and then abolishing it. Personal allowances and the starting rate for a higher rate tax increased in real terms, and the variety of tax reliefs and tax breaks was reduced. Second, in capital gains tax, indexation was introduced in 1982 and extended in 1985; in 1988 all gains rebased to 1989 to avoid taxation of "paper's gains." The corporate tax was mainly restructured in 1984, and the main rate was reduced from 52 percent to 35 percent, whereas the rate on small companies was reduced from 42 percent to 25 percent in the same way as the basic rate of the income tax. Most 100 percent first-year capital allowances were phased out.

---

[59] The lack of revenue consideration may also be attributed to the division of revenue departments. One of the revenue departments, Customs and Excise, is in charge of indirect taxes including the VAT, whereas another revenue department, Inland Revenue, is in charge of other domestic taxes, that is, direct taxation, as the name shows. The Fiscal Policy Division of Treasury, organized in 1968, has attempted to supplement the function of a comprehensive revenue review by regular personnel exchanges with revenue departments (Sandford 1993a, 39). In 1992, the Treasury first accepted that revenue and expenditure decisions should be unified under Chancellor Norman Lamont (Thain and Wright 1995, 235).

[60] Rose and Karran (1986, 179) emphasize this point.

In the VAT, as already mentioned, the double rates of 8 and 12.5 percent were replaced by a single 15 percent to finance the income tax cut. The base was broadened to include hot take-away food and building alterations in 1984; advertising in newspapers and periodicals in 1985, and nondomestic construction (European Court ruling) in 1989. Lastly, the inheritance tax's fourteen rates with a top 75 percent rate were reduced into a single rate of 40 percent in 1988.

These changes should result in several important shifts in tax policy making and the tax system. First, the focus of tax policy making has been shifted away from short-term macroeconomic demand management, rectification of market distortion, and promotion of tax equality (redistribution), which had been dominant in the 1960s and 1970s. The emerging concerns are exclusively related to economic incentives, which the tax system is expected to affect: the tax system has come to be considered a source instead of a remedy for market distortions. Second, the reform of direct taxation was not limited to its system; it affected indirect taxation. From the mid-1970s to the end of the 1980s, the revenue from the VAT almost doubled; it enhanced the revenue from taxes on goods and services and almost filled the gap resulting from the decline of income tax revenue. The shift of revenue reliance from income to consumption was implemented by considering the promotion of economic incentives. Nigel Lawson, who was Financial Secretary from 1979 to 1983 and then Chancellor of the Exchequer from 1983 to 1989, most eloquently tells a consequence of the changes. "The main way in which we were able to leave people more choices was by switching the tax burden from income to spending" (Lawson 1992, 340) and thus, despite the decline in general government expenditures from 46 to 40 percent of GDP (excluding privatization receipts), "[t]he Conservative Governments of 1979–92 cannot claim to have reduced the burden of tax as a proportion of GDP" (Lawson 1992, 339).

Although the VAT revenue certainly helps offset the drop in other tax revenues, increasing reliance on it has nothing to do with the concern to secure revenue or the intention to prepare for a high tax burden. First, all the VAT rate changes, mostly increases, had thus far been ad hoc rather than well-planned measures aimed to supplement the revenue that accompanied the tax cut. For example, in 1974, the year after its introduction, the government reduced the rate to 8 percent to cope with an inflation rate as high as 25 percent. One year later, a higher tax rate of 25 percent was applied to luxuries such as electrical durables, cosmetics, boats and aircraft for private use, and fur coats. But another year later, the rate was cut in half (i.e., to 12.5 percent owing to opposition from manufacturers and distributors of higher-taxed commodities). Second, despite the base-broadening efforts in the 1980s, the VAT system applies a zero tax rate to many items such as children's clothing, food, books, and newspapers; this practice is an exception among the countries that have been members of the EU since the 1970s.[61]

The 15 percent single-tax rate was increased to 17.5 percent in 1991 by Norman Lamont during the John Major administration to reduce the heavy burden of the poll tax. The property tax replaced the poll tax, but the unpopularity of the poll tax made it difficult to introduce the property tax, which would be as high as the poll tax had been. The 17.5 percent tax rate was still below the average of the European standard, and the VAT revenue was still short of the average of the EU member countries and served to restrain the growth of the public sector instead of maintaining its size. This weak revenue-raising power was likely to influence welfare policy, especially during the retrenchment since the 1980s.

The Welfare State

The postwar tax policy was not based on a solid consensus nor was the welfare policy. Therefore, as Glennerster argues, the following view, though widely believed, is mistaken:

[D]uring and immediately after the Second World War the Coalition and Labour governments created a set of new social institutions that were designed to look after citizens 'from the cradle to the grave.'... The invention of Sir William Beveridge, this massive new system secured bipartisan and popular support which was sustained through to the 1970s, when economic crisis and Mrs Thatcher's radical new government began to question whether the economy could afford to sustain such an expensive and outdated system of largess. (Glennerster 1990, 11)

Social spending for education, housing, health care, and social security increased throughout the postwar period until 1979, but a consensus on a large and generous provision had not ever been reached. Glennerster's (1990) own survey of postwar welfare policy until the mid-1970s demonstrates constant fluctuations in a variety of fields. The postwar tax policy changes have been ad hoc, and the postwar development of the welfare state has lacked a solid consensus and thus allowed ad hoc changes. To demonstrate this, the weak foundation of the U.K. welfare state will be

---

[61] For example, Chancellor of the Exchequer Lawson himself admits that the base broadening was an important policy during this period, but not enough (Lawson 1992, 356–8).

illuminated. Then, the meaning of welfare retrenchment under the Thatcher administration will be qualified to explicate how the funding capacity of the government is related to the relatively modest welfare state.

The Weak Foundation of the Welfare State   The 1942 report of the U.K. government, "Social Insurance and Allied Service,"[62] by Sir William Beveridge, the so-called Beveridge report, resulted in the sale of 600,000 copies, even to Adolf Hitler. However, the Beveridge version of the welfare state was never fully accepted in the United Kingdom. The high cost of the proposed scheme and the rigidity of its social insurance principle to cope with future changes were recognized by specialists, including Beveridge himself, when the report was published (Dilnot, Kay, and Morris 1984, 10). There was a gradual erosion and modification of principles in the report (Lowe 1994).[63] After the war, the primary concern of the government changed from the management of a war economy to funding postwar socioeconomic reconstruction, and the Labour Party enthusiastically supported[64] a universal, insurance-based, and minimalist approach. However, many unexpected factors and rapid economic changes facilitated the erosion of the Beveridge approach. Postwar economic recovery and growth during a period of high inflation made the policy implemented under the Attlee government inadequate (Heß 1981). The once appropriate subsistence level quickly fell short of its standard, and a flat rate for subsistence benefits and contributions was abandoned until the mid-1960s. Until the 1970s, the welfare state lacked a comprehensiveness with respect to persons covered and the needs and classification of entitled individuals.

If the ideal of the Beveridge report does not underscore the welfare state, what does? The United Kingdom is statist in public policy making in the sense that making and implementing economic and social policies rely more on governmental organizations than interest groups and industrial organizations when compared with Western European countries. Unlike the strength of the left, corporatist organization, and pro-welfare consensus in

---

[62] "Social Insurance and allied services," Command 6404, 1942 (London: HMSO).

[63] The Beveridge plan also had contradictory philosophical concepts in it. The conflicts were between the traditional concept of the "natural liberty" of "free-born Englishmen" (expressed by the emphasis on a private contract as a natural right) and the Continental concept of the state as an independent organism to which citizens owe certain duties (expressed as universalism) (Lowe 1994, 129).

[64] Scheu (1943) describes in detail how important the Beveridge report was to the British Labour Party.

the other statist organizations, U.K. statism is based on the weakness of industrial capital (in contrast to the strength of financial capital), government mobilization during a wartime economy, and the dismantling of an overseas empire. This "ungrounded statism" (Dunleavy 1989) tends to lead to a policy process that parallels "a reluctant welfare state": "avoiding political obstacles regularly took precedence over exploring new ideas or developing national priorities in a coherent way" (Ashford 1986, 279).

The development of the social security provision, especially its old-age pension, embodies this vulnerability in terms of the conflict between the principles of universalism and targeting (Table 1.1). The targeting principle inevitably leads to an earnings-related provision if we consider that the members of society or citizens are the potential beneficiaries: the provision's coverage excludes the middle- to higher-income earners or is often limited to certain occupational groups, that is, it is earnings-related. But, at the same time, it is possible to make a distinction between a flat-rate and earnings-related benefit provision in the same (targeting) program. Although it generates a flat-rate minimum provision regardless of income level, it can also guarantee earnings-related provision to the well-off. In this regard, universalism faces the dilemma of securing flat-rate universal benefits (i.e., without targeting) to protect the poor while satisfying the middle- to higher-income earners who afford private supplementary insurance.

In the late 1950s, the Labour Party faced this dilemma, and adopted a plan for a superannuation encompassing the population with supplementary pensions based on an earnings-related principle. However, the Labour Party was defeated in the 1959 election, and the plan was not implemented. The program was unpopular because the U.K. white-collar workers were less organized and more privileged from the existing benefit provision than those in the Scandinavian countries, which succeeded in implementing similar reforms at that time (Baldwin 1990, 242). Whereas the existing occupational pension scheme constrains the benefit provision of the U.K. pension system, the three pillars system in Sweden (i.e., social insurance, occupational, and private pensions), when combined with high unionization, guarantees generous benefits.[65] As a result, although the history of the old-age pension dated back to the Old-Age Pensions Act in 1908, the principle of a means-tested provision that dated back to the Poor Law in 1834 had persisted. The introduction of the principle of a secured earnings-related

---

[65] For the U.K. system, see Lynes (1997) and Blundell and Johnson (1999). For the Swedish system, see Wadensjö (1997) and Palme and Svensson (1999).

provision in the old-age program, the State Earnings-Related Pension Scheme (SERPS) was postponed, until the 1975 Social Security Pensions Act.[66] The 1975 act replaced an ad hoc indexation, and the basic pension was to be indexed to whichever was higher – wages or price increases. However, this scheme was short-lived. The 1986 Social Security Act completely reversed the change brought by the 1975 act. The shift from universalism to a means-tested principle was apparent from the significant modification of the SERPS scheme.[67] The Conservative government advocated that the social security system should be consistent with the aims of economic management. This was a clear and major shift in the postwar welfare policy from regarding social security "as a solution" for fighting poverty and insecurity to classifying it as "a problem" that obstructed effective economic management (Barr and Coulter 1990, 274).[68]

The Impact of Neoconservatism   The rule of Margaret Thatcher from 1979 throughout the 1980s was expected to change the welfare state drastically. In the existing literature, however, a close examination of expenditure trends and the contents of structural reforms in a variety of fields gives us a mixed picture. First, public spending on education, health, housing, social services, and social security, that is, broadly defined welfare, continued to increase in the 1980s. An increasing trend (at least there was no sign of stagnation) was observed in all parts of the welfare state without exception. The postwar growth of the welfare state was thwarted in the mid-1970s, but social security expenditure in general maintained the same proportion to the GDP from 1974 to 1987, as shown in Figure 1.1.[69] The retrenchment in the 1980s, therefore, could not lead to direct and immediate cutbacks in the welfare state.

[66] Comparable to the argument here, Fawcett (2000) shows that policy trajectories in the 1950s and 1960s had a fundamental impact on the welfare retrenchment since the 1980s.

[67] This included the calculation of benefits based on a lifetime average earnings instead of those for the twenty best years. (Command 9517, 1985, *Reform of Social Security* [London: HMO: 23]). Bonoli (2001, 250–1) details this process.

[68] The government pointed out five defects in the existing system: the complexity of the system, its ineffective support for the most needy groups, the poverty and unemployment traps resulting from direct taxes and the social security systems, and the smaller role of freedom of individual choice. The poverty and unemployment traps, in most extreme cases, mean that individuals and families will be worse off by earning extra money and being employed, respectively. A more detailed explanation is in Dilnot and Stark (1989).

[69] Le Grand (1990) draws the same conclusion, although the level he reports during this period is a bit different from the level indicated in Figure 1.1 (i.e., around 24 percent, owing to a different definition of social security, or welfare, expenditure in Europe).

Second, despite the continued increase in social security expenditures, policy changes increased inequality. Considering that inequality in original income distribution substantially increased in the 1980s (Jenkins 1996), the effects of tax and social security reforms in the 1980s were expected to magnify the difference between the worst-off and the well-off. In terms of the effect of each social security program as well as the cumulative effect over total income of social security benefits,[70] inequality decreased in the 1970s but increased again up to 1986 (Barr and Coulter 1990, 322–7). Tax reform changes in the 1980s have also increased inequality as a result of the decreasing progressivity in the system (Giles and Johnson 1994). As long as the social security reforms in the 1980s have not been reversed, the enlarged inequality should remain at the same level in the 1990s. Consequently, inequality clearly increased in the 1980s; this tendency has continued in the 1990s without a reversal and is not expected to change in the near future (Hills 1996; Goodman, Johnson, and Webb 1997).

Third, although inequality increased, the change in the 1980s did not necessarily make the richer better off at the expense of the poorer. There has been, instead, a clear shift from universal benefits to more targeted means-tested ones. The share of expenditure for means-tested benefits clearly increased from the mid-1970s to 1987 and 1988 (Barr and Coulter 1990). The same shift was observed from the 1980s to 1990 and 1991 (Pierson 1994, 145). The expenditures for housing benefits also showed the same tendency (Hills and Mullings 1990). In the 1990s, this shift has continued in social security expenditures including those for health care. All these policies reflect a departure from universalism and an affinity for targeting.[71]

The Paradox of the U.K. Welfare State   The paradox of the U.K. welfare state since the 1980s is as follows. The government clearly aims to shift away from universalism, which is popular but expensive, to targeting, which leads to benefit cuts for a wide range of socioeconomic groups, especially middle-income earners. But, the government has failed to cut expenditures. This consequence often leads to the argument that the interests of middle-class people have protected the welfare state from Thatcher's

---

[70] Both are examined to control the sensitivity of the Gini coefficients to economic conditions (for example, the level of unemployment).

[71] According to Radcliffe and McVicar (1997, 108), "the aim of most welfare policy has centered on the desire to move away from universal provision towards increasingly means-tested or targeted benefits and to try to encourage individuals to make provisions for their own personal and family security."

benefit cuts (Le Grand and Goodwin 1987). Does this mean that the policy shift from universalism to targeting was not complete? Before reaching a conclusion, one needs to examine other factors that are expected to influence the level of social security expenditures. The level of expenditures, even in the same program or scheme, is always conditional on socioeconomic situations, such as an increasing aged population and unemployment. For example, a sharp rise in unemployment in the early 1980s was believed to have increased social security expenditures more than expected (Disney and Webb 1990).[72] The Conservative administration from 1992 to 1997 tried to control expenditures, but an increasing number of new pensioners with the improved entitlement conditions and a long period of contributions and persistent high unemployment pushed up the costs of the social security system despite the intentions of John Major (Hill 1999).

More important, the two explanations for the middle-class resistance to welfare state retrenchment and policy inertia under specific socioeconomic conditions do not necessarily contradict each other. The efficiency of targeting social security benefits (i.e., to save the worse-off with lower costs) hinges on how effectively the scope of "targeting" is limited.[73] In the light of this view, the evaluation of the 1986 Social Security Act, which is one of the largest postwar reforms, should be qualified. Even after the act, means-tested benefits have remained a constant proportion of all spending: here, instead of being directed at the poorest and/or highest priority groups such as the sick, disabled, children, and elderly, targeting was based on consideration of economic efficiency in terms of return expected from the same level of benefit provision (Evans 1996). This could be consistent with middle-class interests.

Consequently, in the 1980s, while targeting and the restriction of entitlements were cutting the benefits in specific programs, the state could finance increasing expenditures. This finding closely parallels Pierson's (1994) comparison of the United States and the United Kingdom in the 1980s. Here, the relative robustness of the U.K. welfare state in comparison with the one in the United States can ultimately be attributed to the failure of

---

[72] Disney and Webb (1990) also point out a decline in unemployment from 1986, which also corresponds to the decline in social security expenditures in that year, which was slight but also unexpected.

[73] Atkinson (1993), using cases of several countries including the United Kingdom, demonstrates most social security transfers involve "a degree of conditionality" that ranges "in gladiatorial terms" from universal to targeted benefits.

the Thatcher administration to "defund" it, more specifically, to reduce the government's revenue-generating capacity. The U.S. administration under Reagan financed an income tax cut – more precisely, the simplification and reduction of the tax rate structure – by broadening the income tax base. The United Kingdom adopted a different strategy : financing a "visible" income tax cut by increases in an "invisible" VAT and social security contributions. The Conservative government enjoyed the reputation of being a tax cutter while raising revenue from an invisible tax, and this left the retrenchment of the welfare state more ineffective.

At the same time, however, there was no explicit consensus in the public mind. In a survey of British social attitudes, respondents who supported "increased taxes and more spending on health, education and social benefits" increased from 32 percent (in 1983), to 50 percent (in 1987), to 65 percent (in 1991), whereas the support for the status quo (i.e., "keeping taxes and spending on these services the same as now") decreased from 54 percent (in 1983), to 42 percent (in 1987), to 29 percent (in 1991) (Jowell 1996, 187). Unlike the polls, British voting behavior may imply a more negative attitude toward the welfare state. The radical change in policy orientation brought the long-awaited victory for the Labour Party in the 1997 general election after eighteen years of Conservative reign.[74] While embracing a new macroeconomic policy orientation with a less interventionist and a more laissez-faire style, the Labour Party avoided making a tax increase an issue and abandoned its traditional orientation toward big government. More specifically, it promised to (and after entering office actually did) restrain expenditures and taxes and use more nongovernmental organizations for welfare provision. This new commitment from the Labour Party began after the 1992 general election in which John Major affirmed the Conservative rule after Thatcher. It was not until 1994, under the leadership of Tony Blair,[75] that the new orientation gained credibility among the public. In this

---

[74] An analysis of several different aspects of Labour's victory provides consistent implications that the Labour policy change influenced a campaign style, and this change was an important factor controlling other political and socioeconomic factors to explain the victory (Geddes and Tonge 1997; Denver et al. 1997). In terms of a convergence in each field of welfare and social security policy between the Labour Party and the Conservative Party from 1992 to 1997, see Hay (1999, 117–30); Driver and Martell (1998, 32–86); MacGregor (1998).

[75] Rentoul (1999) starts his description of Tony Blair as a Labour leader compared with his predecessors as follows: "The central question for this chapter is whether Tony Blair belongs in this book at all: is he really the same historical line as the other leaders contained in these pages? He is the most un-Labour of the Labour leaders" (Rentoul 1999,

regard, the New Labour Party is not social democratic, but instead is under a "post-Thatcherite" influence, although its welfare policy orientation is more solidaristic and communitarian than neoliberal.[76]

The welfare and tax policies under the Blair administration from 1997 to 2000 confirm the changing policy orientation of Labour. While targeting lower-income people with children and the elderly and increasing education and health care provisions, the administration has implemented a small tax cut, especially the income tax.[77] Corporation tax rates have been reduced since 1997. The full rate was pushed down from 33 to 31 percent in 1997 and then to 30 percent in 1999 (under Labour), which is an exceptionally low level among industrial democracies. The Advance Corporation Tax (ACT) was abolished in April 1999, and the rate for small companies was reduced from 21 to 20 percent in 1999. The personal income tax cut appeared more drastic. In the 1990s until 1999, the rate change was small – the basic rate was lowered from 25 to 23 percent. But, in April 1999, the lower rate was halved from 20 to 10 percent with the lower rate limit of £1,500 per annual income slashed from the previous £4,300, and, in April 2000, the basic rate was reduced further to 22 percent.[78] As a result, at the turn of the century, the United Kingdom has a three-rate structure of 40, 22, and 10 percent. Increasing tax expenditures apparently target the poor with children and the elderly.[79] The 1999 Finance Act also involved a restriction on the VAT grouping of companies.[80] This will increase both administrative and tax compliance costs but is used as a revenue-enhancing measure.

208). Driver and Martell (1998, 8–17) and Clarke, Stewart, and Whiteley (1998) concur with Rentoul that the novelty of his leadership gained public recognition.

[76] For example, see Driver and Martell (1998, 104–29); Balloch (1998); Gamble and Wright (1999).

[77] Parry (2000) argues that the Labour government's emphasis on the sustainable level of public expenditures strengthened the position of Treasury under Gordon Brown though the government also injected more money to health, education, and social security than the Conservative plan. For a more detailed account of social policy under the Labour government in the 1990s, see Deakin and Parry (2000, Chapters 9 and 10).

[78] Of the basic rate limit, 23 percent has been gradually increased from £20,700 in 1990 to £28,000 per annual income.

[79] Since October 1999, Family Credit has been replaced by the Working Families Tax Credit (WFTC), and the married couples' allowance has been reduced and abolished except for the elderly, but has been replaced by the Children's Tax Credit.

[80] This act aims to increase the discretionary power of Customs and Excise to limit the eligibility of companies applying for members of the VAT groups. If this is implemented strictly, and the eligibility is restricted to the companies subject to the VAT while excluding VAT-exempted countries, all the supplies in the dismantled groups would be taxed.

In the United Kingdom, successive governments have been reluctant to increase the size of the public sector by strengthening its revenue-raising capacity, and the public is not confident to let the government do so. The result is a smaller public sector than the European standard and in sharp contrast to the one in Sweden where the public still supports a large welfare state. Both the United Kingdom and Sweden were governed by the left toward the end of the twentieth century, but they are distinct. The U.K. government orientation is peculiar, even among the EU member countries.

[T]he United Kingdom was the only member country of the European Union which insisted on not being required to honour the Social Charter in the Maastricht Agreement. The agreement of the U.K. Government was that the Social Charter would increase employer costs, which would have to be reflected in enhanced labour costs, which in turn would be detrimental to the U.K.'s competitive position. (Radcliffe and McVicar 1997, 93–4)[81]

The opposite side of this modestly sized welfare state is the moderate revenue-raising power of the government.

France: Resistance to Welfare State Backlash and Regressive Taxation

Big Government Financed by Compulsory and Regressive Taxation

Tax Politics à la **Française**   The French tax system stands distinct from any other industrial democracy; the trend in the French tax policy has been different – even opposite – from other countries. Its tax revenue structure is peculiar – most of the revenue is raised from proportional (i.e., regressive) taxation, that is, from taxes on goods and services and social security contributions (Figure 2.1). In 1965 the proportion of personal income tax to total tax revenue in France was only 10.6 percent whereas the OECD average was 25.9 percent. In 1980, the average in France remained at 12.9 percent, whereas the OECD average increased to 32.0 percent. France made no explicit effort to adopt comprehensive income taxation and increase the personal income tax. It is interesting to note that this characterization of the French tax system in the mid-1960s mirrors the one in the 1990s.

The peculiar tax revenue structure and long conservative rule until 1980 often overshadow other aspects of French socioeconomic policies.

---

[81] Hirst (1999, 95) concurs with Radcliffe and McVicar (1997) in terms of the odd position of the United Kingdom in the EU integration.

First, France has the largest social security expenditure in Europe after the Scandinavian countries. In terms of size, it is a large welfare state even by the Western European standard. Second, although it has not been influenced by other countries' tax policies, France innovated and first introduced several new taxes. It pioneered the use of the imputation system of corporate taxation in 1965 and the indexation of the income tax schedule in 1968. The most notable example was the introduction of the VAT in 1954 – thirteen years before any other industrial country – which was subsequently reformed in a more comprehensive form in 1968 and became the model of the VAT in the EC countries at that time. More recently, it introduced flat-rate taxes on income earmarked for social security expenditures, although it remains to be seen if these taxes will be adopted outside France.

Taxe sur la Valeur Ajoutée – *The Origin of the Regressive Taxation*
Continuing a long tradition of a variety of turnover and sales taxes dating back to 1920, the VAT was introduced in 1954, but services and retail transactions were taxed separately. A 1968 reform abolished a variety of excise taxes on specific goods as well as the tax on services and a local tax (the retail sales tax). Thus the VAT came to cover services and retail transaction. The Ministry of Finance[82] put the reform of the VAT on the political agenda in 1959 at the beginning of the Fifth Republic. The implementation of the reform required almost the entire period of de Gaulle's rule. Until its passage in the National Assembly, six years had elapsed since the first proposal of the reform by the government. The administration conducted a public relations campaign to win support for the reform, which targeted both the public and professionals. Tax councils under the Minister of Finance and Economic Affairs (hereafter Minister of Finance) extensively examined its effect on price changes, estimated the transfers between firms, and determined the tax rate to get the desired level of revenue. This contributed to

---

[82] The MOF, in charge of public finance, has an especially high status even among the bureaucracy. The MOF bureaucrats are more independent from their own minister than those in other ministries, and this is one of the important reasons for the strength of the MOF. First, the Minister of Finance deals substantially with independent directors who head their own divisions in charge of different jurisdictions. There are four secretaries of state, and the Secretary of State for Budget is in charge of tax, and the General Tax Division (*Direction Générale des Impôts*) is in charge of all taxation. But, there is no Secretary General who heads the whole ministry bureaucracy. This is peculiar to the MOF except for the Ministry of Agriculture. Moreover, the selection of personal staff for the Minister of Finance (*cabinet*) requires the approval of the Directors (Suleiman 1974, 254).

making the French system a model for the EC member countries at that time.[83]

Despite an extensive examination of economic activities, the regressive effect of the VAT was underestimated and considered solved inside the system.

In the French view, income may be taxed both when received (income tax) and when spent (sales tax). If a sales tax is levied at differential rates on products of different necessity, the sales tax becomes a progressive tax, bearing more heavily on the rich than on the poor. The value-added-tax, as the French apply it, is a progressive tax on expenditure as a measure of ability to pay (Norr and Kerlan 1966, 71).

At the time of its introduction, the French policy makers had erroneously expected the VAT to be a comparable alternative to the progressive income tax and thus had never seriously attempted to adopt a comprehensive income tax. Their attitude made a sharp contrast with the one of the Swedish policy makers who had already recognized the VAT as a purely revenue-raising measure for redistributive spending *despite* the early institutionalization of the progressive income tax. It was not until 1979 when the French VAT system was reformed to broaden its base that the VAT came to be regarded as a regressive form of taxation, and the rate differentiation came to be considered undesirable (Balladur and Coutière 1981).[84]

Chronic Deficits and Tax Policy Changes Since the 1980s

In the 1970s, the tax level was increasing to finance public expenditures. The additional burden was paid by regressive taxes. The increasing proportion of social security contributions in terms of total tax revenue and GDP were outstanding. The VAT maintained the same proportion to the GDP, although it was slightly replaced by social security contributions in terms of share of the increasing total tax revenue. The progressivity of taxation was pursued mainly by repealing the ceilings to calculate social security contributions and allowing more generous deductions of income tax from wage earners. The government never attempted to comprehend the income

---

[83] For more details of the process and background of the VAT's introduction, see Nizet 1991, chapter 5.

[84] For example, the 1983 Tax Council Report to the president (*Rapport au Président de la République, Conseil des impôts*) explicitly concluded that the VAT system was not neutral but relatively neutral in terms of both income distribution and economic activities, especially in terms of its impact on different sectors of industries.

tax base and apply progressive rates, and the result was an especially weak revenue- raising capacity of the income tax concentrated on a small number of high-income earners with progressive rates. Thus, at the end of the 1970s, all the problems that were to require urgent solutions in the 1990s already existed. A narrow tax base caused by tax exemptions and allowances made the income tax revenue stagnant. The burden of the VAT was increasing as the base was broadened and the rate increased. Social security contributions were heavily levied on both employers and wage earners. There should have been some upper limit to these regressive taxes on consumption.

Although the Socialist government did not immediately change tax policy, three transformations in existing taxes continued from the 1980s into the 1990s. First, the corporate tax rate continued to be reduced. The rate on retained profits had been 50 percent (from 1960 to 1985) but went down to 34 percent in 1991. The rate on distributed profits also decreased from 50 percent to 42 percent in 1991. More neutrality in the corporate tax base was achieved by a variety of measures such as eliminating depreciation allowances. However, together with a lower personal income tax, the tax on corporations vis-à-vis households is higher than in any other industrial democracy owing to the large size of the employers' social security contributions and a tough rule that claims VAT credit on imports.[85]

Second, although the progressivity of personal income taxation was maintained, it continued to have a weak revenue-raising power. Increasing the marginal tax rate ran counter to the major direction of tax policies in other industrial democracies, but, in France, even in the early 1980s, the top marginal tax rate increased from 60 to 65 percent.[86] Although the top rate decreased from the highest 65 percent in 1985 to 56.8 percent in 1991, the progressivity was maintained by applying a variety of tax exemptions to release those with lower income. In the mid-1990s, in terms of income tax, France finally adopted the idea of simplification and rate cut and followed the path taken by other OECD countries in the 1980s. In 1994, under Prime Minister Edouard Balladur, the number of income tax brackets decreased from thirteen to seven. Then, in June 1996, Prime Minister Juppé announced a five-year tax reform plan for decreasing taxes (FF 75 billion almost equating with $14.8 billion) and cutting spending

---

[85] Lienard, Messere, and Owens (1987, 153) mention the same point to show the relatively high burden of French corporations.

[86] Also, it reintroduced the wealth tax in 1981, which major industrial democracies had not reintroduced for the last four decades. The tax was abolished under the Conservative coalition government in 1987 and then reintroduced by the Socialist government in 1989.

for the period from 1997 to 2001. He implemented the reform following the report of a tax commission headed by Dominique de la Martinière in July. The number of brackets in the income tax schedule would remain at seven, but both the top rate and lower rates were reduced accordingly. Various exemptions, deductions, and relief in the personal income tax were eliminated or curtailed gradually or immediately to make the tax base somewhat broader. At the same time, employers' sickness contributions (*cotisation maladie salariale*) decreased from a 6.8 to a 5.5 percent levy on the wages of salaried workers to lower the cost of employment. Long-term capital gains were distinguished from other sales of stocks and taxed at a reduced rate.

The adoption of simplification and a cut in the income tax rate structure in common with other countries curiously made the French tax system even more distinctive. The weak revenue-raising power of the income tax was further weakened. The reform has not significantly changed the characteristics of the French personal income tax – a high marginal tax rate and a narrow tax base (and a low average tax rate) owing to a complex combination of numerous (about one hundred) reliefs and exemptions. The yields of personal income taxation have been continuously lower than in any other major industrial democracy (any of twenty-four OECD countries) in terms of both percentages of total revenue (except Greece) and of the GDP (except Greece and Turkey). Only 48 percent of French households paid an income tax in 1993, and this is unlikely to increase after the reform in 1996 (Blotnicki and Heckly 1994, 1477–8). Consequently, the marginal rate cut in the personal income tax further fortified the low revenue reliance on the income tax, which was around 18 percent of the total tax revenue, even at the time of peak.

Third, the high tax was considered problematic for the first time. The total tax revenue ratio to the GDP increased steeply – by 10 percent – from 1973 to 1984 : the additional burden was concentrated in social security contributions. The previous 5 to 6 percent economic growth rates were almost halved, and public expenditures, especially for social security, continued to increase. "[A]s France chose a rather orthodox fiscal policy and approximately balanced its budget (except in the first years of the 1980s), the tax ratio 'had to' rise" (Maillard 1993, 314).[87] Based on observations

---

[87] A major exception to this tendency was the 1985 budget that aimed to cut the tax level (by 1 percent of the GDP or FF 40 billion) by several measures including the reduction in social security contributions. At that time, the Socialist government was trying to cope with declining electoral support at both national and local levels.

until the mid-1980s, France was classified as a Bismarck type of welfare state with a low budget deficit compared with the United Kingdom or Sweden (Jallade 1988). However, in 1997, France suffered an even larger deficit than other EU countries and even struggled to strike the Maastricht target to lower the deficit. France first responded to the need to solve budget deficits by using existing taxes. In 1995, the standard VAT rate increased from 18.6 percent to 20.6 percent[88] to finance a budget deficit and revenue shortfall from the simplified income tax, which had generated much less revenue than expected. The VAT rate increase was also considered a possible means for financing the social security deficit under the Balladur governments from 1986 to 1988 and from 1993 to 1995.[89] But any further increase in revenue reliance on the VAT became unrealistic. This was counter to the harmonization of VAT rates inside the EU: France had just reduced its higher rate (as high as 33.5 percent) to 22 percent in 1991, to be closer to the standard rate of the European Commission, 18.6 percent, at that time. Moreover, even without the mandate for tax coordination in the EU, just as in Sweden, increasing its reliance on the VAT would be considered intolerable and thus politically infeasible.

In this economic climate, new social security taxes were introduced in the early 1990s to replace parts of the social security contributions and connect the tax system financially with the social security system. Their introduction has transformed both the tax and welfare state in France.

New Social Security Taxes in the Conservative Welfare State

The foundation of the contemporary French social security system was established in 1945. Since then, most social security expenditures, recently up to about 80 percent, were financed by social security contributions (*cotisations sociales*), which are levied proportionally on gross earnings and paid by both employees and employers. The French welfare state has been considered a Bismarckian type in continental Europe in which the social insurance approach has dominated with its employment-based entitlements. Until recently, employers paid approximately two-thirds of contributions for sickness and old age, all contributions for family and housing allowances,

---

[88] There were two reduced rates, 2.1 and 5.5 percent, and a standard rate of 20.6 percent.

[89] I thank Scott Shaughnessy for pointing this out. Balladur considered raising the VAT rate but instead raised the CSG (*la contribution sociale généralisée*) by 1.3 percent in 1994 (Shaughnessy 1994, 552).

and the compensation for work-related accidents and illnesses. The levy on employees was not only proportional and regressive but also degressive because of the application of ceilings on contributions and the deductibility of contributions from the income tax. A high revenue reliance on social security contibutions, more generally, concentration on taxes on wages, caused high employment costs in the conservative welfare state.

In addition, the social security deficit that increased after the mid-1970s has become a politicized issue since the early 1980s. The deficit subsequently continued to increase. The Socialist government recognized the chronic social security deficit by 1982, and a solution was considered within the government.[90] The public was willing to accept a further heavy tax and pay more for maintaining "their beloved social security" (Shaughnessy 1994, 410).[91] Until the mid-1980s, however, the government employed only ad hoc measures – raising the rates of existing social security contributions and levying a 1 percent increase in contributions on the salaries in the public sector. In 1983, the MOF under then Minister Jacques Delors and the Ministry of Social Affairs under then Minister Pierre Bérégovoy decided to introduce an ad hoc 1 percent contribution on taxable income. Because the surplus removed the deficit, this levy was repealed after two years before the parliamentary elections in March 1986 when the governing power changed from the Socialists to the Conservatives. The surplus continued for three years from 1983 to 1985, but was replaced again by a deficit in 1986.

Although the new prime minister, Jacques Chirac, who targeted the presidential elections in 1988, preferred tinkering with the existing taxation to fundamental reform, he appointed a committee of six "wise men" (*le Comité des Sages*) headed by Pierre Laroque, who had been a founding father of the contemporary social security system. When the committee finally reported on a solution for social security in October 1987, a consensus on the necessity of the reform was reached among related interest groups such as unions and professional groups. By March 1988, the decision was made secretly within the government to introduce a new tax to finance social security, which would become a 1.1 percent tax on income.[92] This was to be the first example of a major tax on income earmarked for

---

[90] In 1982, the Secretary of State for the Budget, Laurent Fabius, and, in 1983, Minister of Finance Delors proposed new taxes to finance the social security system. Also, see Shaughnessy (1994, 408–9).

[91] He cites the result of a major opinion survey during this period (Dubergé 1984).

[92] Shaughnessy (1994, 411) cites Pierre-Brossolette (1988, 55) as evidence.

social security among industrial democracies and was named "the general social security tax" (*la contribution sociale généralisée*, hereafter, CSG). In this way, levying a new tax earmarked for social security was put on the political agenda.

The Socialists won in both the presidential and parliamentary elections in 1988, and the rule of a Socialist president and a Conservative prime minister ended. The unified executive did not necessarily provide favorable circumstances for the enactment of the new tax for social security. However, in October 1990, the CSG became part of a government proposal of the budget to the National Assembly (*le projet de loi de finances*) for 1991. Although Minister of Finance Pierre Bérégovoy and the Socialist parliamentary members led by Fabius opposed the CSG, the Minister for Solidarity, Health, and Social Protection,[93] Claude Evin, managed to make it a government proposal based on firm support from President Mitterrand and Prime Minister Rocard. The proposal was attacked in the National Assembly by the opposition including the former Secretary of State for the Budget, Alain Juppé. For the passage of the budget in both the National Assembly and the Senate, Prime Minister Rocard resorted to the confidence vote procedure based on Article 49 of the Constitution.[94] The government demanded that the opposition choose between censuring the government and supporting the policy and won by a slim margin against a censure vote.

The CSG has since been used extensively by both partisan camps. The Conservatives had once opposed it but increased its rates after they entered office. The rate was raised from 1.1 percent to 2.4 percent in 1994 under the new center-right government. This 1.3 percent increase was to be earmarked for a solidarity fund for old-age provision (*fonds de solidarité vieillesse*), that is, for all those retirement and old-age benefits with no *cotisation* of their own. Then, the social security law decided on a rate increase from 2.4 to 3.4 percent effective in January 1997 while broadening the tax base and allowing this additional 1 percent of CSG to be deducted from taxable income under a certain condition. This 1 percent increase in CSG has substituted for 1.3 percent of the health insurance contribution (*la cotisation maladie*) for workers and 1 percent for the retired. In 1996, another social security tax, the social security deficit refund tax (*la contribution au remboursement de la dette sociale*, hereafter, CRDS) was introduced. In the

---

[93] The Ministry of Solidarity, Health and Social Protection was the new name of the former Ministry of Social Affairs. Please refer to footnote 101.

[94] For the confidence vote procedure, see Huber (1996, 1999).

same way as the CSG, this new tax is levied (by 0.5 percent) on almost all types of earned income and is earmarked for the refund of social security debt; it is an ad hoc measure. At the time of its introduction, the CRDS was to be imposed on wages, substitute income such as social security benefits, and investment income until 2009, and on inheritances until 2008. The government also decided that the imposition could be prolonged by five years until 2014.

Ne Touchez Pas Ma Secu!

Since the mid-1990s, the French government has become more reliant on the new social security taxes. Despite their introduction, the social security deficit increased steeply from FF 15.6 billion in 1992 to FF 55.6 billion in 1994. In 1995, therefore, the deficit needed a solution. On October 26, Prime Minister Juppé proposed to reduce the budget deficit (projected to become FF 64.5 billion in the following year). On November 15, he obtained support from the National Assembly for various measures to reform the social security system. Juppé's proposal was an apparent failure of political maneuvering: the labor unions were especially upset about the proposal of a social security benefit cut for workers in the public sector without any prior consultation with the unions (Kesselman 1996, 158–60). They called for a nationwide general strike from late November to December. The strike was joined by major labor unions such as the CGT (*Confédération Générale du Travail*: Communist orientation), a minor part of the CFDT (*Confédération Française Démocratique du Travail*: Socialist and pragmatic orientation) in the national railway company (SNCF), the FO (*Force Ouvrière*: Socialist and Trotskyist orientation), the CGC (*Confédération Générale des Cadres*: white-collar union) and the CFTC (*Confédération Française des Travailleurs Chrétiens*: Catholic union) in SNCF, the Paris transportation authority (RATP), the French electric and gas companies (EDF-GDF), and the postal service (*La Poste*). The public transporation system and the provision of utilities were paralyzed. The labor unrest wracked the country until the social summit on December 21. The government had stood firm at the beginning but was forced to compromise with labor by freezing the reform plan.

In Juppé's announcement, there were, among others, too many controversial proposals against labor unions in the public sector, a massive reduction in retirement payment for workers in public transportation, a decrease in labor's influence on the management board (*caisse*) of the health insurance system, and an amendment in the Constitution to institutionalize a vote on a social security budget in the National Assembly. The reform plan was politicized as a proposal for benefit cuts without any prior negotiation with social partners and thus triggered strong labor protest. In other words, the substance of Juppé's proposal could have obtained labor's immediate support if it had been proposed in a different way.[95] As explained later, almost all proposals were subsequently implemented without major modifications.

In 1996, the total tax revenue to the GDP reached a record-breaking high 45.7 percent, but, at the same time, the social security deficit was expected to grow to FF 48.6 billion instead of the forecast FF 16.6 billion. The combined deficits of social security and general budget were as high as 4 percent against a 3 percent ceiling, which was required by the Maastricht single-currency convergence criteria set by the European Economic and Monetary Union (EMU). The growth rate stagnated, and the deficit became a source of headache for the government. From May to June 1997, President Chirac bet on obtaining a stable majority in the National Assembly and called a parliamentary election. He wanted to win a public mandate to implement a more effective policy to push the deficit down to 3 percent of GDP. But this gamble failed, and Prime Minister Juppé resigned assuming responsibility for the defeat after the first vote in late June. The prime ministership returned to the Socialists, and a new phase of cohabitation in French party politics had started. Conservative President Chirac was forced to face the Socialist Prime Minister Lionel Jospin, who was more eager to decrease unemployment than spending (and thus the deficit) in the election campaign.

At the Amsterdam summit in June 1997, although France had to clear the target of a 3 percent ratio of budget deficit to GDP in 1997, the deficit that year was expected to be 3.5 to 3.8 percent of the GDP. Jospin made clear his priority of deficit reduction after the election as Chirac had done after the presidential election in 1995. In July 1997, Minister of Finance Dominique Strauss-Kahn unveiled a tax package to increase the tax on profitable companies and raise FF 32 billion ($5.26 billion) to reduce the

---

[95] For example, Nicole Notat, then secretary general of the French Democratic Labor Confederation (CFDT), supported a major line of the government proposal though she demanded some amendments (Caillé and Le Goff 1996, 152). In addition to the contents of the plan, the government's lack of prior consultation with the unions and drafting the plan in total secrecy were major reasons for the devastating opposition (Bonoli 2000, 148).

deficit by about 0.3 to 0.4 percent of the GDP.[96] The government implied that the deficit would go down to 3.2 percent, which was very close to the Maastricht target and within a permissible range.

In 1997, therefore, the reduction of both social security and budget deficits was an imminent concern for the new government. Although they were not to solve deficits immediately, the government decided to increase the CSG rate and prolong the CRDS levy as already described. The CSG rate on all kinds of wages, inheritance, investment, and saving increased from 3.4 to 7.5 percent, and the rate on substitute income and social security benefit, from 3.4 to 6.2 percent beginning in January 1998. This additional CSG levy replaced 4.75 percent of the health insurance contribution (*la cotisation maladie*) on wages. As a result, the former 5.5 percent levy for salaried workers was lowered to 0.75 percent, and the former 4.75 percent levy for civil servants went down to zero. For the retired and unemployed, the 2.8 percent additional CSG levy reduced the health insurance contribution from 3.8 to 1 percent. The government made this new levy deductible from the income tax base again. When the CSG was introduced, Rocard had intended to introduce a high rate of 6.77 percent, which would not have been deductible from the income tax base to substitute health insurance contributions and cover universal health insurance coverage. After eight years, the CSG came closer to Rocard's original intention except that most of the CSG has become deductible from the income tax base.[97]

In retrospect, the 1995 winter strike was a drastic protest against the social security benefit cut that had been unexpected from a French labor union organization that was weaker than other Western European countries (Scarbrough 2000, 242). It confirmed nothing except the political mandate to protect social security benefits.[98] The public's resistance

---

[96] The independent Court of Auditors, called by Jospin for France's finances for the first time since 1860, concluded that, without additional measures, the deficit would be 3.6 to 3.7 percent of the GDP (*Financial Times*, July 21, 1997).

[97] I thank Elie Cohen for mentioning this point to me. To finance health insurance costs, the introduction of contributions levied on added values in economic activity (*cotisation sur la valeur ajoutée*) was once considered but lost its relevance, while the CSG rate has increased.

[98] There were many other factors involved in the strike in winter 1995, such as European integration and unemployment. However, the issue of social security was most important in the sense that it was related to other factors that potentially contributed to aggravating the strike. European integration was regarded as a threat to maintaining a high welfare provision and a cause of unemployment that had already been high due to the employment costs related to the heavy burden of employers' social security contributions.

reflected the French people's attitude to social security – they supported a generous benefit despite its accompanying high burden. The subsequent increase of the CSG implies that the French have accepted the increasing tax as long as the state provides the benefits that have become their vested interest and are not to be challenged.

Tax Financing of Social Security: Is the Bismarckian Welfare State to Be Replaced by the Beveridge Without Strong Labor?

The CSG has great revenue potential.[99] When it was introduced in 1991, 1.1 percent of the CSG was proposed as a trade-off for the social security contributions. Replacing parts of the social security contributions with the CSG in 1997 resulted in a net increase in revenue.

Technically the CSG is a large-scale income tax earmarked for social security expenditures. Social security *contributions* in many countries are counted as a part of general revenue but are considered by the government as distinct from *taxes*. Generally speaking, the financial authority does not like an earmarked tax simply because it is likely to decrease its discretion. The introduction of a *tax* earmarked for social security has often been discussed in industrial democracies but has not been implemented except in France.[100] In this regard, the introduction of the CSG and the subsequent rate increase were very curious considering the power of the French fiscal authority. The MOF had once opposed the CSG and, after its introduction, periodically showed a reluctance to the CSG rate increase for macroeconomic reasons but generally came to support it. One of the reasons is that the CSG has increased the government's control over the social security budget, which had been under the influence of social partners (i.e., employers and employees). The Ministry of Employment and Solidarity,[101] not the MOF, is directly in charge of the revenue from the CSG, but the MOF still welcomes the shift in control over the social security budget from the social partners to another ministry, especially when the government budget

---

[99] With more than FF 55 billion from 1 percent of the CSG, the 7.5 percent of the CSG from 1998 yielded more revenue than the approximately FF 290 billion from the income tax existing in 1996. In an interview on November 5, 1997, the MOF official was already confident about the CSG's revenue-raising capacity.

[100] For example, it was politicized in Japan in the late 1980s and in the United States in the early 1990s when the introduction of the VAT was proposed in each country.

[101] The French ministries change their names as frequently as the ministers change. This ministry is the same as the Ministry of Social Affairs previously mentioned.

deficit is of urgent concern.[102] Increasing deficits also explained the ultimate acceptance of the CSG by the labor unions, although its introduction was destined to decrease their leverage over the social security budget. The labor unions had long argued that the social security deficits were derived from an excessive need to finance noncontributory benefits by social security contributions and that the government was responsible for the deficits (Palier 2001a, 12). Therefore, when the CSG, earmarked for noncontributory benefits, was proposed by the government, the labor unions had no way to refuse it.

Although it is imposed on "income," the CSG is distinct from the income tax. The existing income tax has a narrower base than the CSG and thus has weaker revenue-raising power.[103] The French government did not attempt to improve the existing income tax by broadening the base of the existing income tax in the same way as the CSG (i.e., to include earned, transfer, and capital incomes). Although the CSG is considered a tax on income, it is clearly distinguished from the existing income tax with progressive rates, which is regarded as having little room for improvement.[104] The original idea at the time of the introduction was to combine the flat-rate CSG and the existing (progressive) income tax as a tax on income. Strictly speaking, however, it has become difficult to maintain that the CSG is a tax because, in the past two increases (1 percent in 1997 and 4.1 percent in 1998), the CSG has been deductible from the income tax base. If the CSG is defined as an income tax, the deduction is technically impossible. The CSG's partial deduction from the income tax base represents feasible judgment in tax politics but not strictly in tax theory.[105] The French government

---

[102] This point was confirmed in an interview with an MOF official on September 18, 1997.

[103] The weak revenue-raising power also results from a low level of tax compliance. In a chapter on France in a study of comparative income taxation, Gest (1997, 46) writes: "French tax payers do not like taxes, and they say they don't....Many tax payers still consider tax evasion as legitimate and the amount involved in tax evasion is indeed not inconsiderable."

[104] When I asked an MOF official why the French government has not attempted to broaden the income tax base for more revenue raising instead of introducing the CSG, he answered, "because it is a bad tax." There is a clear distinction between the existing income tax and the CSG in the minds of policy makers even though both taxes are imposed on an income base. This is not just because the CSG is earmaked for social security expenditures. (Interviews with an MOF official, November 1997).

[105] Aside from the financial aspect, there are a couple of reasons to define the CSG as a tax instead of a contribution. First, the CSG rate increase is decided by the National Assembly in the same way as other taxes, whereas social security contributions are decided

continues to maintain that the CSG is a tax not a contribution. As a result, the CSG is treated as a personal income tax in the national accounts, but the government distinguishes this from the existing income tax.[106]

The second impact of the CSG on the French tax revenue structure is to decrease the high social security contributions characteristic of the continental European countries based on the social insurance principle (Scharpf 2000). The CSG diffuses the existing high burden on wages and thus pushes down employment costs. Although the total burden of social security contributions has continued to increase, the employers' contribution has stagnated since the mid-1980s. As a result, in 1993 about 60 percent of total contributions were paid by employers, whereas in 1965 almost 80 percent had been paid by them. The CSG was effective in coping with the high unemployment problem by decreasing the high employers' social security contributions when budget deficits prevented the government from expanding the employment opportunity to increase public spending. More important, the public recognizes that the burden for financing social security has shifted from a wage to a wider income base. The French people usually know how much their employers pay for their social security;[107] this is in sharp contrast with the Swedish situation in which high social security contributions are hidden from the public eye. As exemplified by the government report on the problem of unemployment and high employment costs, the CSG has been regarded as the financing

by government decrees. In the same way as the CSG, new social security taxes, such as the CRDS and social levy on property income (*prélèvement social*), are decided by legislation.

[106] In the revenue statistics of the OECD countries, it is classified as an individual income tax instead of social security contributions. However, the CSG has not been understood well outside France because the CSG is a tax peculiar to France. For example, several officials complained that even those in the EU headquarters who push tax harmonization tend to regard the CSG as social security contributions (interviews with officials in November 1997). At the same time, however, if the CSG is defined correctly as a tax on income, it faces another problem resulting from European integration. On February 15, 2000, the European Court of Justice criticized that France illegally taxes French income outside the country. If the CSG was a social security contribution, it could be legally collected from the income abroad. But if it is defined as a tax, and the French Constitution actually defines it as such, it means that the French government extends the imposition of the income tax outside France against the agreement among member countries.

[107] This is because the payment strip (*bulletin de paye*) widely used by accounting programs has two equally large divisions to show salary paid to employees and payments by employers to the government and social security fund. I am grateful to Jean-Pierre Jallade who mentioned this point to me.

measure for social security, which is consistent with maintaining employment opportunity.[108]

The biggest change that the CSG has brought, however, is to increase the government's control over the social security budget. The consitutional amendment to pass the social security budget in the National Assembly was included in Juppé's proposal in November 1995. After a constitutional change at the beginning of 1996, which increased the CSG rate from 2.4 percent to 3.4 percent, the National Assembly for the first time in its history deliberated over a law to finance social security (*Projet de Loi de financement de la Sécurité Sociale*). Since 1945, financing the social security system had been under the control of the government and its social partners, that is, labor unions and employers' associations on the managing board of the social security fund. Separating the social security budget from the ordinary budget and bringing both budgets for deliberation in the National Assembly first appeared to be a nonpolitical and technical change because the government at that time was forced to abide by the Maastricht target of budget deficit reduction (Lamaignère 1996, 1059). But the successive replacement of social security contributions by the CSG has drastically decreased money that flows into the social security fund managed by the board of social partners. When the government decided that 4.1 percent of the CSG would substitute for the health insurance contribution after 1998, it became apparent that this was a radical and revolutionary change to finance social security.[109] All the new social security taxes now flow into a general revenue fund under the exclusive control of the government and are examined by the National Assembly. The influence of the government and legislature over the social security system increased at the expense of social partners. Financing health insurance seems to have changed the nature of the CSG to finance noncontributory benefits. Although health insurance benefits are noncontributory-based, they are regarded as much closer to contributory benefits in the sense that most of the population is expected to benefit from them.[110] In this regard, the CSG has brought a direct financial link between general tax revenue and social security under the government's control.

---

[108] Groupe "Perspectives économiques," 1994, "Coût du travail et emploi: une nouvelle donne," chapitre IX (Paris: Commissariat général du Plan).

[109] See "La CSG au coeur du débat pour une nouvelle fiscalité" (*Le Monde*, September 11, 1997); "CSG: Plus de pouvoir d'achat avec plus d'impôt!" (*Nouvel Observateur*, September 18, 1997); "CSG Opération danger" (*L'Express*, September 18, 1997).

[110] I thank Bruno Palier for drawing my attention to this point.

Postscript: Changes in the New Millenium?

Facing the turn of the century, the French government enjoyed an increasing tax revenue as a result of its effective revenue structure. With the effect of a booming economy, the upsurge in tax revenue means that France now boasts a very strong revenue structure and effective government control of the social security system. Financing social security by a tax (i.e., the CSG) contradicts the social insurance approach in the Bismarckian welfare state and appears to veer toward the tax-financed, universal welfare state.[111] Will France go further in the direction of a tax-financed Beveridge-type welfare state? There are clear differences between France and the existing universal welfare state in Scandinavia.

First, in terms of the management of the social security system, France has had a parallel with the social partnership in the corporatist arrangement, but labor's power to organize the working population has declined.[112] From 1985 to 1995, the percentage of organized workers to total working population by labor unions dropped by 37.2 percent and went as low as 9.1 percent. This is a much sharper decline and lower rate than in other industrial democracies. For example, during the same period, the U.S. rate dropped by 21.1 percent to 14.2 percent, the U.K. rate by 27.7 percent to 32.9 percent, the German rate by 17.6 percent to 28.9 percent.[113] This may also derive from the fact that labor unions play a different political role in French politics than they play in Scandinavian class politics. The French labor unions long held a legitimate place in social security policy making and thus represented the interests of salaried workers in general instead of the interests of narrower-based workers (Palier 2001a, 9; 2001b, 100). This large constituency for the social security system is most likely the middle class, and, thus, as long as their interests are protected under a new arrangement, the declining influence of the labor unions will be more

---

[111] In a comparative study of European welfare states based on the size of expenditure (percentage of GDP) and the method of financing expenditures (taxes or contributions), Bonoli (1997) pays special attention to the implementation of the CSG and Bonoli and Palier (1998) present more spcifically the transformation of the French welfare state from the Bismarckian type to the tax-financed Beveridge type.

[112] This tendency can be attributed to several factors, such as the inherent ideological division in the union movement, the return of the Conservatives to office, the effect of globalization, and the increasing state intervention through employment in the public sector (Kesselman 1996; Groux and Mouriaux 1996).

[113] Le Monde (November 6, 1997). The data are publicized by the International Labor Organization (ILO).

politically accepted. It is worth noting that the decision to increase the CSG rate in 1997 was unexpectedly easy considering that this was the largest rate increase that had ever been made. With the CSG, as already explained, the labor unions are destined to lose much leverage over social security, and they have resisted the CSG introduction and each rate increase, but in vain. In this regard, "the strike movement of autumn 1995 served only to reveal the last throes of a privileged core of workers and a union oligarchy dependent on a centralized state" (Milner 2000, 56).

Second, a reliance on regressive taxation leads to revenue-raising power, but the left is still reluctant to raise revenue from regressive taxation even for the purpose of social security expenditures. There is opposition inside the Socialist Party to the CSG and VAT. This is diametrically opposed to the enthusiasm of the Swedish Social Democrats for financing a welfare state by regressive taxation.

Third, although the CSG has been extensively used by the government and accepted by the public, this may not imply that there is a consensus on the tax-financed welfare state. Although the government regards and confirms the CSG as a tax, it is still equated with social security contributions in the public's mind. The more apparent symptom is the exemption of the CSG from the income tax base as already explained. The CSG replaces social security contributions that are, in principle, to finance contributory benefits, and it also finances noncontributory benefits. The social insurance principle appears to have been challenged and transformed by the CSG, but it is still distinct from the universal approach to providing benefits regardless of contributions. Consequently, the recent transformation in the French welfare state is likely to challenge conventional wisdom about the Bismarckian welfare state (Palier 2000),[114] but even if France were to go further in the direction of a tax-financed welfare state, it would still be different from the Beveridge-type universal welfare state in Scandinavia.

Conclusion

This chapter disputes the idea that under a long, common history and tradition, an integrated Europe facilitates the convergence of tax and

---

[114] More explicitly, the Bismarckian social security system in France has been structurally changed. Three prominent policy changes are the introduction of the CSG, parliamentary deliberation about the social security budget, and the 1988 introduction of new noncontributory benefits to guarantee a minimum level of revenue for all above 25 (RMI: *Revenue Minimum d'Insertion*) (Palier 2000).

welfare policies. Three European countries – Sweden, the United Kingdom, and France – have not only preserved but increased the cross-national variation in their tax systems and welfare states.

Sweden is a typical case in which the Social Democratic policy orientation has dominated, that is, a large social security expenditure is financed by the strong revenue-raising power of a government reliant upon regressive taxation. This case of a typical mature welfare state constitutes strong counterevidence to the idea that both progressive taxation and generous welfare provision are imperative for a mature welfare state. The United Kingdom, which fell short of being a universal welfare state, has endured the strongest attack of welfare retrenchment since the 1980s. This resistance to welfare backlash is due to the state's funding capacity. The United Kingdom introduced the VAT only to enter the EC in the early 1970s, but this has become a powerful revenue machine that no policy maker expected at the time of introduction. Sweden and the United Kingdom make an interesting contrast in terms of the influence of European integration. As shown in their decision not to participate in the Euro at its inception, both countries have kept a distance from the integrated Europe. But the influence of integration has contributed to preserving the moderate welfare state in the United Kingdom, whereas Sweden has constructed one of the most mature and universal welfare states in the world by keeping its distance.

Contrasting the French case with both the United Kingdom and Sweden illuminates the importance of state funding power for the expansion of a welfare state. France has had a long conservative rule and experienced leftist rule since the 1980s, but this relatively weak presence of the left in the past has not prevented its welfare state from growing. An important difference between France and Sweden is the consciousness of policy makers of the revenue-raising power of regressive taxes. Interestingly, the Swedish Social Democratic policy makers were more eager to use the regressive VAT to raise revenue for redistributive spending, whereas the French conservative incumbents were more apparently concerned with the VAT's regressivity and wrongly believed that it could be solved within the tax system. The contrast between the United Kingdom and France supports the importance of state funding power independent of the influence of the left rule as well as of the labor movement on welfare state development. With an early institutionalization of regressive taxation as well as the new flat-rate social security taxes, France is one of the rare countries that has not experienced the intense welfare backlash in Europe. At the turn of the century, France boasts a strong revenue-raising power and preserves its high social security expenditure as does Sweden, a distinct type of welfare state.

Even in relatively homogeneous cases in Europe, the argument that a mature welfare state is closely connected to a larger reliance on regressive taxation is confirmed. In the following chapters, cases outside Europe will be examined to further confirm this argument.

3

Contrasting Paired Comparisons in Oceania and North America

From the mid-1980s to 2000, four industrial democracies introduced the VAT for the first time. Their introduction of the VAT (New Zealand in 1986, Japan in 1989, Canada in 1991, and Australia in 2000) can be regarded as a response to chronic budget deficits, which have become a common problem in industrial democracies since the mid-1970s. The Australian introduction of the VAT has made the United States the only country among eighteen OECD countries without the VAT. Each of these countries has a modest-sized welfare state and has not had an effective revenue measure to finance it. Despite their current low tax levels, however, these governments' efforts to explore new revenue sources have met formidable opposition except in New Zealand. This chapter compares the experiences of Canada and New Zealand with their neighbors: the United States and Australia, respectively.

Divergence and Convergence in the United States and Canada

Both the United States and Canada are typical Anglo-American countries whose tax revenue is heavily reliant upon income taxation. A quick comparison between the U.S. and Canadian tax revenue structures (Figure 1.2*a*, *b*, *c*, *d*) reveals that the two countries have shown both convergent and divergent patterns over the last three decades. In 1965, the Canadian tax level was closer to the average of the eighteen OECD countries, and the U.S. level was fourth from the bottom; in 1980, both became lower-tax countries, especially the United States, the second from the lowest; in 1995, while Canada restored its relative rank, the United States became the country with the lowest tax level (for more detailed changes, see Figure 3.1). More interesting, the same pattern of changes is observed in their social security

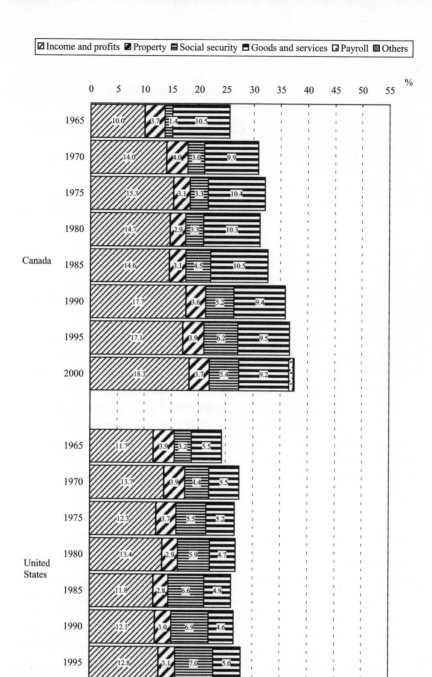

Figure 3.1. Tax revenue as percentage of GDP – Canada and the United States, 1965–2000. *Data for 1999. *Source*: OECD 1997b.

expenditure as percentage of GDP during the same period (Figure 1.1). The Canadian social security expenditure once dropped to the same level as that in the United States in the mid-1970s but has now increased its proportion closer to the average level. The U.S. proportion is consistently lowest together with those of Australia and Japan.

In 1991, Canada introduced the VAT, which is called the GST, whereas past U.S. attempts to introduce it have been thwarted. Canada slightly increased its total tax level in the 1990s, but the revenue from taxes on goods and services has been almost the same (Figure 3.1), and the VAT introduced in Canada is far from replacing a part of income tax revenue. The total taxation is still at a low level, and the size of the Canadian welfare state remains modest.

The Tax Reform Process in Canada

In the Canadian case, replacing the existing manufacturers' sales tax (MST) with the GST, the Canadian form of the VAT, was an important aim of tax reform. Nevertheless, this apparently legitimate goal did not help the Canadian government, and "[t]he GST was one of the most unpopular policies implemented by a federal government in Canada's history" (Brooks 1992, 1).

Proposals for MST Reforms Under the Liberal Government   In 1920, Canada introduced a turnover tax and then, in 1924, converted it to the MST. The Canadian MST had the same deficiencies as its counterparts in other countries, that is, a narrow tax base that had eroded almost one-third of total consumer purchases, distortions of business behavior to separate taxed manufacturing from marketing and other activities, and imposition of the tax on business transactions. During the Liberal governments from 1955 to 1984 (with a short interruption by the Conservatives), reform of the MST was proposed six times by assigned committees or government documents – in 1956 (the Carter Committee), 1967 (the Carter Commissions), 1975 (the Green Paper), 1977 (the Brown Paper), 1982 (the White Paper), and 1983 (the Goodman Committee). The government had proposed to replace the MST with the WST, that is, to replace an inferior general consumption tax with another inferior one, but the Goodman report in 1983 finally abandoned this position, and, for the first time, mentioned the VAT. This report changed the reform toward the VAT at the federal level together with the existing retail sales tax (RST) at the province level and supported a tax mix of a general consumption tax and an income tax at both federal and province levels. More specifically, the government also rejected the option that "the federal government abandon the federal sales tax and turn this room over to the provinces, presumably in exchange for a larger federal share of the personal income tax field."[1] This proposal was not implemented by the Liberal government, which was replaced by the Progressive Conservatives in the following year, but the Conservative government followed the major reform direction of this report.

Tax Reform Proposal and Implementation   In September 1984, the Progressive Conservative government was formed as a result of a landslide victory of the Conservatives over the Liberals in the general election. The adverse economic situation forced the government to release the *Agenda for Economic Renewal*, and Prime Minister Brian Mulroney and Minister of Finance Michael Wilson attempted to push a budget deficit cut, deregulation, liberalization, and privatization. Tax reform was considered a part of this agenda, and the government proposed to replace the MST in 1986 with a business transfer tax (BTT), a subtraction type of the VAT.

In the proposal based on the *White Paper* in June 1987, the tax reform process was divided into two phases. Phase I of the reform involved simplifying the corporate and personal income tax systems. Because of the influence of the U.S. comprehensive tax reform, the government decided to implement a broader and structural reform instead of confining it to the sales tax reform. This measure was also fortified in Phase II. In corporate taxation, for example, while the tax base was broadened, the tax rate was slashed from 36 percent in 1986 to 33 percent in 1989 for a standard rate; it was cut even more to 28 percent in 1991 (Phase II). In personal income taxation, base broadening was facilitated by reducing deductions and tax credits, and a rate structure was simplified from ten brackets ranging from 6 to 34 percent to three brackets of 17, 26, and 29 percent. The top rate, which combined a federal and an average province maximum rate, was then reduced from 53 to 45 percent. In terms of a general consumption tax, Phase I included only traditional and ad hoc revenue enhancement from the existing MST by broadening the base and increasing the tax rate. Replacing the MST with a multistage general consumption tax was a part of Phase II. The Phase I

---

[1] Report of the Federal Sales Tax Review Committee, submitted to the Honourable Marc Lalonde, Minister of Finance (1983, 52). This part is also cited by Brooks (1992, 25), who analyzes the impact of the report.

reform was smooth and quick. All the deliberations and hearings were held, and the legislation was passed in fall 1987. The reform became effective as early as January 1, 1988.

The reason the government divided the reform into two parts was to avoid the politicization of the unpopular part of tax reform, that is, the sales tax reform before the general election, which was eventually called for November 21, 1988. The government wanted to win public support in the elections through the popular part of the income tax cut. Then, with a more solid mandate, it would push the introduction of the unpopular new tax on general consumption. The Japanese government adopted the same strategy in 1986 as described in Chapter 4. This strategy did not work well in either case: in Japan the government failed to implement the proposal of the VAT, and in Canada the government failed to deflect the public censure of the unpopular new tax.

In the Canadian case, replacing the inferior MST with an alternative tax that ensured the same level of revenue won public support, but the VAT was never a popular alternative. In the *White Paper* in 1987, the government proposed three alternatives to the MST: the VAT at the federal level with an invoice method (i.e., the same type as in the EU countries); the VAT at the federal level with a subtraction method, which was the same as the BTT that had been proposed previously;[2] and the unified VAT, which would combine and merge the existing general consumption taxes, that is, the federal MST and provincial RST. The unified federal and provincial VAT was not very feasible due to different tax bases and rates of the existing RST at the province level. Even with exemption of groceries and medical services announced by Minister of Finance Wilson in fall 1987, the VAT was still to impose flat rates on a broad base and was inconsistent with each provincial government's use of discriminatory tax rates and tax exemptions (Brooks 1992, 30–1; Whalley 1990, 83–4).

The GST was unpopular, but it managed to pass mainly owing to political maneuverings. Immediately after the government's decision not to integrate the RST and the VAT in April 1989, it began work on the technical paper and issued the details of the VAT system called GST. The finance committee of the House of Commons (chaired by Donald Blenkarn) called hearings and deliberated on the paper from November 1989. Here the tax rate was reduced from 9 to 7 percent for political feasibility. Based on the

---

[2] For this alternative, the government for the first time used the name GST, but later gave this name to the first option of the EU-type invoice method VAT, which was actually introduced.

new technical paper with other small changes, the legislation was drafted by the government in October. Since the Progressive Conservatives held a majority of the House of Commons, the legislation was passed after only two months (i.e., in December 1989). In the Senate where hearings were held from May 1990, the Liberals held a slight majority. During the summer, when the risk of blocking the bill had grown, Prime Minister Mulroney, using his right, filled fifteen vacancies in the Senate, but still the Liberals held a majority of fifty-two over forty-six Conservatives. Then Mulroney decided to use a 123-year-old section of the Constitution that has never been used and added eight persons to the Senate. After many disputes and conflicts,[3] the GST bill was passed by a vote of fifty-five to forty-nine on December 13, and the GST became effective beginning on January 1, 1991.

The passage of the GST aroused extensive public debate over the constitutionality of the decision in terms of the relationship between the House of Commons and the Senate and also between the federal government and the provinces. The Canadian Senate is an unelected legislative chamber, which is very exceptional among industrial democracies: all the members are appointed on a regional basis by the governor-general as representatives of the monarch, that is, the prime minister. Although "an unelected body (the Senate) should not indefinitely deny the will of the elected House of Commons, . . . public opinion polls indicated that the majority of Canadians continued to oppose the GST and favoured the Senate blocking the bill" (Brooks 1992, 40). The provinces, and, more precisely, the attorney general of Alberta and intervenors from three other provinces challenged the constitutionality of the government enactment of the GST, but the constitutionality was upheld by the Supreme Court in June 1992.

The GST was expected to liberalize the economy by its neutrality effect on economic activities and to reduce deficits of 3 to 4 percent of the GDP at the federal level. But, the recession deepened after the introduction of the GST. The GDP declined by 1.7 percent in 1991 and increased slightly by 0.7 percent in 1992. More important, the inflation rate increased to 5 percent at the end of 1991 and then to 6.8 percent at the beginning of 1992. The Consumer Information Office that was set up after the introduction of the GST announced that the impact of the GST on the inflation rate increase had been limited (Brooks 1992, 42).

[3] For details, see Frith (1991).

Despite a leadership change from the unpopular Mulroney to Kim Campbell, the Tories in Canada encountered an historic defeat in the 1993 election. The GST was an indirect but important reason: the public pointed to the GST and free trade as reasons for the deepening of the recession. In addition, the Progressive Conservative Party had the misfortune of winning only two seats, which was a disproportionately small share considering a 16 percent vote share and the emergence of a new political power in Alberta and Quebec, where they had done well in the previous election.[4] In the 1988 election, the Progressive Conservatives had won by persuading the public of the importance of free trade to revitalize the economy and also by avoiding the politicization of the sales tax reform issue. After five years, the recession made the Progressive Conservatives pay back on these issues. Jean Chrétien formed a cabinet, and the Liberals dominated all ministerial positions.

The Cost of Late Introduction: The VAT Weakened by Opposition The GST in Canada is a weak VAT. Its 7 percent rate at the time of introduction was the lowest next to that of Japan among the eighteen OECD countries and has shown no sign of a significant increase. Among the eighteen OECD countries, it is exceptional for the adoption of zero-rating on basic goods – basic groceries, prescribed drugs and medical devices, most agricultural and fish products, purchases for food production, and imported goods. Other examples include the U.K. and Irish systems, which are less extensive than those in other European countries, and the Australian system. Zero-rating reduces the disadvantage of tax exemption (for small traders below an annual turnover of CAN$30,000 as of 2000) in trading of taxed goods or with taxed firms and thus preserves tax exemption practices and narrows the tax base. The GST system's efficiency was lost by tax exemptions and zero-rating as well as by tax credit (for low-income earners). Considering that all luxury goods and entertainment that are consumed by the rich are also taxed, the introduction of the GST brought a milder increase in regressivity (Hamilton and Whalley 1989), but it encountered strong public opposition. This has been a typical consequence of the late introduction of the VAT among industrial democracies, as was observed in Australia and Japan.

---

[4] Alberta had become the power base of the growing Reform Party. In Quebec, a separatists' party, *Bloc Quebecois*, had gained public support as the attempt for constitutional reform was thwarted. For details on the election, see Frizzell, Pammett, and Westell (1994).

In Canada, the federal government introduced the GST while the provincial governments were raising revenue from another general consumption tax, the RST, without harmonizing a tax system at the federal and provincial levels. In 1994, the House of Commons standing committee on finance did an extensive review of alternatives to the GST including its abolition, expenditure cuts, and reduction of federal transfers to the provinces. It concluded that the GST and provincial sales taxes should be replaced by a national invoice-method VAT.[5] The late introduction, however, matters on this point, too. Both the federal government and general government (including at the provincial level) experienced budget deficits after the mid-1970s. This experience made it difficult for a federal and provincial agreement for a unified general consumption tax to occur. The centralization of tax policy making in the Department of Finance with an administrative arm of Revenue Canada has not offset decentralization during fiscal federalism.

The adverse economic situation also worked against the introduction of the GST in Canada because it aroused public suspicion about a new burden. This point is illuminated by the difference between New Zealand and Canada. As explained later, the New Zealand government used economic difficulty as a legitimate reason for reform in seeking the liberalization of the economy and a small government. Unlike New Zealand, the Canadian government failed to assure the public that the government was pushing economic liberalization and would not expand the public sector. In other words, the consequences in Canada were to be expected from its late introduction: difficulty raising revenue and public suspicion about a new tax burden.

The Canadian Welfare State Caught in the Middle of Neoconservatism and Universalism

Both the United States and Canada possess strong propensities toward the liberal welfare state of Esping-Andersen's typology (1990). They are relatively late comers among contemporary welfare states. Moreover, since the 1980s, the neoconservative approach has gained power in both countries. However, the Canadian welfare state, especially compared with the United States, has not been under extensive retrenchment. Neither has it shifted

---

[5] For more details on subsequent developments, see Department of Finance, 1996, *Towards Replacing the Goods and Service Tax.*

toward a universal welfare state, which finances high expenditures with high tax. The result is a welfare state at an impasse that suffers from both public suspicion of retrenchment and high deficits.

Although Canada is a liberal welfare state, it also involves an element of universalism. Myles (1996, 118) argues that Canada has all the elements of the three basic models of the welfare state – a residual *social assistance* model of means-tested benefits for the poor, an industrial achievement model of *social insurance*, and a citizenship model of *universal* social benefits – whereas the United States has both former elements but lacks the universal one. Canada adopted welfare programs relatively later than other countries, even later than the United States, which institutionalized the basic programs during the New Deal. Canada enacted unemployment insurance in 1940, introduced family allowances in 1944, and passed the Old Age Security Act in 1951. Social transfers increased by the introduction of various programs from 1965 to 1971 have made Canada distinct from the United States with fewer social security expenditures (Myles 1996, 121).[6] As a liberal welfare state, it uses a means-tested program like the guaranteed income supplement (GIS). But it also brings universal health insurance and the Canada and Quebec pension plan (C/QPP), which is an earnings-related social insurance plan.

Despite these differences inherent in the two North American countries, in the mid-1980s when the Progressive Conservatives entered office, Canada appeared to follow the path of welfare retrenchment, as was evident in two other Anglo-American countries, the United States and the United Kingdom. In the 1984 election campaign, the Progressive Conservatives were silent about the necessity of expenditure cuts, although the budget was in chronic deficit. Once in office, they advocated neoconservative reform. The government immediately appointed a task force (with Erik Neilson as chair) and asked it to review federal social programs, obviously searching for potential candidates for cutbacks. However, due to strong opposition, in 1986, only two years after the advocacy of neoconservative reform, it abandoned welfare retrenchment. The Neilson task force issued a report that contributed no radical cutbacks and privatization of the programs (Mishra 1990, 74–5). The inevitable choice for the government was then a tax increase, which led to the GST proposal as already described.

In this regard, Canada appeared to be locked between liberalism and universalism in a world in which other welfare states have made their

---

[6] Myles relies on Guest (1985) for this periodization.

ideological orientation distinct. This will not be surprising if we consider that the two major parties are not very ideologically distinct. An international expert survey by Castles and Mair (1984) locates the Liberal Party as a centrist party closer to the ideological right and the Progressive Conservative Party as a moderate right party closer to a centrist position. In other words, as far as party politics was concerned, there was a certain degree of consensus on the status quo of the welfare state. This expectation from party politics is also consistent with public opinion. In the opinion polls, public support targeted programs for low-income people and universal programs, which are the main components of universal welfare states, although the percentages favoring tax increases to maintain the programs are lower than the percentages of supporters for programs (Crane 1994, 138–9).

Since the general election in 1993 in which the Progressive Conservatives were severely defeated, welfare policies with numerous social programs along with Quebec sovereignty have been the focus of public debate. The fate of social programs gained special attention from policy makers. During chronic budget deficits, the debt reached almost 70 percent of GDP. It was problematic owing to the aging of the society, with more than 10 percent of the population over age 65. This level is lower than the Western European standard; however, a peak is expected to come in the 2030s when more than 20 percent of the population will be elderly. This was caused by a revenue shortfall as well as increasing expenditures. Unlike other industrial democracies that have increased income tax revenue by bracket creep during high inflation, Canada has instead restrained income tax revenue by full indexations.[7] Consequently, Canada has not raised revenue as extensively from an income tax as other industrial democracies and has also failed to shift revenue reliance from an income tax to a consumption tax.

The changes in the 1990s appear to predict the long-term decline of the Canadian welfare state. First of all, some changes during the Progressive Conservative government period have been effective. The change in 1988 to introduce an income test for the aged with incomes of more than CAN$54,000 is one example. But this cut-off point was only indexed to inflation that exceeds 3 percent per year and "[t]his strategy of 'social policy by stealth'" has been widely used to have the long-term effect of spending cuts (Myles 1996, 136). Second, and more important, since the budget in 1995, it has become apparent that the government intends to cut federal

---

[7] This system continued until 1982; since 1985, the income tax was indexed only for more than 3 percent of inflation per year.

social programs as well as transfers to the provinces that support welfare provision.[8]

In 1994, the Canadian growth rate was the highest among the G7 countries. The shape of the economy was much better, but the government still suffered from a huge deficit and debt. The deficit declined from 5.9 percent of the GDP in the 1993–4 fiscal year to 5.0 percent in the 1994–5 fiscal year, but the debt had already accumulated. The government attempted to reduce and then eliminate the deficit from the 1995–6 to 1997–8 fiscal year budgets. As a result, the debt-to-GDP ratio, which had been as high as 71.2 percent of the GDP in the 1995–6 fiscal year, started to decline significantly during the 1996–7 fiscal year for the first time in more than twenty years. At the turn of the century, it was expected to fall below the 50 percent level by the 2004–5 fiscal year.[9] The budget was balanced in the 1997–8 fiscal year for the first time since the 1969–70 fiscal year and then was expected to be balanced (and actually was) for five years in a row for the first time for fifty years.[10] This is an exception among the G7 countries. The balanced budgets were achieved by spending cuts without tax increases along with government promises. Then, in the 2000–1 fiscal year budget, the government announced the Five-Year Tax Reduction Plan aiming to restore full indexation of the personal income tax and reduce the middle tax rate from 26 to 23 percent. In the general election in November 2000, the governing Liberals won a safe majority, 172 out of 301, and were praised for their policies much more than in the election in 1997. Seeking a smaller government is apparently a desirable goal of both the government and the public. The weak revenue-raising capacity at both the federal and province levels went hand in hand with the long-term decline of the Canadian welfare state.

American Exceptionalism: A Low Tax Burden and the Centrality of the Income Tax

In many ways, the tax state and the welfare state of the United States are peculiar when compared with other countries. The U.S. tax reform in 1986 initiated a global trend of income tax simplification. The reform financed a tax cut using base-broadening measures in the income tax system and was revenue neutral in itself. Considering the modest size of its welfare state, there has been no urgent need to introduce alternative tax measures

[8] For more details, see McGilly (1997, 26).
[9] Department of Finance, Canada, *The Budget in Brief 2000*, February 28, 2000, 9.
[10] Department of Finance, Canada, *The Budget in Brief 2000*, February 28, 2000, 8.

to compensate for income tax cuts, most notably, a general consumption tax at the federal level. Despite an apparent propensity for a low tax level reliant upon income tax throughout the postwar period, tax reform debates in the United Sates, including the one over the introduction of the VAT, have been very active. For example, it is easy to find several collections of tax proposals by scholars for the last decade (Boskin 1996; Slemrod and Bakija 1996; Krever 1997). The public attention to taxation has also been high. Tax revolts have been frequently observed in most of the states and have symbolized an important aspect of interest group politics (Smith 1998).

In the evolution of the federal income tax from 1861 to 1913, "income taxation represented not an expression of real economic democracy through a reduced burden on the poor and middle classes, but a rejection of the far more fundamental institutional change" (Stanley 1993, 230–1). More specifically, the income tax was enacted by the Republicans with the hope of taming grassroots dissenters while securing revenue. This was diametrically opposite to the institutionalization of income taxation by the Social Democratic state such as in Sweden. During the postwar period, tax policy has been one of the dominant issues on the public agenda and embodies the dispute over economic liberalism.[11] Income taxation, which is a major revenue source, has been used by policy makers for a variety of purposes for serving their constituencies. Thus, it came to lack the consistency whose restoration was an important aim of the tax reform in 1986. This centrality of the income tax went along with political institutions sensitive to popular pressure (Steinmo 1993).

As clearly exemplified by its low tax level, the U.S. tax state is traditionally small. This is closely related to its welfare state, which has been considered less interventionist and thus "liberal" in Esping-Andersen's typology. This link, in the U.S. case, is especially important because of tax expenditures, which are defined as tax exemptions, allowances, credits, and reliefs for specific socioeconomic purposes.[12] In other words, a smaller tax revenue than the size of the nation's economy not only means less direct expenditures but also implies more indirect expenditures, which work for the same socioeconomic purposes as welfare expenditures. This "hidden welfare state" has expanded such tax expenditures quietly (with less political opposition than direct expenditures) during the last nine decades, that

---

[11] For details of postwar tax policy making and its characterization, see Pollack (1996), Steuerle (1992), Strahan (1988), and Zelizer (1998).
[12] For a more detailed definition and the current state of OECD countries, see OECD (1996).

is, a much longer period than the expansion of welfare programs (Howard 1997).[13] The existence of tax expenditures serves to promote income equality more than expected from the small size of direct expenditures and will promote an understanding of the detailed mechanism of the U.S. welfare state. To clarify the characteristics of the weak funding base of the liberal welfare state, the next section examines the tax reform in 1986 and looks at the periodic proposals for the VAT over the last decades that have missed serious scholarly attention. Failing proposals for the VAT illuminate the central place of the progressive income tax that corresponds to the U.S. "hidden welfare state."

Proposals of the VAT Although a proposal for the introduction of the VAT at the federal level has not yet come close to passage in the U.S. Congress, it is unfair to say that policy makers have made little effort toward its introduction. On the contrary, it has been proposed once every ten years.

The first proposal for the VAT was made by President Richard Nixon between 1969 and 1972 when the introduction of the VAT became mandatory among the EEC countries. In September 1969, Nixon named a presidential commission headed by John H. Alexander, who was a tax specialist and his old law partner, and asked it to examine the federal tax on business and find a means to reduce it.[14] From the beginning, the VAT was considered a candidate to substitute for the reduction of the corporate income tax and thus was welcomed by the business community. The necessity to balance the 1971 fiscal year budget (from July 1970) had been one of the important reasons why Nixon asked the Treasury Department to make a comprehensive proposal of the VAT. In addition, it was believed the VAT would facilitate U.S. exports and help the trade balance. As the possibility of a surplus in the 1970 and the 1971 fiscal budgets emerged, however, the legitimacy of the VAT proposal was reduced. Moreover, the Alexander task force itself was reluctant about the VAT because it was still a new tax that had just begun to be adopted in Europe, and thus it was hard to know its effect on economic activities.

A survey by George Gallup in spring 1972 reported that among 1,614 adults, 51 percent were against a national sales tax, whereas 34 percent were for it, and 15 percent had no opinion.[15] The Advisory Commission on Intergovernmental Relations, consisting of federal, state, and local

---

[13] Howard (1997) examines four major tax expenditures for home mortgage interests, retirement pensions by paid employers, earned income tax credits, and targeted jobs tax credit.

[14] *New York Times*, September 19, 1969 (page 1, column 3).

[15] *New York Times*, August 27, 1972 (page 20, column 1).

government officials, also opposed the VAT because Nixon proposed to use the revenue from the federal VAT to reduce almost half the burden of state property taxes and finance expenditures for education. Democrats opposed the introduction of the VAT owing to its regressivity and forced Nixon to disclose the detailed tax reform plan before the presidential election that year: before the election, the possibility of introducing the VAT in the 1973 fiscal year was denied. In November, the VAT was rejected by Nixon, who had been just reelected. He maintained that the strong revenue-raising power of the VAT went against his policy of keeping federal spending in line.[16]

The second proposal was made in 1980 as a part of the bill HR 5665 (Tax Restructuring Act of 1979), sponsored by Senate Finance Committee Chairman Russell Long and House Ways and Means Committee Chairman Al Ullman. The VAT was put on the public agenda at the beginning of 1979. The debate in Congress substantially started on October 22 when Ullman announced the proposal of the VAT. The bill was introduced to the House of Representatives on April 2, 1980. However, it was not enacted before the end of the 1980 Congress and was not introduced again.

The major characteristic of the second proposal was an emphasis on the revenue shift from income to consumption taxes. More specifically, the introduction of the VAT was proposed as a part of a structural change in the federal tax system, that is, shifting the heavy revenue reliance on income taxation to a general consumption tax and solving budget deficits including the one for social security. The final section of the bill was called "Limitations on the Growth of Federal Spending" and presented a target for keeping all federal spending (including spending for agencies excluded from the budget) to 22.6 percent in 1981 and 20 percent in 1986.[17] While restraining federal spending, the VAT revenue was intended to finance social security expenditures for which no target for a spending cut was set. More specifically, the VAT revenue was planned to flow into social security trust funds to reduce the burden of social security payroll taxes such as old age and survivors insurance (OASI), disability insurance (DI), and health insurance (HI).[18]

The 10 percent rate of the VAT was not introduced mainly because it had not obtained strong support from the Congress or the Treasury.[19]

---

[16] *New York Times*, November 20, 1972 (page 25, column 4).

[17] Brecher et al. (1982, 7–8) illuminate this point as a major characteristic of the proposal.

[18] *Congressional Quarterly*, October 27, 1979: 2424.

[19] Treasury Secretary G. Williams Miller did not explicitly oppose the VAT but pointed out the problems expected from its introduction. These problems were essentially the same as

Despite the desirable economic effects of the VAT advocated by Ullman – encouraging capital formulation, balancing trade, and solving the budget deficit – the VAT was also expected to cause inflation and increase regressivity instead of increasing economic productivity.[20] In retrospect, it is simply wrong that the VAT would encourage exports and investment and thus have a competitive advantage.[21] Its economic neutrality only means less distortion. In the same vein, it was an exaggeration to label the VAT as a price increase tax (i.e., its introduction usually causes a modest inflation for a short period). The European experience had not been long enough to give accurate information for the evaluation of the VAT, and this worked against its introduction.

Aside from the preceding reasons, however, these results were to be expected from the traditional heavy revenue reliance on income taxation and the low tax level in the United States (see Figures 1.2 and 3.1). The proposal to expand the public sector was not politically feasible, and revenue-raising power was used exclusively as a means of substituting for other taxes or avoiding deficits instead of financing an increasing revenue need. Thus, it was hard to make the VAT proposal in the United States legitimate if the government could secure tax revenue and maintain fiscal discipline under the existing tax system.[22] The reform was instead aimed at the existing income tax and was implemented in 1986 during the second term of the Reagan administration.

The 1986 Reagan Tax Reform   In 1981 during the first term of his presidency, Ronald Reagan enacted the Economic Recovery Tax Act, which was

the ones raised by the opponents (Hearings Before the Committee on Ways and Means, House of Representatives, Ninety-sixth Congress, First Session on H.R. 5665, November 8, 14, and 15, 1979, Part One: 6–57).

[20] For example, see *Congressional Record*, 96th Congress: 2124–5 (February 8, 1979); 24167–8 (September 12, 1979); 25653–4 (September 21, 1979); 26614–16 (September 27, 1979); 29059–64 (October 22, 1979); 29136 (October 23, 1979); 2708–9 (February 12, 1980). Also, see *Congressional Quarterly*, March 17, 1979: 446; October 27, 1979: 2424; January 12, 1980: 66.

[21] Tanzi (1995, 143) points out that this erroneous belief often becomes an important reason for politicians to support the introduction of the VAT.

[22] Steinmo (1993, 143–4) makes this point very convincingly by showing that Ullman was not reelected in the 1980 election owing to the unpopularity of the VAT proposal. His colleagues knew that his proposed VAT was a strong means to reduce deficits, but they did not support his proposal publicly. The existing income tax policies, especially tax credits and special treatments, were used to obtain and secure electoral support. Thus, no lawmakers wanted to take the risk of upsetting the electorate.

popularly called a supply-side tax cut. The United States was in recession and experiencing high inflation, but the government wanted an income tax cut without paying a financial compensation even though the government also had a budget deficit. The Tax Equity and Fiscal Responsibility Act in 1982 and the Deficit Reduction Act in 1984 as well as the social security payroll tax increase in 1983 were responses to revenue loss caused by the supply-side tax cut. Indexations of income tax brackets, personal exemptions, and standard deductions became effective in 1985 as specified in the Economic Recovery Tax Act, and this facilitated the revenue loss further. This is an important background for the 1986 Tax Reform Act (Sandford 1993a, 117). In other words, the restraint over a revenue increase caused by a nonpolicy change (i.e., inflation) led to base broadening and simplification of the income tax.

The 1986 reform has institutionalized a tax system that raised stable revenue (and thus was less likely to be expanded or shrunk by nonpolicy changes such as economic conditions or the behavioral adjustments of taxpayers). For this purpose, the income tax system was reformed comprehensively, that is, a simple and low tax rate structure was combined with a broad base. From the release of Treasury I in November 1984, the tax reform package evolved into Treasury II, the House Ways and Means bill, and the Senate Finance bill, and then was passed as the Tax Reform Act of 1986 in October 1986. President Reagan, Treasury, and both houses of Congress sponsored the reform package at each stage and pushed the reform enactment. Since the reform brought sweeping and radical changes to the tax system, there were many political maneuverings to cultivate the opposition and form a consensus (Birnbaum and Murray 1988; Conlan, Wrightson, and Beam 1990). It has been exceptionally free from the active exercise of pressure of social interests that evaded the income tax base: the influence of experts was apparent in the ideal of the reform, that is, making the progressive rate structure flat with tax base broadening (Pollack 1996, Chapter 8). As a result, the characteristics of the U.S. tax system – a heavy reliance on income taxation and a restrained revenue-raising power – have been fortified and consolidated.

Replacing fourteen brackets ranging from 11 to 50 percent with two brackets of 15 and 28 percent was the most radical simplification of the income tax rate structure that the OECD countries had made thus far during the postwar period, and other countries followed the United States. The base-broadening measure to supplement revenue loss from the tax rate cut was comprehensive. Capital gains are treated as part of the income tax base and thus come under the same top rate of 28 percent from the previous 20 percent. Exclusions include dividends ($100 per capita), 10 percent of the income for two-earner married couples, and unemployment compensation. The corporate tax top rate has been reduced from 46 to 34 percent, while base broadening such as the abolition of investment tax credits has also been achieved. The combination of a tax rate cut and base broadening is the reason the subsequent reforms in the 1980s brought a less regressive effect than they appeared to be bringing.[23] More important, this combination explains why the United States could implement a revenue-neutral reform in income taxation, that is, finance an income tax cut with an income tax increase without introducing another tax such as the VAT. Since 1986, the personal income tax rate structure has become complicated. For example, in 1999 it had four to five brackets from 15 to 39.6 percent for different individuals; unmarried, married, filing jointly, and head of household. The corporate tax structure has been complicated by the phasing out of low tax brackets. However, the basic characteristics of the U.S. tax system have remained the same as described here.

A Health Insurance Proposal and the VAT in the 1990s   National health insurance reform was a major policy agenda in 1993. In September of that year, at the end of 103rd Congress, President Bill Clinton presented the Health Security Act, which aimed to extend national health insurance coverage to all Americans. The flames for reform, however, rapidly disappeared for a year owing to the Republican seizure of majorities in both houses of Congress in the mid-term election in 1994. The introduction of the VAT was brought onto the public agenda as the health insurance reform became politicized. When the health insurance reform did not succeed, the VAT introduction was thwarted.

Obviously, enormous costs were expected to accompany extending coverage to more than 35 million uninsured. The only way to institutionalize a national health insurance system without an increasing deficit was to secure a financial source for it. The VAT was considered a promising candidate

---

[23] Gravelle (1992) judges the equity effect of the 1986 tax reform from the perspective of the effects of the 1981 tax cut and the payroll tax increase in the 1983 social security act, which also appeared to be regressive reforms. He concludes that, in terms of vertical equity effect (redistribution from the rich to the poor), the reform should increase the progressivity in the short run (a five-year horizon) but would reduce it in the long run – after the adjustment of the people to tax changes. The reform is expected to increase horizontal equity (treating people with the same income in the same way).

to fulfill this purpose. The combined reform might be regarded as the first step to a tax-financed welfare state from the modest-sized U.S. welfare state heavily reliant upon the progressivity of a tax system for redistribution. An examination of the process, however, illuminates a more complicated relationship between health insurance reform and the VAT. Although health insurance reform dominated the public agenda from the end of 1993 to the 1994 midterm elections, the introduction of the VAT had already lost support from policy makers as well as the public at an early stage.

In February 1993, Clinton first mentioned the possibility of using the revenue from the VAT to finance his proposed national health insurance but backed away immediately and called it "a 'radical change' that could only be looked at in years ahead."[24] For the White House, the VAT was an attractive financial source that could pay the cost of health care, which was estimated to be from U.S.$50 billion to U.S.$100 billion. The economists supported the VAT's introduction. As already mentioned, its neutrality in economic activities and revenue-raising power to achieve a deficit solvency were the main reasons for their support.[25] Unlike the 1986 tax reform, however, they fell short of influencing the policy debate this time. Despite the urgent need for a financial source for the health insurance reform, in December 1993, an adviser to the President, Stanley Greenberg, said that White House officials had rejected a proposal to finance health insurance costs with a new VAT after poll results showed that the VAT was unpopular.[26] In other words, well before the health insurance reform plan had been shelved by the Republicans' victory over the Democrats in the 1994 midterm election, the administration had already given up the idea of introducing the VAT and was left without a reliable financial measure for the health insurance reform.[27]

Existing studies attribute the failed health insurance reform to U.S. political institutions (Steinmo and Watts 1995) or policy inertia and legacy (Hacker 2001) rather than the content of the proposal and policy debate at that time. In spite of differences in emphasis and details of explanations, the analyses agreed that the influences of the past (including events and

[24] *New York Times*, April 15, 1993 (Page 1, Column 6).
[25] For example, Lester C. Thurow, an economist at MIT, wrote an article in the *New York Times* encouraging its support (*New York Times*, June 8, 1993).
[26] *New York Times*, December 8, 1993 (page 20, column 1).
[27] Pollack (1996, 150–60) presents the details of a variety of proposals of broad-based consumption taxes in the early 1990s but also concludes that it is difficult to see the introduction of such a tax in the foreseeable future.

institutions shaped in the past) determined the consequences and, in this regard, are path-dependent. Among such institutional factors, the lack of revenue-raising capacity should also attract serious attention: how has a small tax state coexisted with a liberal welfare state in the U.S. context?

A Liberal Welfare State Consistent with a Small Tax State The foundation of the U.S. welfare state occurred during the interwar period as a product of the New Deal of Franklin Roosevelt. In 1935, old age insurance, unemployment insurance, and social assistance programs such as old age assistance, aid to dependent children, and aid to the blind were set up, and, in 1937, public housing was started. During the postwar period, however, the increasing productivity of the economy and a rising living standard first lowered the need for the further extension of welfare coverage. Even during the campaigns for the "Great Society" and the "War on Poverty" under the Johnson administration, social programs were created to provide equal work opportunities for all (exemplified by the Economic Opportunity Act in 1964) or to target the needy (like Food Stamps). The extension of universal coverage beyond these measures involved only those for the aged. They included the Medicare Act in 1965, which guaranteed health insurance for everyone over 65, increased old age benefits from 1969 (for three years by 23 percent), and the indexation of benefits against inflation. The United States has established earnings-related income security for the old and the unemployed but has lacked universal coverage even in fields such as health insurance (except for those over 65) and family allowances.

The United States started some social assistance programs early, such as Civil War pensions whose benefits and coverage exceeded those of social insurance programs in other countries at the turn of the century and pensions for mothers with dependent children as early as the 1920s. Thus, Skocpol (1992) considers the small welfare state such as the United States to be the result of a failure to replace these early programs with universal ones. Policies during the early period influenced the capacities of the state and social identities and the capability of political actors; then these factors, which she broadly defines as political institutions, influenced policies in the subsequent period.[28] Comparison with Canada illuminates the fact that the United States failed to find an opportunity to convert existing programs to universal ones as Canada had done since the 1960s (Myles 1996).

---

[28] Noble (1997) also attributes the reason to broadly defined political institutions that include electoral politics and the organizations of business and labor.

Along with political institutions and policy legacy, state funding capacity is indisputably linked with the current state of the U.S. welfare state.

The U.S. government's funding capacity is traditionally lower than expected from the size of nation's economy (i.e., its total tax revenue as a percentage of the GDP has always been lower than that of most industrial democracies). This weak funding capacity appears to have been used to restrain public expenditures since the 1980s. The Reagan administration cut taxes and sought a smaller government by reducing the funding of it. By the 1990 Budget Enforcement Act, the Congress had decided to offset increases in spending for some entitlements by decreases in those for others. This tendency has not been reversed since 1992 when the presidency was returned to the Democrats after twelve years of Republican rule. Bill Clinton introduced a substantial increase in the earned income tax credit (EITC), tax expenditures that are an important component of the "hidden welfare state" (Howard 1997), but failed to institutionalize a more generous social security program as exemplified in the failure to introduce the national health insurance system described earlier. Clinton was forced to retreat from his original intention to expand welfare coverage: the existence of a budget deficit has worked for those in opposition to an active government role (Pierson 1998). Clinton's idea of a New Democrat that advocated a more active role for the government was not accepted by the Democratic Congress.[29] The public has opposed replacing the existing programs with privatized ones.[30] This also has made politicians shy away from a cutback in major programs and mitigated the welfare retrenchment. Yet, it does not constitute pressure for a shift toward more universal coverage. Weak funding capacity has been assumed to be a precondition for policy makers and the public to consider the future of the welfare state.

In the United States, the introduction of the VAT was considered an option for tax reform and was even proposed. Aside from the cases introduced here, even at the time of the 1986 tax reform, the introduction of the VAT was one of the alternatives in Treasury I, which was the first reform plan issued by the Treasury. In the late 1990s, it was considered a serious alternative for reforming the U.S. tax system.[31] However, the VAT proposal was destined to die because of lack of political support. The right likes the VAT for its neutrality in economic activities but suspects that its

---

[29] For more details of this process, see Ferejohn (1998).

[30] In terms of the public attitude toward social policies, see Cook and Barrett (1992) and Jacobs and Shapiro (1998).

[31] For example, see American Bar Association Tax System Task Force (1997).

revenue-raising power will allow the expansion of public spending and take it out of control. The left welcomes the VAT as a new revenue source but dislikes its regressive effect on income redistribution. Neither camp whole-heartedly supports the VAT, and the reason for this relates to the small size of the U.S. welfare state. The right believes that the revenue-raising capacity of the VAT, if it were once introduced, could not be controlled and thus would expand public expenditures. In the United States, there is no centralized fiscal authority that dominates the power to check the budget size. In such a situation, the best strategy for the right to maintain a small public sector is to tighten the size of tax revenue itself (Suarez 1999, 12). The left does not believe that welfare provision from a greater tax revenue would compensate for the VAT's regressivity. The U.S. total tax revenue is the lowest in terms of proportion to the national economy among the eighteen OECD countries. Thus, without a drastic increase in tax level, it is impossible to compensate for the regressivity in the tax system with social security expenditures. As a result, there is little support for the introduction of the VAT as far as domestic politics are concerned. Here, the underly-ing logic for the attitude toward the VAT is directly opposite the one in Sweden where the VAT has been regarded as a revenue-raising measure to achieve neutrality over economic activities and supply enough revenue for redistribution through a social security system. The size and strength of the U.S. economy mitigate against the need for tax coordination during globalization. Thus, it is unlikely that the United States will introduce a national VAT that integrates a retail sales tax at the state level in the near future.[32]

The End of Parallels? Comparing New Zealand and Australia

Both New Zealand and Australia are considered small welfare states of a peculiar type defined as a "radical welfare state" (Castles and Mitchell 1993: see chapter 1). Both countries have recently experienced several parallel changes in political economy, which are likely to influence their type of welfare state. First, in terms of partisan politics, the Australian Labor Party (ALP) entered office in 1983 and almost simultaneously the

[32] Sales tax, ranging from 3 to 7 percent, is used in forty-five states and the District of Columbia as of 1998 with the exception of almost half of such consumption items as food and services. This inconsistent system is not a good model on which to base a federal VAT (William G. Gale, "Don't Buy the Sales Tax," Policy Brief, March 1998. http//www.brook.edu/comm/Policy Briefs/pb031/).

New Zealand Labour Party (NZLP) in 1984. The rise and fall of labor politics have shared several events since the mid-twentieth century. The ALP formed a majority government at the national level as early as 1910 after two short-lived minority governments in the 1910s and was also in office during most of the 1940s. The NZLP came late compared with the ALP but entered office in 1935 for the first time and remained a governing force until 1949. This is "the longest running majority, democratic socialist, national government in the English-speaking world" (Castles, Gerritsen, and Vowles 1996, 4). However, during most of the postwar period until the mid-1980s, both the ALP and the NZLP were in opposition. Exceptions were the Nash NZLP government in the late 1950s and the Whitlam ALP government and the Kirk and Rowling NZLP governments, which governed almost simultaneously in the early 1970s. All these earlier governments were relatively short-lived and lasted about three years.

The lack of political fortune of these two parties is striking if one considers that both continued to have stable electoral support from between 40 and 50 percent of the valid total votes throughout the postwar period. In this regard, as Castles (1985) points out, both countries were, at least until 1980, anomalies in social democratic politics. Both the ALP and the NZLP rarely occupied office despite a well-organized and strong labor movement in terms of unionized membership and electoral support for them.[33] The difficulty of translating popular support into electoral strength in both countries may be explained by their election systems with some contingent political factors. For example, in Australia the vote split under the preferential voting system worked against the ALP. In New Zealand, the NZLP was less successful than the National Party in translating votes into seats in the first-past-the-post system. Consequently, their simultaneous rule in the 1980s is regarded as a significant change in party politics as well as a common political background for tax reform in both countries.

---

[33] Castles (1985, 41) presents a very illuminating and interesting comparison in terms of the average electoral vote share and years in office from 1950 to 1980 among Australia, New Zealand, Norway, Sweden, and the United Kingdom. The contrast is striking. Whereas Australia and New Zealand have a 45.6 percent and 43.9 percent vote share and three years and six years in office, respectively, Norway has 44.1 percent and twenty-two years, Sweden 45.7 percent and twenty-six years, and the United Kingdom has 43.0 percent and twelve years. Castles's information is based on Mackie and Rose (1982). Castles also shows relatively high union membership shares: 44 percent in Australia and 35 percent in New Zealand, which is comparable to the United Kingdom's 44 percent in 1977.

More important, immediately after entering office, both parties launched major economic reforms that aimed to promote efficiency by liberalizing trade, slimming the public sector by privatization and financial policy, and deregulating the labor market. In other words, the social democratic parties had an opportunity to influence policies for the first time since the 1940s. They implemented neoliberal reforms in the two countries and suddenly switched from import-substituting, closed economies to paragons of neoliberalism, which occurred after the achievement of a high level of industrialization.[34] A market ideology was the fashion among industrial democracies in the 1980s, as typically exemplified by neoconservative revolutions in the United States and the United Kingdom, but this move by the ALP and the NZLP was unexpected.[35] Their reforms, especially the more sweeping one in New Zealand (Orchard 1998, 112), have attracted much scholary attention (Easton 1989; Sharp 1994; Massey 1995; Evans et al. 1996; Walker 1989). The reform ideology, "Rogernomics" (named after Roger Douglas, Minister of Finance of the fourth Labor government), was a subject of importance in itself.

During the postwar period until the mid-1980s, the revenue reliance on income taxation in both countries was certainly the highest in terms of the proportion to total tax revenue. In New Zealand, it is still highest, that is, comparable to the level in the high-tax Scandinavian countries (Figure 1.2). The New Zealanders use income tax as extensively as the high-tax countries despite a much lower total tax level. The reason lies in the weakness of the revenue-raising capacity of other taxes, primarily general consumption taxes and social security contributions.

Reflecting a much smaller total tax revenue, the idea of the welfare state in both countries is diametrically opposed to the Swedish idea to redistribute wealth through a social security system.

Benefits could be residual rather than universal, because they were only required by those with no labour market connection; benefits could be flat-rate rather than earning-related, because they were only a secondary safety net below stipulated minimum wages. (Castles and Shirley 1996, 91)

[34] For a detailed comparison of the two, see Ellis (1998).
[35] Both the ALP and NZLP, while classified as social democratic parties, have ideological positions somewhat closer to the liberals. According to the expert survey by Castles and Mair (1984), both the ALP and the NZLP are classified as social democratic parties whose ideological score range is from 2.3 to 3.8 in a range of 0 (ultra left) to 10 (ultra right). The ALP's score was 3.1, the same as the Italian Socialist Party (PSI), and New Zealand's was a margin of 3.8, the same as Denmark's counterpart.

Despite the residual nature of the welfare state, however, both Australia and New Zealand, as social laboratories, had begun to develop welfare programs even earlier than most other industrialized countries. Australia and New Zealand adopted a compulsory old-age pension scheme with substantial universal coverage in 1908 and 1898, respectively.[36] The timing of the adoption in New Zealand followed the earliest, in Germany, 1889. The Australian scheme occurred almost at the same time as Sweden's in 1913 and the United Kingdom's in 1908 (but the funding of the U.K. system was complete as late as 1925). Around the turn of the twentieth century, New Zealand was regarded as the world leader of the social security system, and Australia was one of the most advanced welfare states.

During a crucial period until the 1960s, the ALP had not been in power as long as the NZLP (from 1935 to 1949). The social democratic rule in New Zealand during the Great Depression parallels more the Swedish experience. Its development in New Zealand was apparently ahead of the Swedish version until the 1940s. New Zealand established a base for social security provision by the passage of the Social Security Act as early as 1938.[37] The Swedish Social Democrats "used the period from 1932 to 1945 to implement the bulk of the social policy that New Zealand pioneered in 1891–1898 (plus the family policy of 1926), and then used the post-war period to construct a true welfare state in much the same way as New Zealand had done in the period between 1935–1940" (Davidson 1989, 2). Their paths crossed and then diverged: whereas Sweden continued to increase welfare spending, New Zealand reduced it from the late 1960s. The New Zealand welfare state since then has become similar to the one in Australia, which focused on full employment and wages.

Why were both Australia and New Zealand, and then New Zealand only, forerunners of the welfare state and why have they now fallen behind? One key to answering this question lies in tax policy. "[R]edistribution through taxation policy had virtually ceased in Sweden [by the mid-1960s], and recompense made through the positive transfers . . . was basically measures [sic] of horizontal equity," whereas the New Zealand tax system "remained a progressive and vertically redistributive system, independent of the effect

---

[36] Hicks, Misra, and Ng (1995, 337) detail the adoption of social security programs across industrial democracies.

[37] According to Jones (1997, 43), "[u]niversal, non-means tested benefits for all of the aged, at levels that are generous by comparison with a number of countries, and non-contributory but means-tested benefits for the non-aged that were paid without time limits, became its distinctive and expensive features."

of the positive transfers" (Davidson 1989, 230). This divergence in welfare state development constitutes an important parallel with the distinct tax system. Behind it are different ideas about redistribution: New Zealand's reliance on the tax system and Sweden's extensive use of a social security provision. In this context, the introduction of the VAT in New Zealand in 1986 is worthy of serious attention. Will this serve to increase the tax level and thus public expenditures in the same way as the early institutionalization of regressive taxes in Sweden?

The Process of Tax Reform in the 1980s

In both Australia and New Zealand after the 1950s, the tax system had kept abreast of the rising revenue need for increasing public expenditure and changing industrial structures and economic activities. Tax policy had rarely been on the policy agenda but, in the late 1970s, the heavy reliance on personal income taxation, illegal tax evasions, and the abuse of existing income tax avoidance and exemption measures became the center of public criticism. The erosion of the existing indirect tax base (especially the wholesale sales tax in New Zealand introduced in 1933) was a different side of the same problem. The reform of corporate income taxation was also demanded.

The problems were not new and had been recognized in the small circle of policy makers. Examples included the Ross Committee Report on Taxation in 1967,[38] the Report of the McCaw Task Force on Tax Reform in 1982 in New Zealand,[39] and the Asprey Taxation Review Committee in Australia in 1975.[40] Australia simplified its tax rate to a three-rate structure in 1977, and New Zealand, to a five-rate structure in 1978. Neither country, however, enacted a major reform until the mid-1980s. The Australian Fraser Liberal Party government had attempted to introduce a retail sales tax in 1978 and 1981 but did not implement it. Robert Muldoon, who was Prime Minister and Minister of Finance of the National Party government in New Zealand from 1975 to 1984, was overtly reluctant to implement reform and took ad hoc measures to reform the public finance system.

In the early 1980s, tax policy was rapidly politicized together with the urgent economic problems; large deficits both in the national government

[38] *Report of the Committee on Taxation in New Zealand,* 1967.
[39] *Task Force on Tax Reform,* 1982 (Wellington: Government Printer).
[40] *Taxation Review Committee Full Report.* 1975. AGPS, Canberra.

budget and in trade were caused by growing expenditures and the declining international competitiveness of a "banana republic," respectively. New Zealand had a budget deficit of 8.9 percent of the GDP in the 1983–4 fiscal year (which declined to 1.9 percent in the 1987–8 fiscal year); the unemployment rate was 6.2 percent in 1983 and 5.8 percent in 1984, and there was a foreign exchange crisis immediately after the 1984 election. In Australia, the general government deficit was 7.0 percent of the GDP in 1984, and the unemployment rate was 10.6 percent in 1983 and 9.0 percent in 1984. In both countries, the restoration of a tax base was essential to close the gap between revenue and expenditure. A major tax reform that would stimulate the economy was needed. Increasing exposure to the global economy, symbolized by lifting the control on exchange rates, required the tax system to promote international competitivenes.

Under these circumstances, the ALP won a majority in the election in 1983, and the NZLP won a stable majority in a snap election in 1984. In August 1995, the treasuries of both countries decided to enact major tax reforms. The paths of both countries, however, began to diverge at this point.

New Zealand   Despite the subsequent implementation of radical reform, the NZLP said little about taxation in the 1984 Election Manifesto. This was not a result of electoral strategy but rather an inevitable consequence of a snap election leading to the formation of the Labour Party government for the first time in ten years.[41] Tax reform, especially the need to broaden the tax base, was first politicized in the economic summit of the NZLP in September that year. In the budget statement in November 1984, three major objectives of tax reform – horizontal equity, less distortion over resource allocation, and a simple system of taxation – were stipulated. The statement also announced the introduction of New Zealand's version of the VAT, that is, the goods and services taxes (GST), which would replace the existing wholesale sales tax (WST).

The tax reform was proposed as an indisputable part of "Rogernomics": Rogernomics pushed massive deregulation and changed a "command economy" with a fixed currency exchange rate to a less-regulated economy. Support for the GST was regarded "as a test of confidence in the government"

---

[41] Only specific tax issues were politicized in the election. For example, "concern over tax issues – particularly an anti-avoidance measure introduced in 1982 to confine tax losses from farm tax concessions to owner operators – was a strong motivation for many people who shifted their allegiance from the governing National Party to the fledgling New Zealand Party" (Dickson 1989, 139).

(Jesson 1989, 74) and became "a highly visible target for opponents" of the broad economic reform (Douglas and Callen 1987, 211). The subsequent process was smooth and fast, however, although the introduction of the GST was delayed from April to October 1986 mainly for administrative preparation. In March 1985, the government issued the *White Paper on Goods and Service Tax* as a base for legislation and the *GST the Key to Lower Income Tax* to explain the role of the GST in the entire reform package. Then *Statement on Taxation and Benefit Reform* detailed the entire reform package in August 1985. Under the GST coordinating office, started in June 1985, the public campaign continued for eighteen months until 1986, exemplified by a pamphlet entitled "A Fairer Deal," which was distributed to every household.[42] Economists also became involved in the tax policy debate to broaden public understanding on the GST.[43] For tax compliance, free booklets were distributed to tax accountants to facilitate the understanding of the new tax filing system among prospective tax units of the GST, mostly retailers who were not in the existing WST system.[44] The GST advisory panel[45] "reviewed almost 1500 submissions from the public and reported effective simplifications for small businesses and accommodating arrangements for importers and exporters" (Douglas and Callen 1987, 218)[46] and issued recommendations. The GST bill, which was introduced to the House of Representatives, was then referred to the Finance and Expenditure Select Committee and passed in December 1985.

From the first proposal in November 1984 to mid-1985, thus, the public support for the GST increased from 25 percent to 35 percent (Douglas and Callen 1987, 218). In addition to the public relations campaign, there are several reasons why the GST was accepted smoothly. First, the reform was a clear tax mix shift. Ten percent of the GST was introduced with a

---

[42] This explained in plain language that the introduction of the GST would not adversely affect life because the government would provide compensation for its regressive effect on income distribution.

[43] For example, economists at the Institute of Policy Studies at Victoria University published two booklets that explained the GST (Scott and Davis 1985; Teixeira, Scott, and Devlin 1986).

[44] As a result, tax compliance with the GST proved better than expected. The government had estimated that 180,000 tax units would file the GST, but actually about 280,000 began to file. This gap meant NZ$1 billion more revenue: tax compliance has been much better than with the WST and income tax. Interview with a Treasury official, March 29, 1998.

[45] The GST advisory panel was chaired by Donald Brash, an economist and businessman, who had been a former National Party candidate.

[46] Sandford (1993a, 67–8) characterizes the setup of such a panel as an "innovation."

personal income tax cut that amounted to about 20 percent of total revenue and the reduction of the top income rate from 66 to 48 percent. Because even people earning an average income had been included in the highest 66 percent tax bracket, this package was welcomed by the public. Second, the newly introduced GST was regarded as a more consistent and efficient system, exemplified by the adoption of a single rate and a small number of exemptions. Third, smaller exemptions (i.e., taxation on basic goods such as food and clothes) were applied, and those with lower incomes were compensated *outside* the GST system.[47] One example was through family support, which was a new tax refund based on consideration of family circumstances. All other benefits increased by 5 percent to compensate for the expected price increase by 5 percent.[48] More important, this tax refund, although it is classified as a tax expenditure in other countries, is classified as a public expenditure in New Zealand.[49] This helped the government to persuade the public that the regressivity of the GST would be compensated by welfare expenditure. Fourth, the GST was also price inclusive from the beginning except for business transactions. This made New Zealand an exception among the countries that introduced the VAT after the mid-1980s and contributed to avoiding public antipathy toward the new tax as an additional burden to the net price.

In December 1987, again Roger Douglas proposed a similarly radical reform including a single nominal income tax rate. This resulted in the deferral of the entire proposal in January 1988 and led to his resignation in the subsequent December. As the economic condition deteriorated and the unemployment rate increased, support for Rogernomics had already

[47] The government made this decision after learning about the United Kingdom's difficulty in restoring a tax base that had been narrowed by exemptions. The recommendation to keep the GST as simple as possible and then alleviate the regressivity outside (instead of inside) the system was from Cedric Sandford, then a director of the Institute for Fiscal Studies in the United Kingdom (see Chapter 2). Douglas appreciated his advice (Douglas and Callen 1987, 215). This author's interview with Sandford (September 1997) confirmed this.

[48] Since 10 percent of the GST was to replace the WST with five rates ranging from 10 to 50 percent on the narrower base, Treasury expected a 5 percent price increase.

[49] An official in the Inland Revenue explained that this is a welfare benefit paid through the tax system and thus is regarded as a public expenditure (interview, April 1998). Stephens explains that this is due to transparency and is based on the government proposals in 1991 (Stephens 1997, 503–4). In my interview, the official estimated that gross social security benefits expenditures (including tax expenditures such as family support) were more than 14 percent of the GDP, and net social security expenditures (excluding tax expenditure) were about 12 percent of GDP (interview, April 1998).

waned. The revised reform package in February 1988 dropped the single income tax rate and instead adopted 24 and 33 percent as a two-rate structure. The full imputation system of corporate taxation, a corporate tax reduction, establishment of a controlled foreign corporate tax system, and the GST rate increase to 12.5 percent were also included. This package was implemented without substantial compensation, and the GST rate was raised to keep the promise of the Minister of Finance to reduce deficits to 1 percent of GDP. However, the tax reform effort by the Labour Party, which continued even after the departure of Douglas from the government, abruptly ended with its defeat in the 1990 general election.[50] This was also the end of Rogernomics. The analysis of an opinion survey of the 1990 election concluded that declining support for Rogernomics had become apparent especially when compared with the 1987 election in which the NZLP had won a second term (Vowles 1993, Chapter 6).

Most interesting during the Rogernomics period is that the boundary between the National Party and the NZLP blurred in terms of social security policy: the liberal ideology of Rogernomics contributed to the impression in the public mind that the NZLP was a challenger and the National Party a defender of the welfare state. While public spending and social security spending increased in real terms, "spending *per recipient* has, in fact, fallen for most categories of welfare entitlement" (Rudd 1990, 88). Rogernomics involved targeting welfare provision, which apparently contradicts the left ideology of the Labour Party, but the welfare issue had little impact on the voters' defection from it in the 1990 election (Vowles 1993, Chapter 8). The dominance of economic consideration in Rogernomics was criticized within the left wing of the NZLP. There was a continuous and unresolved conflict between the supporters of traditional welfare policy, including Prime Minister Lange, and reformers, such as the Treasury and Minister of Finance Douglas (Jesson 1989, 104–10). In the second term, thus, the Labour government embarked on the reconsideration of its orientation as exemplified by the Royal Commission Report on Social Policy in April 1988. But no substantial change was made (Koopman-Boyden 1990). Consequently, the Labour government decided not to impose Rogernomics on social policies nor provide a cover of social protection in a rapidly deregulating society. In the 1990 election, the voters were certainly disappointed

---

[50] For example, the introduction of a capital gains tax was confirmed in July 1988 and implemented after Douglas under Minister of Finance David Caygill. The introduction, which was withdrawn before the 1990 general election, was kept away from the policy agenda by Labour's defeat in the election.

with the lack of competence of Rogernomics for economic management – an unemployment rate as high as 12.6 percent in 1990. But they at least reserved judgment on the future concept of the welfare state.

Australia The Australian tax reform in the 1980s under the Labor government has several parallels with its New Zealand counterpart. The tax reform package in September 1985 decided that the personal income tax rate structure would be simplified by slashing the number of brackets from five to four with a reduction of the top rate from 60 to 49 percent: this decreasing progressivity would be offset by base broadening, which was to affect those with higher incomes. The package also included the introduction of a fringe benefit tax and a full imputation system of corporate taxation. However, unlike the New Zealand case, the Australian government's attempt to shift revenue reliance from an income tax to a consumption tax was thwarted by a complete withdrawal of the proposal of the VAT. The tax reform in 1988 was centered on a corporate tax system including a rate reduction from 49 to 39 percent. It included a measure to improve the existing wholesales tax by narrowing the tax base without replacing the incomplete WST with a broad-based consumption tax.

The process of the rejection of a broad-based consumption tax in Australia was without political drama. Immediately after the 1984 election, after the first Hawke government from March 1983 to December 1984 that had done little for tax reform, the government of the Australian Labor Party, headed by Bob Hawke, launched the tax reform under Treasurer Paul Keating. In July 1985, the government called a tax summit following the election pledge made by Hawke and responding to criticism by the Liberal Party in opposition to a previous proposal by the ALP for a capital gains tax. Representatives of all vested interest groups, local governments, labor unions, business associations, and welfare and women's groups participated.[51]

A draft white paper was distributed, and the government, while analyzing the existing tax problems, presented three alternative reform plans based on fairness, efficiency, and simplicity of taxation. Option A was a proposal exclusively for a base broadening of the income tax; Option B combined the base broadening of the income tax and a broad-based 5 percent retail sales

---

[51] This summit followed the example of the economic summit held in New Zealand in April 1983, which succeeded in reaching a consensus on economic reform. But, in Australia, economic reform was not as politicized as it was in New Zealand, and tax reform was neither regarded nor defined as a part of it.

tax with 10 percent of the existing wholesale tax on selected goods; Option C was the government's preference, which combined the base broadening of the income tax and a 12.5 percent of retail sales tax with a broad base plus income support measures for those with lower income. The outright withdrawal of Option C, including a broad-based consumption tax, was decided by the initiative of Prime Minister Hawke, who had a strong connection with labor unions at the expense of Treasurer Keating's wish to preserve that option (Sandford 1993a, 100). Then, the government combined one principle of Option A with some base broadening and the rationalization of the existing WST that symbolized the principle from Option C without a new tax. This was the final tax reform plan that Treasurer Keating submitted to the House of Representatives. The number of income tax rates was reduced to five with a 49 percent top rate. Base broadening was achieved by introducing taxes on capital gains and fringe benefits, listing some special tax measures, taxing employers' contributions to superannuation funds, and so on. Without introducing a more consistent single-stage general consumption tax than the existing WST, the reform in Australia was much more limited than the one in New Zealand.

The withdrawal of the introduction of a tax broadly based on retail sales made the entire reform package in Australia in 1985 lose revenue neutrality and thus did not ease the deficit-ridden budget.[52] Subsequently, the ratio of budget deficit to the GDP (which had been at a peak of 4.1 percent in 1983–4 and 3.1 percent in 1984–5 immediately before the tax reform) plummeted to zero in 1987–8 largely because of expenditure cuts. In other words, the Australian government took the risk of "using a tax cut to force the pace on expenditure cut reductions" and won, unlike Reganomics in the United States (Evans 1988, 28–9). However, the spending cut was not enough to decrease the income tax, and, in the early 1990s before the Liberal-National coalition returned to office, Australia had high marginal income tax rates and high revenue reliance on income tax. The continuous scaling back of tax rates since the mid-1980s resulted in four rates of 21, 38, 46, and 47 percent in 1991. There were two options for reform – increasing corporate income taxes as in the United States and Canada or introducing the VAT as in New Zealand and the United Kingdom (Sandford 1993a, 103). Neither was considered politically feasible: an increase in the corporate tax was

---

[52] Evans (1988, 28) explains the excess tax cut by labor politics. As the exchange rate began to float and the rate depreciated, a real wage decline was required for international competitiveness. Thus, the government needed to compromise with the trade unions with an income tax cut.

against the efforts of economic reform since the 1980s, and the introduction of the Australian version of the VAT (i.e., GST) carried a stigma.

The GST returned to the public agenda in 1991 when the Liberal and National parties issued a proposal for tax reform called *Fightback! Taxation and Expenditure Reform for Jobs and Growth*. It advocated a 15 percent VAT called GST like the one in New Zealand.[53] In the 1993 election campaign, Prime Minister Keating, who, as treasurer of the Hawke government, had once proposed the introduction of a broad-based consumption tax, criticized the opposition's tax proposal. Although public criticism of economic policies appeared to make this election unwinnable for Labor, the incumbent party won the election. One of the important reasons was the unpopularity of the tax proposal by the Liberal-National coalition. John Hewson, who had masterminded the tax reform plan, resigned from leadership of the Liberal Party. Thus, the broad-based consumption tax and especially the VAT became politically stigmatized, and the new tax became a hot potato that no politician wanted to touch.

Subsequent Changes in the 1990s: A Revenue Machine for a Small Tax State

New Zealand: Decline of a Welfare State with a Strong Revenue Machine?
The diverging consequences of tax reform in the 1980s have made the tax structures and tax levels of both countries change (Figure 3.2). For example, in 1985, the proportion of personal income tax to total tax revenue was 45.2 percent in Australia and 59.8 percent in New Zealand. In 1996, the gap between the two countries had significantly narrowed – 41.2 percent in Australia and 43.5 percent in New Zealand. Will New Zealand follow the path of the Western European countries that introduced the VAT before the 1960s with less opposition? New Zealand uses the VAT extensively to raise revenue; thus, New Zealand is different from the other countries that introduced the VAT late where a tax rate increase is repressed by public opposition. However, it is also different from the countries in Europe that introduced the VAT early: New Zealand uses a strong revenue machine to decrease budget deficits and reduce the burden of other taxes instead of

[53] The proposed GST excluded medical service, education fees, and residential rents. In the 1992 revised version, food was also exempt. It aimed to replace not only the WST but also the state payroll tax, petroleum product excise taxes, and custom duties. The enhanced revenue from the GST was also expected to finance an income tax cut. The compensation for the regressive effect of tax reform was also included in the proposal.

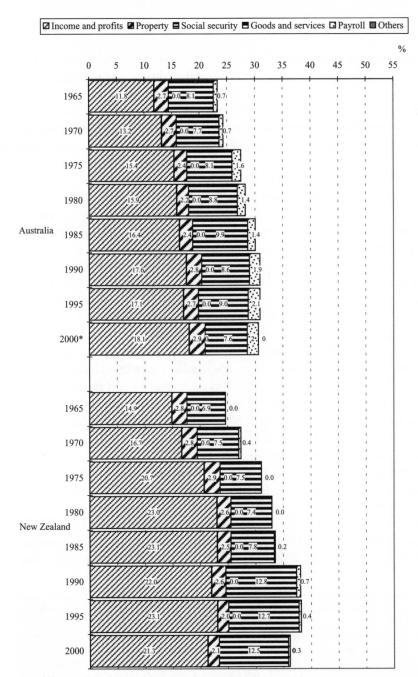

Figure 3.2. Tax revenue as percentage of GDP – Australia and New Zealand, 1965–2000. *Data for 1999. *Source*: OECD 1997b.

expanding the public sector. As Figure 3.2 shows, the total tax revenue of New Zealand has increased and then stagnated since the introduction of the GST in 1986. In the 1990s, an income tax cut has been implemented gradually in four steps, from the 1996–1997 to 1999–2000 fiscal years; in the resulting schedule, the highest 33 percent and lowest 15 percent are the same, and a 21 percent reduced rate is applied to a majority of middle-income earners. This income tax cut results in decreasing the tax level while maintaining the revenue reliance on consumption.[54] Consequently, the funding capacity of the government has been used to restore fiscal balance rather than to expand the public sector significantly, unlike the situation in the early introducing countries. This tendency is illuminated by a welfare retrenchment from the late 1980s to the 1990s.

As mentioned already, New Zealand had been a forerunner of the welfare state and then changed to a peculiar type of wage earners' welfare state in which emphasis was put on a full employment policy and regulations of wages and labor relations. In the 1950s and 1960s, with a relatively good economic performance, the welfare state protected well "the 'typical' family headed by an able-bodied, unionised, award-covered, waged, working male" (Rudd 1997b, 244). In the 1970s, social security expenditure increased from 5.69 percent of the GDP in 1971–2 to more than 11 percent in 1980 and 1981. This resulted from expanding coverage by new major programs – the accident compensation scheme in 1974, the statutory domestic purposes benefits (DPB) in 1975, and the national superannuation in 1977 that was inflation-adjusted and tax financed generously.[55]

Welfare expansion in the 1970s made New Zealand closer to a universal welfare state, but this was also met by economic recession with high unemployment, low economic growth, a high inflation rate, and large budget deficits (Rudd 1997a; 1997b). Benefit cuts had already been made in the late 1970s in the DPB (in 1977) and in superannuation (in 1979) under the National government. They continued under the Labour government that

---

[54] The New Zealand government published the first comprehensive review of the GST system in March 1999 (Policy Advice Division of the New Zealand Inland Revenue Department, 1999, *GST: A Review*). Although the government has suggested raising the threshold for tax exemptions to decrease tax compliance costs, it is generally eager to broaden the tax base by considering a tax on imported services. It has also examined the possibility of lifting tax exemptions on financial services. Inclusion of these two kinds of services depends on the actions of other countries. In this regard, the New Zealand tax system is expected to become further globalized and affirm a shift to revenue reliance on consumption.

[55] These programs aimed to cover personal injury for single parents (including unmarried mothers) and death from accidents for the elderly.

was formed in 1984 through the imposition of severe eligibility criteria and substantial retrenchment of benefits. In 1985, an income test was applied to superannuation, and the eligibility age was raised by five years to sixty-five. More important for dismantling a radical welfare state were abandoning a full employment policy, lifting labor relation regulations, and rationalizing the tax system to promote work incentives. Inside the Labour government, the welfare policy was always under dispute. Minister of Finance Douglas and the Treasury opposed the establishment of the Royal Commission on Social Policy in 1986 by which Prime Minister Lange tried to reorient the welfare policy by distinguishing it from Rogernomics' sweeping liberalization and laissez-faire approach (Easton 1989, 174–5). Aside from the influence of the growing number of needy and unemployed during the prolonged recession and the increasing aged population, thus, the expenditure level was maintained by the government's reluctance (Toder and Himes 1992, 350; Wells 1996, 226–7).

Shifting revenue reliance from income to consumption first helped the Labour government maintain the public sector size in the late 1980s during the recession. But, in the 1990s under the National government, the efficient funding capacity was focused on solving budget deficits and reducing accumulated debts. As a result, the budget deficit that had persisted throughout Labour's reign turned into a surplus under the National government in the 1993–4 fiscal year for the first time in fifteen years. The buildup of debt that had risen from 31.6 percent of GDP in 1984–5 to a peak of 51.6 percent in 1991–2 stopped (Wells 1996, 229).

If the Labour Party had remained in power in the 1990s, however, would New Zealand have followed a path similar to other early introducing countries, that is, would it have expanded the public sector without concentrating on a financial source for fiscal solvency? Although it is impossible to answer this "if" question, there is evidence to believe that the Labour government in the 1980s had not intended to cut welfare as much as the National did in the 1990s, but neither planned to employ a more universal approach in welfare. The Labour government was reluctant to increase targeting but fell short of shifting toward a universal provision. Compensation measures for economic liberalization were implemented, but income inequality has increased since the formation of the Labour government in 1984 to the 1990s (Roper 1997). Together with labor market deregulation by the Employment Contract Act under the fourth Labour government, a general level of social protection seems to be lifting in New Zealand (Castles and Shirley 1996, 104). The full employment policy based on protection in

147

the closed economy may not be held under economic globalization.[56] The effort for economic liberalization together with the welfare retrenchment under the National government from 1990 has pushed New Zealand in the direction of a minimal welfare state.[57]

New Zealand's easy introduction of the VAT is an anomaly. The economic liberalization reform since the 1980s helped the government cut the link between a strong revenue machine and an increasing total tax level; thus, the government could assure the public that it would not increase the total tax level. This point will be further clarified when the New Zealand case is compared with the introduction of the VAT in Australia in 2000.

The Australian Introduction of the VAT in 2000   In the 1996 election, the Liberal-National coalition won the election with the promise that it would not introduce a GST during the first period in office. However, in 1997, Prime Minister John Howard brought the GST back onto the public agenda. He was helped by political luck: from late 1996 to early 1997, a firm support coalition for tax reform, including the GST, emerged between unexpected partners – business and welfare. For the business community, the tax reform in 1985 had included, in retrospect, the worst of all possible worlds – incomplete business tax reform and preservation of the inefficient WST. In other words, if the government had proposed a general consumption tax separately, the new consumption tax might have obtained support at least from business interest groups.[58] Business interests were to make

---

[56] Mabbett (1995, Chapter 8) makes a good contrast with the Swedish case in which the strong labor unions have exercised influence over redistribution policies of the government.

[57] Rudd (1997a, 258) shows that, based on government statistics, social welfare expenditure as a proportion of GDP increased from 11.27 percent in the 1984–5 fiscal year to 14.44 percent in the 1989–90 fiscal year. Social welfare expenditure as a proportion of government expenditure increased from 29.10 percent to 40.45 percent during the same period. However, under the National government, the proportion of GDP dropped to 13.9 percent, and the proportion of government expenditure dropped to 38.6 percent in the 1995–6 fiscal year. This stagnation continued to the end of the century. For a summary of numerous retrenchments, see Rudd (1997b, 251).

[58] In 1985, the business groups opposed the base-broadening measures that were the fringe benefits tax and the foreign tax credit system and thus opposed the reform alternative (Option C) that combined a general consumption tax with these measures. In the final proposal, the government decided to introduce a full imputation system that was favorable for business interests and made them accept these base-broadening measures that were also included in the adopted reform alternative (Option A). In this regard, the most decisive factor for business opposition to Option C was an inclusion of these base-broadening measures instead of a general consumption tax. The combination of the proposals in the three alternative options was likely to lead to the rejection of the reform alternative

both corporate and personal income taxation more efficient and integrate numerous indirect taxes into the GST. Graems Samuel, President of the Australian Chamber of Commerce and Industry (ACCI), expressed support for the introduction of the GST and persuaded Robert Fitzgerald, president of a major welfare group, the Australian Council of Social Service (ACOSS), to agree to support it. The support of the ACOSS for the GST was cautiously based on two conditions – removing income tax shelters and distortions and maintaining the existing spending level, especially the one for social security.[59] The ACOSS rotated from opposition to support because it recognized the difficulty of raising revenue under the existing tax system and became more confident of compensating the regressivity of the VAT by expenditure as budget deficits decreased.[60] Both business and welfare interests agreed that the income tax reform would broaden the tax base and the GST would raise more stable revenue. The ACOSS-ACCI tax reform summit on October 3–5, 1996, agreed to introduce the GST on the condition that its revenue would be used for increasing social security expenditures. About four months after the summit, the Business Council of Australia (BCA) joined them. In early 1997, when Howard put the tax reform on the public agenda, therefore, there was much less risk than before. The formation of the business-welfare coalition worked "to break the political 'log jam' over tax reform," that is, "the unwillingness of both major parties to contemplate tax reform or to increase the revenue base."[61]

In addition to the unexpected business-welfare alliance, two factors encouraged the coalition government to advance the reform further. One

including a general consumption tax (i.e., Option C) by business groups (Evans 1988, 18–21). There is a different explanation (Groenewegen 1988).

[59] For more details about the ACOSS's position, see "A Fair Tax System for a Fair Australia: Documents for the National Tax Summit 3–5 October 1996," ACOSS Paper No. 82, Second edition, March 1997; "Tax Reform Pack," an information and policy paper by the Australian Council of Social Service, September 1997.

[60] The Treasury had informally informed both labor unions and welfare groups including the ACOSS about the necessity of revenue security in 1985 when it attempted to introduce the GST under the Labor government, but no groups had been persuaded (interviews with a Treasury official, March 1998). However, from 1993 to 1994, looming budget deficits under the Labor government made the welfare group more conscious of the importance of revenue security. The deficit reduction under the Liberal-National coalition government since 1996 made it confident of the possibility of compensation if a regressive revenue-raising machine such as the GST were introduced. The ACOSS admitted that it had come to support the GST because it had changed its perception of budgetary conditions and the tax system (interviews with an ACOSS official, March 1998).

[61] "Outcomes of the ACOSS-ACCI Tax Reform Summit 3–5 October," Report to the community welfare sector, October 9, 1996.

was the Asian economic crisis triggered by a currency crisis in 1997. The Australians believed they could only prevent its spillover by further economic reform including that of taxation. The other factor was a bracket creep in the income tax system that could not be remedied by an ad hoc measure such as an indexation and, thus, made any substantial reduction in the income tax impossible. Another important incident to facilitate reform was the High Court decision in 1997 to deny the constitutionality of the states' imposition of a franchise tax on commodities, that is, an excise tax on production.[62] The indirect tax reform was necessary to create a new fiscal relationship between the Commonwealth and states that were denied a major source of revenue from excise taxes.

In February 1998, the Treasury, which had conceived of the GST's introduction since the 1970s, for the first time formally advocated the necessity of the introduction of the GST.[63] The Treasury, however, did not expect that Howard and Treasurer Costello would ask for the electorate's mandate for reform in the election of the House of Representatives and half the Senate.[64] In June 1998, the coalition government decided to spend AU$10 million on a campaign to get public support for tax reform, and, in July, the government decided to include only the GST introduction with income tax reform in a preelection tax package preceding business tax reform. The major points of the tax package on August 13, *A New Tax System*, were to replace the WST with a 10 percent GST with exemptions for health, education, child care, and nursing homes; to abolish several state taxes such as stamp duties; and to lift diesel fuel excises for off-road use by farmers and miners. The package also had large personal income tax cuts, especially for low- and middle-income earners; compensation for pensioners,

---

[62] For example, see Abelson (1998, 4). However, Section 55 of the Constitution, which says, "[l]aws imposing taxation, except laws imposing duties of customs or of excises, shall deal with one subject of taxation only," could also threaten the constitutionality of the GST on numerous goods and services. The government tried to clear up this problem by defining everything taxed under the GST as "supply." But, the legal advice of the Australian Government Solicitor was that the validity of the GST under Section 55 was contingent upon whether the High Court adopted a "more generous approach" in interpreting this section (*Australian Financial Review*, June 29, 1999).

[63] "Wholesale Sales Tax: Sixty-Eight Years On," *Economic Roundup* (a quarterly journal of the Treasury): 33.

[64] Interviews with a Treasury official, March 1998. Howard and Costello had their own reasons for implementing the reform. Howard had been a proponent of the GST since the late 1970s, and Costello wanted the success of major reform to stabilize his future leadership in the Liberal Party after Howard.

unemployed and self-funded retirees; a crackdown on the use of trusts with tax exemptions; fringe benefits tax reform; and a comprehensive review of the business tax. An improvement (that is, AU$1.2 billion surplus over an AU$1.1 billion deficit) in the 1997–8 budget bottom line was encouraging for the government, which had been required to sell a large income tax cut. In the election on October 3, the Liberal-National coalition maintained a majority in the House of Representatives, although it reduced votes and seats in both houses. Improving economic conditions, despite the prolonged Asian financial crisis and Labor's failure to present more attractive tax reform alternatives, as well as the involvement of its leader, Kim Beazley, in the failed proposal of the GST in 1985, all worked for the coalition government. The coalition government won a mandate to introduce an AU$18 billion tax package to Parliament. On December 3, the coalition government introduced sixteen tax bills to Parliament.

There were several points of serious dispute. First, business and welfare groups differed about planning the new system. The business community advocated a simple system of the new GST for a more competitive and open economy, whereas the welfare group emphasized the exemption of food. Although the research by the government and economists or economic organizations in the private sector presented a moderate estimate of the regressive effect on income distribution and smaller price increases and job loss by the GST, the ACOSS published more pessmistic predictions.[65] The demand for increasing the number of tax exemption items resulted in the formation of a coalition of religious, welfare, and consumer groups to make basics such as food, clothing, and housing GST-free at the end of March.[66] Increasing pressure for widening the number of exemptions drove the coalition government into a difficult position; however, at the same time, it also damaged outright opposition such as that of the Labor Party, which had promised to block the GST in the last

---

[65] The government pointed out that the ACOSS's own research predicted that low-income earners would not be worse off under the GST, and the ACOSS president, Michael Raper, replied that one-third of low-income earners would still be worse off (*Australian Financial Review*, February 5, 1999). ACOSS relied on the economic modeling by Chris Murphy of Econtech, which predicted few regressive effects if only restaurant and take-away food were included in the GST.

[66] These groups include the ACOSS, the Uniting Church, the Brotherhood of St. Laurence, the Womens Electoral Lobby, the Australian Catholic Healthcare Association, the Australian Consumers Association, the Australian Pensioners and Superannnuants Federation, Anglicare, the Catholic Social Welfare Commission, St Vincent de Paul, and some elements of the Salvation Army (*Australian Financial Review*, March 30, 1999).

election.[67] Another conflicting issue was the financial relationship between the Commonwealth and the states. A part of the GST revenue would go to states in exchange for repealing the state taxes, such as stamp duties and bank taxes,[68] and would replace the financial assistance grants that constituted almost 40 percent of the state revenue. Although increasing room for discretion was favorable to the states, lifting the protection for financing them from the Commonwealth increased concern.[69] Along with the Australian Local Government Association, the opposition parties – the ALP and Democrats – opposed the repeal of the Financial Assistance Grants Act, that is, the transfer of responsibility for local government financial assistance from the Commonwealth Treasury to the states.

Although the coalition government won the mandate in the House of Representatives to pass the GST bills in the Senate, the coalition needed the support of the Democrats or the two independent senators[70] to control a majority and pass the tax reform bills. The government wanted to secure time for safe passage in the Senate but did not want to give enough time for nongovernmental parties to bring major modifications. After failing to obtain support from one independent senator,[71] the focus of the deliberation

---

[67] While maintaining absolute opposition to the GST, the ALP leader, Beazley, repeated that if the ALP won the next election and inherited the GST introduced by the coalition, the party would not repeal it because it would be practically impossible (*Australian Financial Review*, April 16, 1999).

[68] Abolishing state payroll taxes was deferred despite business' expectation that the GST revenue would make it possible.

[69] For example, they demanded compensation for newly taxed goods and services such as public housing, an increase in the compensation for the transition from the wholesale tax to the GST, and the extension of a transition period in which the government would provide any compensation and protection for the states (*Australian Financial Review*, April 8, 1999).

[70] More precisely, the balance of power was transferred from the two independent senators to the Democrats after June 30, that is, after the new Senate was to be sworn in as a result of the last election.

[71] Of the two independent senators, Mal Colston expressed conditional support immediately after the election; Brian Harradine expressed concern for the impact of the GST on low-income earners. The budget of the 1999–2000 fiscal year was delivered on May 11. AU$5.4 billion of surplus owing to the increased tax revenue receipts enabled the government to include AU$965 million for new spending measures, which fulfilled all the coalition's pledges in the last election. To gain Harradine's support, the government added AU$200 million to a family assistance scheme (to raise the eligibility threshold for tax benefits from the age of 18 to 21) and then a total $1.5 billion in the first year for a 1 percent increase in pensions (in terms of male total average weekly earnings), but in vain. Although Treasurer Costello denied that the new compensation was aimed specifically at winning Harradine's support for the GST, the government had promised at the election a significant allocation in the budget for Harradine's home state of Tasmania.

then turned to the negotiation between the government and Democrats for an amendment to the GST bills. The Democrats insisted on the exemption of basic food from the GST against the wishes of the Treasury.

During this deadlock, Prime Minister John Howard and Treasurer Peter Costello started to compromise with the Democrats' leader, Meg Lees, and economics spokesman, Senator Andrew Murray. Since opinion polls showed that a majority of voters were still opposed to the GST itself, but not necessarily the entire reform package, there was reason for the coalition government to compromise. New points in the final agreement were made on May 28. The exclusion of basic goods was a major point. A more than AU$4 billion revenue loss from the exclusion of basic food made it impossible for the federal government to transfer all the funding to the states. As a result, the Commonwealth was to provide assistance to balance the state and territory budgets during a transition period instead of outright abolition of the state taxes.[72] A crackdown measure on tax avoidance such as the 20 percent alternative minimum company tax was also included to finance the loss. The new package also meant a drastic reduction in tax cuts for taxpayers in the AU$50,000–AU$75,000 annual income brackets by keeping them in the top bracket of 47 percent, although the annual tax cut amounted to AU$12 billion. The income tax system would still maintain a certain amount of progressivity without a tax mix-switch from income to consumption.[73] The new tax rate structure scheduled from July 1, 2000, is progressive and goes against the global trend of a high marginal income tax cut (Table 3.1).

Exemption of food, more precisely, zero-rated food, inevitably would make the system more complicated[74] and result in preparing a long list of tax-exempted items, comparable with the ones of Canada, Ireland, and the

[72] More specifically, the government decided to reconsider nine state taxes that had been promised to be abolished because of inefficiencies. Only the bed tax and stamp duty were repealed by the original dates, but the abolition of an additional seven taxes was postponed. The abolition of bank account debits was postponed until 2005, and financial institutions' duty was postponed by six months from January to July 2000. Other taxes may not be taken away in the foreseeable future.

[73] In addition to concessions on diesel fuel taxes that made the package more "green," compensation measures such as lowering the eligibility age from 60 to 55 for a bonus of AU$2,000 for self-funded retirees were decided.

[74] An example was whether roasted chickens would be taxed or not. Because meals were not to be exempted from the GST, take-away roasted chickens at fast food shops were to be taxed whereas the whole roasted chickens sold in supermarkets were to be tax-exempt. The Democrats opposed a tax on roasted chickens at fast food shops owing to lobbying by takeaway industries. The line was finally drawn between taxed and tax-exempted roasted

Table 3.1. *New and old income tax rate schedules in Australia*

Old Tax Rates		New Tax Rates	
Old[a] taxable income	Tax rate %	New scale[a] taxable income	Tax rate %
AU$0 - AU$5,400	0	AU$0 - AU$6,000	0
AU$5,401 - AU$20,700	20	AU$6,001 - AU$20,000	17
AU$20,701 - AU$38,000	34	AU$20,001 - AU$50,000	30
AU$38,001 - AU$50,000	43		
AU$50,001+	47	AU$5,0001 - AU$60,000	42
		AU$60,001+	47

[a] In addition, a low-income rebate of up to AU$150 continues to apply.

Source: Australian Treasury's homepage (http://www.treasury.wa.gov.au/).

United Kingdom.[75] However, other measures were devised to encourage tax compliance and thus secure a broad tax base. A 10 percent flat rate is high enough when compared with the introduction of the VAT in New Zealand, Japan, and Canada since the mid-1980s. A tax return must be filed every month by big businesses with an annual turnover of more than AU$20 million, whereas businesses with up to AU$20 million are allowed to file returns quarterly. The tax exemption point is low enough; all enterprises with an annual turnover of AU$50,000 or more must register under the GST system, and the registration of smaller traders with less than AU$50,000 is optional. Unregistered businesses are unable to claim tax credits that correspond to the GST charges from their suppliers.[76] Because of these modifications, the tax package was expected to cost an additional AU$1.4 billion in the 2000–1 fiscal year, resulting in a net tax cut of as much as 1 percent of GDP, and to use the budget surplus.[77]

chickens by deciding that "hot food for consumption" would not be tax-exempt and defining "hot" as "above room temperature."

[75] A wide range of health and education goods and services were also added to the list of tax exemptions. Rules for exemption of food in Australia are summarized according to manufacturing and trading units. On farms, the GST applies to producing animals and other plants (except horticulture); in factories, manufactured foods for human consumption are tax free; at the retail level, the GST applies to restaurant/takeaway or specified taxable items including prepared meals, confectionery, bakery products, savoury snacks, ice cream, and biscuits; and all other (unspecified) foods for human consumption are tax free (*Australian Financial Review*, June 24, 1999).

[76] Because almost all firms and distributors are likely to have registered trading partners, this system encourages registration, facilitates more firms that would otherwise be unregistered to be registered for the GST, and increases the consistency of taxation.

[77] *Australian Financial Review*, May 29, 1999.

The bulk of the GST bills passed in the Senate committee on June 25, and the complete package passed on June 28. The GST was to be effective from July 1, 2000. On the following day, Prime Minister Howard announced that the coalition government had finished the tax reform, the most important reform among five pillars of economic reform in the last two decades (the other four were financial deregulation, tariff cuts, labor-market reform, and fiscal consolidation). But, together with the business tax reform (lowering the corporate tax rate from 36 to 30 percent by the 2001–2 fiscal year and introducing a competitive capital gains tax regime) that was later implemented, the GST cost the popularity of the Howard government.[78]

Did the Wage Earners' Welfare State Survive Only in Australia? The Australian welfare state is smaller than the OECD standard. From the mid-1940s to the mid-1970s (in some areas to the mid-1980s), the Australian welfare state promoted equality by a centralized wage maintenance system, high employment rate, means-tested and flat-rate social security provision, high private home ownership, and a male breadwinner model. The economic crisis since the mid-1970s overturned this system, and the economic reform since the 1980s could not restore it. Increasing income inequality during the 1980s was reported, but the market wage redistribution in Australia was still more equal than in other liberal welfare states such as Canada, the United Kingdom, and the United States (Cass 1998, 49). Also, even in the 1990s, there was a view that the Australian welfare state maintained income equality by a compressed income distribution as well as a progressive tax system reliant upon income taxation and the direct transfer from the rich to the poor (Whiteford 1998). Compared with New Zealand where "the Employment Contract Act marks the end of the wage earners' welfare state" (Castles 1996, 106), Australia has had a less intense deregulatory and liberal reform and a better relationship between the Labor Party and unions. Together with the maintenance of progressive taxation, along with this view, the wage earners' welfare state has been preserved better in Australia than in New Zealand.

As far as redistribution through a social security system is concerned, however, the situation in the 1990s is such that

Governments, caught between the twin pressures of an ageing population and declining revenues, have found it extremely difficult to formulate rational and

---

[78] Geoffrey Lehman, "Income tax cuts may save Howard," *Australian Financial Review*, June 26, 2000.

comprehensive policies. The problem becomes even more obdurate when longer-term considerations are blanketed by a concern to eliminate budget deficits at all costs, manifested in extreme form in the federal government's 1996 Budget strategy. (Borowski, Encel, and Ozanne 1997, 15–16)

Whether the Australian way will achieve income equality in a manner that is quite different from other countries remains to be seen.[79] But, as exemplified in the new system of GST, the fight against the regressivity of the tax has been assigned the higher priority at the expense of state funding capacity; thus, the government is not ready to expand or even maintain the public sector. In this regard, a universal welfare state focused on middle-class interests will not be "the Australian way."

Conclusion

The first question to conclude this chapter is: why was the VAT adopted much more smoothly in New Zealand than in Australia, Canada, or Japan (as introduced in Chapter 4)? The New Zealand case appears to be an exception because the late introduction of the VAT is more likely to face strong opposition and difficulty in increasing revenue from it. There are several plausible reasons for the easy introduction. New Zealand is a unitary state (as opposed to the Australian and Canadian federal system) with a unicameral parliament (as opposed to other countries' bicameralism). Governing without a written constitution as in the United Kingdom is called "elected dictatorship" (Palmer 1987). In addition, the NZLP won a safe majority by a landslide in the 1984 election; the National Party suffered because its supporters switched to the New Zealand Party that had just formed as a new right-wing party.[80] The first-past-the-post single-member district system

---

[79] There are two opposing views on the future of the Australian welfare state. For example, whereas Schwartz (1998) argues that social democratic protection of labor through enterprise bargaining and an arbitration system survived the Liberal rule in the 1990s, Juankar and Kapuscinski (1997) stipulate that the labor market reform in the early 1990s by the Labor government itself failed. Pierson (1991, 190) also cites the latter.

[80] The 1984 election had a very high turnout rate of 91.9 percent. Compared with the 1981 election, the NZLP increased its votes from 39 percent to 42.6 percent, and the National Party decreased from 38.3 percent to 35.9 percent. Despite this small shift of vote shares, the NZLP got fifty-seven seats; the National Party, thirty-seven; and the Social Credit Political League, two. This larger swing in seats than votes was explained by the fact that the New Zealand Party, without gaining a seat, absorbed a significant number of votes from the National Party in the urban single-member election districts. For a more detailed explanation of the process leading to and the consequences of the snap election, see Douglas and Callen (1987, Chapter 4).

at that time[81] allowed such a dramatic shift in support from one party to another. Before the government's proposal, however, the introduction of the VAT had been regarded as next to impossible, even in New Zealand.[82]

The most important factor is the peculiar political economic background for the proposal of tax reform in New Zealand – the serious economic crisis that completely changed the meaning of the reform. The deregulation and globalization of the economic system were considered solutions for the crisis and became important reform aims.[83] Not only did both the base broadening of the income tax and the introduction of the GST fulfill these aims but also "[r]eform of the tax system was an integral part of economic restructuring and liberalization" (Stephens 1993, 46). The neutrality of the VAT on economic activities would facilitate the deregulation of the economy, and the simplicity of taxation would provide easier tax coordination with other countries. In addition, the regressivity of the VAT would be outside the tax system by compensation measures. This differed from the Australian case. This persistence of the liberal economy ideology in the reform was derived from the strong leadership of the Minister of Finance, Roger Douglas, assisted by a strong Treasury, the best partner for Rogernomics.[84] The Treasury, which had converted its social democratic Keynesian policy orientation to one of market liberalization since the late 1970s, was a strong and reliable partner for Douglas in pursuit of

---

[81] The introduction of a German-style proportional representation system was decided in subsequent referenda in 1992 and 1993.

[82] For example, Douglas and Callen (1987, 207) succinctly write: "More than one media commentator pointed out in the 23 months between the first announcement of GST in the 1984 Budget and its implementation on 1 October 1986 that historically any Government which introduced a major tax found itself out of office at the next election."

[83] For detailed accounts of the reform, see Evans et al. (1996) and Silverstone, Bollard, and Latimore (1996).

[84] Even before entering office, Douglas was influenced by the presence of a Treasury official (Oliver 1989, 18–23) who had been assigned as an adviser in the opposition leader's office since 1975. Although the Treasury never explicitly recommended the VAT over the retail sales tax, its investigation of general consumption taxation in other countries unambiguously introduced the VAT's superiority, and he changed his mind because of it (Douglas and Callen 1987, 209). As early as 1980, Douglas himself proposed a 10 percent broadly based retail sales tax with an income tax cut as a "shadow minister of finance" in his radical alternative budget, which caused him to lose his seat on the front opposition bench under Bill Rowling as NZLP leader. In 1983, under the new leadership of David Lange (who subsequently became prime minister), Douglas, again as a "shadow minister of finance," submitted a proposal, which pointed up the economic disincentive of high marginal income tax rates and proposed the base broadening of the retail sales tax or the introduction of the VAT with about a 15 percent rate (Sandford 1993a, 64).

economic reform.[85] During the reform, the Treasury's power was further strengthened.[86] It issued two briefing papers that determined the major direction of reform. *Economic Management* in 1984 became the framework for economic reform (Goldfinch 1997), and *Government Management*, issued after the 1987 election and referred to as the New Zealand model, proposed to restructure the public sector. (For detailed accounts, see Boston et al. 1996.)[87]

Consequently, in New Zealand, because the VAT was proposed under a liberal, market-centered ideology, the public did not suspect that their tax burden would increase in the future and were satisfied with compensation outside the tax system. This is in sharp contrast to Canada and Japan (as introduced in Chapter 4), where the government could not guarantee restraint over future tax burdens; this inevitably made it impossible for them to propose compensation measures for the regressivity. The Canadian and Japanese governments attempted to make an income tax cut precedent over the VAT introduction to cultivate public opposition, but this attempt to deflect the public's attention further increased public suspicion about an increasing tax. Unlike the early introducers, New Zealand has increased its revenue from the VAT but has not shown significant signs of increasing

---

[85] In retrospect, dedication to the liberal ideology is more important to explain the distinctiveness of the New Zealand tax reform than a strong and unified fiscal authority if compared with Australia and Japan. Whereas, in Australia, a split in the Treasury in 1976 and the accompanying formation of the Ministry of Finance broke the monopoly of information (Sandford 1993a, 84, 97–8; Arnold 1990, 386–91), the Japanese Ministry of Finance, which had a jurisdiction and control comparable to the NZ Treasury, encountered difficulty introducing the VAT (Chapter 4). A critical difference between the Japanese fiscal authority at that time and its counterpart in New Zealand is a consistent policy orientation to emphasize the government's role in keeping its distance from the market ideology.

[86] The power over public and private finances, economic planning, and advice on social policy was especially fortified by policy changes such as the Public Finance Act and the Fiscal Responsibility Act in 1989 (Boston et al. 1996, 6).

[87] In the new recruitment system of the bureaucracy, employees have a short-term contract between chief executive officers (department heads) who are employed for a fixed term by ministers in the jurisdiction (State Sector Act in 1988) instead of pursuing a longer-term career in the public sector. This allows the easy use of experts outside the administration, permits relative freedom to change jobs in the public sector as well as between the private and the public sectors, and provides for use of the "best people for any particular purpose" (Sandford 1993a, 69). It also allowed the promotion of a market-centered liberal ideology in the Treasury together with the massive shuffle of personnel at the time of the reform (interview with a financial official in April 1998). Since the mid-1960s, the Treasury has recruited people with postgraduate degrees, often from foreign universities, and employed a significant number of economists from abroad on short-term contracts (Boston 1992, 197).

the total tax level (i.e., revenue as percentage of GDP).[88] In this regard, the argument presented in Chapter 1 is fortified by the New Zealand case.

Findings are summarized as follows from the cases of three countries that have introduced the VAT between the 1980s and 2000 (New Zealand, Canada and Australia) and one country without the VAT (the United States). First, all four countries have had small social security expenditures and thus have been far removed from the universal model of the welfare state. Second, even if three of them have introduced the VAT after their governments experienced chronic budget deficits, their tax revenue structures that rely upon an income tax have been preserved. The delayed attempt to institutionalize more effective revenue-raising measures resulted in preserving the small size of the tax and welfare state. In New Zealand where the introduction was smooth, the VAT revenue has significantly increased, but it has been used to finance an income tax cut rather than to expand public expenditures. In Canada, the introduction was difficult enough to incur costs for the governing party at that time. Both the tax rate and revenue from it have been compressed by public antipathy toward the tax, and tightened control of the total tax level and expenditures is the consensus at the turn of the century. In Australia, although the system has just been introduced, the VAT is unlikely to become a reliable revenue machine owing to a wide range of exemptions and persistent opposition to a tax mix switch from income to consumption. Thus, the Australian tax system most likely goes well with a small welfare state. Finally, and most important, the United States, which relies heavily on an income tax without the VAT, has increased its tendency for a lower tax and a marginal welfare state. The cases here, as small tax and welfare states, illuminate the sharp contrast with the European cases of the variety of mature welfare states discussed in Chapter 2.

---

[88] It may be too early to argue from the changing trend of the total tax level but the attitude of the New Zealand Treasury is clearly toward a small government. In my interview in April 1998, when I mentioned that the New Zealand total tax level is relatively low, a Treasury official answered, "No, it is still too large." I showed a list of the total tax levels among eighteen OECD countries in 1995 and pointed out that the New Zealand burden was below the average. His answer was, "Look. The United States has a much smaller burden." The U.S. total tax level was the lowest among the eighteen countries.

4

Another Pattern of Path Dependence

A COMPARISON BETWEEN JAPAN
AND THE NEWLY DEVELOPING
ECONOMIES

The cases of the seven industrial democracies discussed in Chapters 2 and 3 demonstrate that the development of a tax state and a welfare state is path-dependent upon the development of the state's funding capacity. The focus is on a revenue reliance shift from income to consumption before the government's experience of chronic budget deficits. In newly developing countries, however, the pattern of path dependence of the tax revenue structure is different from the one in the industrial democracies, because it has been common knowledge which tax is effective to raise revenue and how to administer it. A comparison between Japan and newly industrializing Taiwan and South Korea in this chapter will explicate how a different pattern of path dependence explains the different development of the funding capacity of the welfare state.

The Diffusion of the Value Added Tax into Newly Developing Economies

Mobilizing financial resources and raising tax revenue are important tasks for newly democratizing and industrializing countries. The failure to finance the public sector results in deficit finance and excessive money printing. Both are undesirable for developing economies, which often suffer from balance-of-payment problems and exposure to more competitive and industrialized economies. Whereas industrialization provides potential resources for the government to extract tax money, democratization makes social groups and private organizations express their demands and ties the hands of the government with respect to the democratic policy-making process (Bates and Lien 1985). Despite the increasing demands and pressures from society, political institutions in developing countries are less

160

capable of articulating interests and setting priorities about policy alternatives than older institutions, and their administrative organizations are still immature. However, compared with dictatorships, new democratic regimes are not necessarily inefficient in collecting taxes and extracting resources (Cheibub 1998).

The reason for this lies in their tax systems and more precisely in the distinct way they develop tax systems. Industrialization in newly developing countries does not accompany a tax system that is more reliant upon income taxation, such as the industrialized countries used extensively during the postwar high-growth period. The erosion of the income tax in industrialized countries was caused by the democratic pressure to increase tax loopholes and the increasing complexities of economic activities caused by globalization that resulted in a revenue reliance shift from income to consumption or a stagnation in the growth of total tax revenue. Learning from the experiences of the industrialized countries, the newly developing countries, without following the same path as their predecessors, have come to rely on a tax on consumption without enhancing revenue from income taxation. Whereas the industrialized countries started from a preliminary form of taxation, such as tariffs, and proceeded to an increasing reliance on a comprehensive income taxation and then the VAT, the newly developing countries have tended to change from a preliminary form of taxes on consumption, such as tariffs, directly to the VAT. However, the VAT diffusion does not represent a revenue reliance shift from income to consumption. Instead, unlike in industrial democracies, it has served to fortify the existing revenue extraction from consumption.

Evidence has been obtained from data that are comparable with the eighteen OECD countries presented in Chapter 1. Figure 4.1*a, b, c, d* presents the available data on the transformation of tax revenue structures in nine newly developing countries. They include four countries in the south of Europe that are the original members of the OECD: Greece, Portugal, Turkey, and Spain; two cases of successful new industrializers: South Korea (OECD member since 1996) and Mexico (since 1994); and three former Socialist countries: Czech Republic (since 1995), Hungary (since 1996), and Poland (since 1996). The tendency among them is obviously influenced by the characteristics of three Latin countries, that is, a reliance on an indirect consumption tax, but it also shows that there is no indication of an increasing revenue reliance on income taxation. Instead, the revenue from the taxes on consumption has become an important revenue source for the last decades. Why is this? The intensifying tax competition

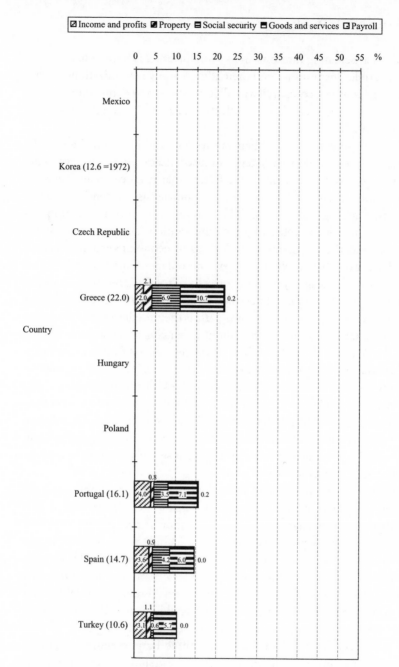

Figure 4.1a. Total tax revenue as percentage of GDP among four OECD countries in 1965. *Source:* OECD 1997b.

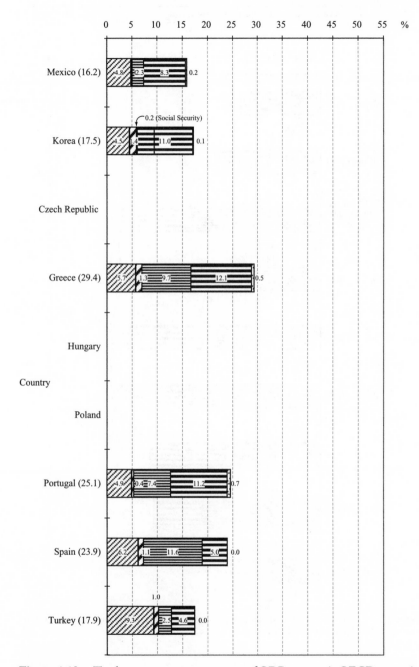

Figure 4.1b. Total tax revenue as percentage of GDP among six OECD countries in 1980. *Source:* OECD 1997b.

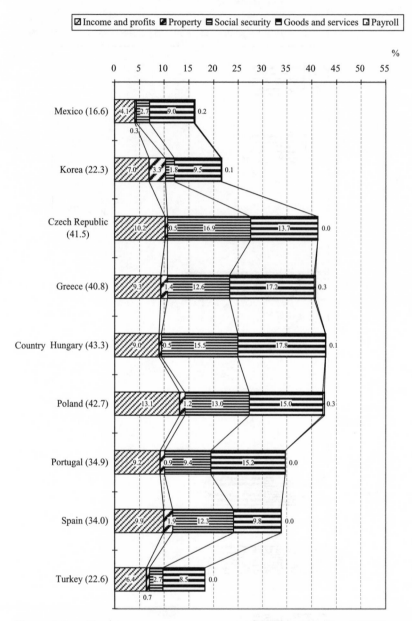

Figure 4.1c. Total tax revenue as percentage of GDP among nine OECD countries in 1995. *Source:* OECD 1997b.

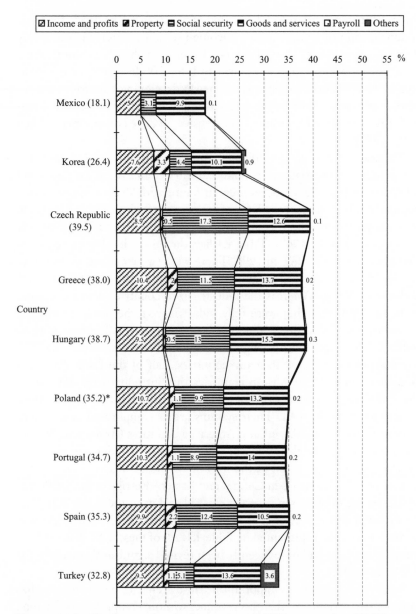

Figure 4.1d. Total tax revenue as percentage of GDP among nine OECD countries in 2000. *Data for 1999. *Source:* OECD 2001a.

that is happening with the globalization of the economy has made the institutionalization of comprehensive income taxation uninteresting to newly developing countries (Thirsk 1991, 66). In addition, the administrative costs of income taxation are not low (Virmani 1988, 20). Instead of comprehensive income taxation, in many cases, newly developing countries have replaced the inferior form of general consumption taxes or excises and duties with the VAT. This has resulted in extensive revenue enhancement (Tanzi 1991; 1992).

Because some newly developing countries are now regarded more appropriately as industrialized economies, I will examine the situation around 1990 to compare their tax revenue structure with that of industrialized countries. The timing of the VAT adoption was much earlier among them than in the industrialized countries, that is, those that had been already industrialized in the 1960s. Table 4.1 lists the newly developing countries that already had the VAT in 1990. There were two countries in Asia, seventeen in Latin America, including the Caribbean and Central America, and five in Africa. Whereas the industrialized countries began to implement the VAT after they were fully industrialized, the newly developing countries introduced the VAT at the beginning or middle stages of their industrial development. Although integration of excise taxes into the VAT has not been completed in many countries, half of the Latin American countries and the four African countries that introduced the VAT since the 1980s have a limited scope of excise taxes, which is the result of their integration into the VAT. Their systems are as complicated as the older ones in Europe: only three Latin American countries (Argentina, Bolivia, and Brazil) have a single (standard) rate without zero-rating and exclusion of basic items. The spread of the VAT may also be observed among the former socialist countries in Central and Eastern Europe in the 1990s followed by the disappearance of the East bloc during the Cold War. The information on them as of 1998 is presented in Table 4.2 in the same way as the information is presented in Table 4.1. All of these VAT systems have multiple tax rates and have recently been revised significantly to apply for EU membership.

Early VAT adoption is important because it enables newly industrializing countries to enhance their tax revenues without comprehensive income taxation. Since the late 1970s, it has become common knowledge that the VAT is a strong revenue machine and a feasible alternative to income tax as a revenue source. Information about the details of the system have been available, and lessons from the experiences of industrialized countries have

Table 4.1. *VAT introduction and rates in newly industrializing countries*

Country	Year of VAT Introduction	Standard Rate as of 1990
Asia		
Korea	1977	10.0%
Taiwan	1986	5.0%
Latin America		
Argentina	1975	13.0%
Bolivia	1987	11.0%
Brazil (states)	1967	20.5%
Chile	1975	18.0%
Colombia	1974	10.0%
Ecuador	1970	10.0%
Peru	1982	14.0%
Uruguay	1973	22.0%
Costa Rica	1975	10.0%
Dominican Republic	1983	6.0%
Grenada	1986	20.0%
Guatemala	1983	7.0%
Haiti	1982	10.0%
Honduras	1976	7.0%
Mexico	1980	15.0%
Nicaragua	1975	10.0%
Panama	1977	5.0%
Africa		
Madagascar	1969	15.0%
Niger	1986	17.0%
Senegal	1990	20.0%
Togo	1984	14.0%
Tunisia	1988	17.0%

Source: Cnossen 1991, Table 5-1.

been spread in publications by practioners and academia as well as through international economic organizations such as the IMF and the World Bank. The VAT is effective for reducing the possibility of malcompliances and corruption concerning revenue collection, which have been frequently

Table 4.2. *VAT introduction and rates in former socialist countries*

Country	Year of VAT Introduction	Standard Rate as of 1990
Bulgaria	1994	22%
Czech Republic	1993	22%
Estonia	1991	18%
Hungary	1988	25%
Latvia	1992	18%
Lithuania	1994	18%
Poland	1993	22%
Romania	1993	18%
Slovak Republic	1993	23%
Slovenia	1999	20%

Source: The information is obtained from OECD 1998c, Table 1-1.

observed in developing countries (Rose-Ackerman 1999, 45–46, 51–52, 87). "[B]oth the IMF and the World Bank targeted tax and customs systems" (Rose-Ackerman 1999, 184) in anticorruption policies. Thus, newly developing countries utilized the late-comers' advantages in designing their tax systems. As a result, they have tended to develop directly from inferior forms of indirect (consumption) taxes to the VAT without striving for the institutionalization of comprehensive income taxation.

More important, the total tax level of these countries has increased for the last decade but not as drastically as the changes among the eighteen industrialized countries between 1965 and 1980 when they experienced rapid economic growth. Despite the early adoption of the VAT in terms of the stage of industrialization, these countries have not expanded the public sectors as much as the industrialized countries have. This is likely to lead to a different pattern in the development of both the tax state and the welfare state from the one in the industrialized countries. To illuminate this point, Figure 4.2 shows the relationship between social security expenditure and a tax revenue structure in four newly industrializing countries outside Europe (South Korea, Argentina, Chile, and Mexico). First, it is very difficult to see a common pattern between tax revenue structure and social security expenditure as was true in the industrialized countries. All the countries have a low revenue reliance on income taxation and a higher revenue reliance on the consumption tax. A high tax level is associated with a higher revenue

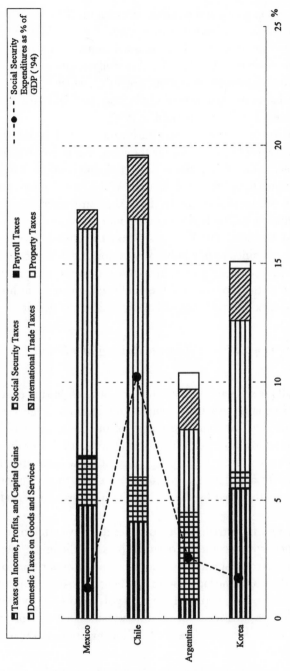

Figure 4.2. Tax revenue structure and level of social security expenditures as percentage of GDP. See a definition of SSEXPT in Appendix. *Source:* Shome (1995) and ILO.

169

reliance on taxes on goods and services (of which the VAT is a major part) and a higher social security expenditure in Chile; thus, Chile is most similar to a universal welfare state. But the substantial content of its social security system is much closer to a liberal and residual welfare state as exemplified by the privatization of the pension system. Argentina, which has an especially low revenue reliance on income tax and a low tax level, is regarded as being closer to a universal welfare state (Huber 1996).

The next two sections will compare the introduction of the VAT in Japan (an early industrialized country outside the West) and in South Korea (one of the most successful cases of newly industrializing countries) and examine their difference in tax politics behind the VAT's introduction. Although both countries are located in the far East, their introduction and use of the VAT are different. The Japanese case is more comparable to the cases of Canada and Australia. The VAT was introduced after a chronic budget deficit that accompanied strong public opposition and difficulty extracting revenue from it. The Korean case, in contrast, involved less political opposition owing to the repression of the public will under an authoritarian regime and the lack of experience with a chronic budget deficit.

Japan: Strong Opposition to Revenue Raising in a Small Welfare State

Japan is a small tax state and welfare state. Because of Japan's postwar tax policies, its tax revenue structure is similar to that of the Anglo-American countries. Inevitably, the funding capacity of the government is weak as represented by its low tax level, which is comparable to that of the United States, and its higher revenue reliance on income tax without effective revenue measures. In addition, the government's effort to institutionalize a welfare state was thwarted by the end of the high-growth period in the mid-1970s.

Among the four industrialized democracies that have attempted to shift revenue reliance from income to consumption since the mid-1980s, Japan encountered the strongest and most persistent public opposition to the introduction of the VAT. The Japanese government poured the most time and energy into its introduction (i.e., three proposals from 1979 to 1988 when the introduction was finally decided).[1] The amount of time involved in the government's attempt to introduce the VAT is comparable to the Australian

---

[1] The description of the Japanese case in this section is based on Kato (1994, Chapters 3–6).

case. The intensity of opposition was as strong as in Canada, although the Japanese long-term incumbent party, the Liberal Democratic Party (LDP), did not lose office because of the VAT as was the case with the Progressive Conservatives in Canada. There was no inferior general consumption tax before the VAT in Japan: the public had long accepted the commodity taxes on luxury goods and goods damaging to health (i.e., tobacco and alcoholic beverages), which the VAT was to replace. The government was required to present a reform agenda to introduce the VAT rather than to rationalize and integrate the existing indirect tax system. In other words, the revenue reliance shift from income to consumption was politicized not only by an almost 50 percent reduction of its reliance on income tax to total revenue but also by a systemic change in the tax system.

A Looming Budget Deficit and the First Proposal of the VAT in the 1970s

The first proposal of the VAT in Japan was put forth in 1978 when both the Government Tax System Research Council and the LDP Tax System Research Council recommended the introduction of the VAT, which was called a "general consumption tax (*ippanshohizei* literally in Japanese)" in the 1980 fiscal year. This proposal and its subsequent demise had three important background factors: the Ministry of Finance's interest in the VAT, the budget deficit that had emerged since the mid-1970s, and the risk taking of then Prime Minister Masayoshi Ohira.

The Japanese Ministry of Finance (MOF) has always been a powerful bureaucratic organization. It has dominated the management of public finance (both tax revenue and expenditure) and the regulation of financial markets, and exercised significant influence over other ministries through its budget allocation.[2] Close observation of the postwar history of public finance demonstrates that the MOF's wide jurisdiction, as well as its concern with budgetary control, has produced a peculiar fiscal orientation. "[I]n order to maintain discretionary power over the budget, the MOF tries to keep

[2] The MOF's power was expected to decline after the interruption of the LDP's thirty-eight years of one-party predominance in 1993. Administrative reform was decided in 1997 to be implemented fully in 2001. Budget making is expected to be controlled more by the cabinet (and thus by incumbent politicians), and the supervision of financial markets has been separated into a new agency, although the real consequence remains to be seen. The MOF's power to regulate financial markets was also strong though it had a higher policy priority over public finance management (Mabuchi 1994). This power has been also weakened by the financial market crisis since the early 1990s and the subsequent administrative reform.

the budget tight enough to use its leverage on expenditures, but also tries to make it loose enough to leave room for discretionary power over new programs" (Kato 1994, 70). The MOF's concern with the modest tightness of the budget was consistent with the restraint on revenue by cutting taxes during high-growth periods when Japan often enjoyed double-digit annual growth rates of the GNP and large natural increments in tax revenues.

The MOF studied the VAT in the then EEC countries in the early 1970s without imminent concern for its implementation in Japan. But this soon led to more serious concern because the Japanese government experienced budget deficits, that is, it started to issue deficit bonds as a special exception to the public finance law in place since the 1975 supplementary budget. The VAT was considered an attractive revenue source because of its ability to raise stable revenue with a small percent increase in the tax rate (Kato1994, 71–80). The VAT, if implemented, was very likely to change the ideal of comprehensive income taxation held by tax specialists, including those in the tax bureau of the MOF, since the Shoup Mission put in place by the U.S. occupational forces established the Japanese postwar tax system in 1949.

Although the VAT was desirable for the MOF, it was certainly a hot potato for incumbent politicians. As a surprise for the MOF bureaucrats who had presented the VAT as a tax reform alternative, however, Prime Minister Ohira immediately brought the VAT onto the public agenda and publicized his intention to introduce the VAT even before the general election in 1979. Ohira had been deeply involved in the issuance of deficit bonds since the 1970s both as a minister of finance and the incumbent LDP's Secretary-General and thus felt deeply responsible for this. The opposition from the public as well as his own party forced Ohira to shelve the proposal well before the election on October 7. Nevertheless, the LDP lost the election. Since a variety of opinion polls had reported a conservative resurgence, the electoral loss was apparently attributed to Ohira's straightforward proposal of the VAT as a means to solve budget deficits, that is, to increase the tax. Owing to existing factional rivalries inside the LDP, non-mainstream factions demanded the resignation of Prime Minister Ohira and supported another candidate, Takeo Fukuda, as LDP President as well as Prime Minister.[3] After forty days of conflict, Ohira managed to secure his premiership for a second term with the help of the biggest Tanaka faction, but the intraparty disharmony increased. In May 1980, the absence of many

[3] The LDP president automatically became prime minister owing to the one-party dominance of the LDP from 1955 to 1993.

LDP Diet members from nonmainstream factions caused the unexpected passage of a nonconfidence motion submitted by the Socialist Party. Faced with the choice of his own resignation or dissolution of the Diet, Ohira chose the latter and proceeded to the second general election in a year. It was to be held simultaneously with the scheduled election of the House of Councilors.

No one could have imagined the consequence of his choice. In June, during the election campaign, Ohira died of spasms and constriction in a coronary artery that allegedly had been caused by "unimaginable mental stress." Upon his death, ironically, the whole LDP, including those in non-mainstream factions who had been against Ohira, began to cooperate to fight for the election. The LDP's support rate had already recovered from a slump in the 1970s and, thus, in the 1980 general election, moved by the formal funeral of Ohira, the voters introduced a new era of conservative dominance. It ended the close parity in numbers between the LDP and opposition parties in the Diet. The LDP won enough seats both in the House of Representatives and in the House of Councilors to restore a stable majority.

Consequently, between 1979 and 1980, the VAT had twice been stigmatized in the two general elections. First, after the general election in October 1979 the Diet issued a resolution on "fiscal reconstruction," stipulating that elimination of deficit bonds should not depend on a revenue increase from a "general consumption tax," which was the name given to the Japanese version of the VAT at that time. Second, after the general election in 1980, the MOF was considered responsible for the hardship and death of the late Ohira. Although Ohira himself had been eager to introduce the VAT, the MOF became the focus of public censure for its responsibility in driving Ohira into a fatal proposal for a tax increase.

From Fiscal Reconstruction to the Proposal of the Sales Tax

After Ohira, Zenko Suzuki was elected prime minister from the same faction. The LDP members were tired of the intense factional strife and did not want to increase ill will between factions; thus, they appointed Suzuki, whom no one expected to become prime minister. Suzuki, using this unexpected opportunity, launched a major policy agenda – administrative and fiscal reform. This major policy agenda, which dominated Japanese politics until the late 1980s, had inherited Ohira's strong will to solve budget deficits. However, it adopted a different strategy – "fiscal reconstruction without a tax increase." This was a rejection of a tax increase such as a general consumption tax while advocating the deficit solvency of the government budget by an expenditure cut. Yasuhiro Nakasone, then the director general of the Administrative Management Agency, appointed a special commission to recommend a plan for administrative reform. To secure the position of the next prime minister, Nakasone, as a small faction leader, needed to affirm his influence and reputation by cooperating with Suzuki to promote the major policy agenda. The commission was headed by a prominent business leader, Toshio Doko, who had criticized the inefficiencies of the public sector.

Although the agenda was set and the commission was organized independently of bureaucratic influence, the new agenda did not necessarily oppose the intention of the MOF to have an expenditure cut at the same time as a tax increase for fiscal solvency. From the beginning of the administrative reform, the MOF actively intervened. For example, in the budget making for the 1981 fiscal year, the MOF proposed to impose a ceiling, a limit, on almost all expenditure items with a few exceptions and cautiously redefined administrative reform as an austerity policy. Doko resisted this exclusive redefinition, arguing that the purpose of the reform was to find and remedy inefficiencies in the public sector, but his efforts were in vain. The Doko commission ultimately succeeded in advancing reforms such as the privatization of three major public corporations, but the MOF also succeeded in imposing an across-the-board ceiling on the budget.

Budget making under the constraints of a zero ceiling in the 1981 fiscal year and a minus ceiling in the 1983 fiscal year made the issuance of deficit bonds unavoidable owing to revenue shortages. Suzuki resigned to take responsibility for failing to stop the issuance of deficit bonds by the 1983 fiscal year, and Nakasone followed Suzuki as prime minister in 1983. By 1984, there had been no explicit decrease in the budget deficits. To supplement revenue, the MOF proposed an ad hoc increase in the corporate tax, arguing that this was not categorized as "a tax increase" by a permanent measure. As a result, until the mid-1980s, after several years of an austerity policy, the incumbent politicians were eager to find a new financial source to curry the favor of constituencies. The public now began to suspect that it was impossible to make ends meet in the government budget with only austerity measures.[4] From spring to summer 1984, one major business association,

---

[4] For example, *Jijitushinsha* opinion polls demonstrated the rapid change in the public perception of the introduction of a major indirect tax on consumption. In December 1982, only

Keidanren, which Doko had once headed, mounted a major campaign to criticize the greater tax on enterprises other than industrial democracies at the expense of international competitiveness. The MOF opposed this, based on relatively low statutory tax rates, but Keidanren said that, considering less generous special tax measures, the Japanese corporate tax was high. Although their debate was not resolved, the business had to rethink the option of introducing the VAT as an alternative to a corporate tax increase.

Prime Minister Nakasone put the VAT on the public agenda first in the mid-1980s,[5] but, unlike Ohira in the late 1970s, he was more concerned about attracting public support for tax reform. He won a second term as the LDP's President and Premier for the first time since the 1970s and wanted to have a major policy campaign for his second term after the administrative reform of the first term. The tax reform proposal suited his political ambitions. No structural tax reform had been enacted after the reform based on the Shoup Mission in 1949 despite the persistent public discontent with an income taxation. Salaried workers whose income taxes had been subtracted at the source without a tax return alleged that their income tax base had been comprehended more fully and that tax exemptions had been less generously applied than to the self-employed. Because the LDP failed to secure an organized and stable support base in the urban election districts with many salaried workers, an attractive tax reform for them was good for the stability of the LDP rule as well as for the Nakasone administration.

The preparation for tax reform continued inside the administration from 1985 to early 1986. However, Nakasone's agenda setting was distinct from the MOF's long-term wish of tax reform. This was a fragile marriage of convenience between them. The MOF desired revenue enhancement while increasing the consistency of the tax system. For this purpose, it selected a tax mix switch from an income tax whose tax base was eroding to a broad-based consumption tax that would guarantee a stable and large revenue. Although it accepted Nakasone's proposal to reduce the nominally

29.0 percent of respondents answered that the introduction of the tax would take place in the future, whereas 27.0 percent did not answer so. However, in December 1983, 42.2 percent answered for the future introduction, whereas only 23.3 percent did not.

[5] In the debate about the 1985 fiscal year tax revision in December 1984, the MOF proposed to repeal the application for tax exemptions on savings and impose a commodity tax on office automation equipment. Both proposals were censured by special interest groups and the incumbent LDP and were blocked. With no means left for revenue enhancement, the MOF's proposal, pushed by the urgent need for revenue, directed the attention of some incumbent politicians to the VAT. Almost at the same time as the MOF's failed porposal, Prime Minister Nakasone, for the first time, proposed structural tax reform.

high progressive tax rates and decrease the complexities of the system, the MOF was also concerned with securing a revenue source for an income tax cut: the VAT was thus an imperative part of the reform. However, Nakasone was more concerned about making the income tax cut attractive to the public and, thus, was willing to introduce an incomplete form of a broad-based consumption tax, such as a manufacturers' sales tax or retail sales tax if it would be more acceptable to the public than the VAT. Nakasone had apparently been influenced by the Reagan tax reform, which had just started in the United States, especially its attractive ideals of fairness, simplicity, neutrality, and later growth, which led to a marginal rate cut and simplification of income taxation. Nakasone advocated similar ideals of fairness, justice, and simplicity and emphasized the reduction of the income tax.

Nakasone was very persistent in selling the reform to the public. In the interim report of the Government Tax System Research Council on April 25, 1986, which was the first publication about the approaching tax reform, only the income tax cut was emphasized. The report did not show the size of nor the financial sources for the income tax cut, that is, the repeal of tax exemptions for savings and the introduction of a broad-based tax on consumption. The Government Tax Council had already deliberated on these measures, and Nakasone was informed by the MOF of some of their technical details:[6] without the VAT a large income tax cut would have been impossible to implement. But, Nakasone resisted publicizing the details of a tax increase to finance an income tax cut because he expected simultaneous elections in the House of Representatives and the House of Councilors. In the elections on July 6, 1986, the LDP won a record-breaking share of seats: in the House of Representatives it won 300 out of 512 seats, and in the House of Councilors, 72 out of 126 seats. During the election campaign, Nakasone tried to quell public suspicion of the tax increase and made a pledge not to introduce a large-scale indirect tax that the people and the party opposed.

Thus, after the election, the income tax cut became a fait accompli, and the introduction of the VAT was to be blocked legitimately, that is, based on the election pledge of the Prime Minister. Nakasone first clung to his election pledge, and line members of the LDP with weak electoral bases were ready to resist the VAT, fearing public antipathy toward the new tax. However, the LDP politicians with longer tenures who had accumulated

---

[6] *Nihon Keizai Shimbun*, February 5, 1986.

tax policy experience were aware of the tight budgetary conditions and thus helped the MOF persuade Nakasone to accept the VAT and then repressed the line members' opposition. In December 1986, as a result, finally both the party and government tax commissions proposed a tax reform plan. This included ¥ 4.6 trillion in income and corporate tax cuts with a corporate tax rate reduction, compression of the number of personal income tax brackets from fifteen to six, repeal of tax exemptions on small-lot savings (Maruyu system), and 5 percent of the VAT called sales tax (*uriagezei* literally in Japanese). Before February 1987, seven tax bills had been submitted to the Diet.

Between December 1986 and April 1987, when the tax bills were shelved, the potential problems and concerns about the VAT's introduction were revealed. First, interest groups and industries actively demanded tax exemptions of some goods and services. There was, then, the same problem as in the Australian case, about definitions of goods and services to be exempted. For example, if food were exempt from the VAT, should ships for fishing and machines used by farmers also be exempt in addition to the containers for food, such as bottles and bins? Second, smaller firms and traders also demanded tax exemptions. Because of their size and small share in total transactions, this was considered a relatively easy compromise for the government. The exemptions appeared to be the best way to avoid the additional costs of tax compliance, and the increasing possibility of the tax authority's investigation of their business incomes. But, the businesses that had won exemptions subsequently became concerned about exclusion from transactions and exchanges with taxed businesses because they could not issue documents for their traders to use for tax credits. The government tried to cope with this problem by making small-business exemptions optional, but the chaos could not be extinguished. Moreover, whereas the distributors were concerned that a tax might be imposed on them without being added to prices and thus without being transferred to consumers, the consumers were concerned that distributors would increase prices more than the amount of the VAT. Thus, the concerns about the introduction of the tax were not necessarily consistent among businesses or between businesses and consumers, but all worked to block the VAT.

After having met the revolt of their own local branches who feared the adverse influence of public opposition to the VAT in unified local elections, the LDP government finally shelved all tax bills. In the summer of 1987, the government agreed with the opposition parties on a more modest version of income tax reform including the compression of tax brackets from fifteen to twelve. Of course, in tax reform, the introduction of the VAT was excluded.

Introduction of the VAT and Its Consequence

Despite the public's absolute rejection of the VAT in 1987, the VAT was introduced at the end of 1988 and became effective in 1989 under Prime Minister Noboru Takeshita. The reasons for the final introduction of the VAT in Japan may be summarized in several points when compared with the blocked proposal of the VAT under the Nakasone administration. First, the cooperation of tax experts among the LDP politicians and the MOF was fortified. Takeshita was one of such tax experts inside the LDP who was in close communication with the MOF, whereas Nakasone had preferred strong leadership and tried to minimize bureaucratic influence. Thus, there was no room for disagreement within the administration. Second, related interest groups had learned from the chaotic opposition to the sales tax during the Nakasone administration. The government's effort to explain the details of the VAT system in 1987 had been rewarded with a better understanding of the VAT on the part of the public. This significantly decreased their antipathy to the unknown new tax and contributed to their reluctant acceptance of the VAT under the Takeshita administration.

Third, and most important, the government agreed to more acceptable aims for tax reform than a tax mix switch from income to consumption, that is, rectification of tax inequity (i.e., by income tax reform) and preparation for the aging of society (i.e., by securing tax revenue from the VAT). These aims did not necessarily embody the content of reform. The proposed income tax reform did not involve sufficient base broadening to rectify tax inequities such as the one under the U.S. Reagan administration. And the VAT revenue was not earmarked for welfare expenditures nor did it accompany a major compensation package for the poor. However, these aims served to weaken the worst image of the VAT, regressivity, and did win, though reluctantly, the public's acceptance. Despite strong opposition from the Socialist and Communist parties, the LDP passed the tax bills in December 1988.

Finally, 3 percent of the VAT, which used a subtraction method without invoice and was currently being called a consumption tax, was introduced in April 1989. Several devices to alleviate political opposition resulted in reducing the consistency of the system and narrowing the tax base. The tax exemption point in terms of the amount of annual sales was set high for exemptions of many small traders (less than ¥ 30 million of annual sale). Marginal tax reduction, in proportion to total annual sale, was allowed for small traders (less than ¥ 60 million of annual sale). A simplified rule of tax calculation was applied to businesses with less than ¥ 500 million. Tax returns were required twice a year, every six months. The low tax rate together with these tax exemptions and protections for small traders meant less revenue, but these measures aiming to "protect" small traders did not lead to a significant revenue loss. Although the proportion of small traders to the total number of tax units was high, the proportion of their sales to the sales of all traders was small. In other words, these devices were politically feasible and inexpensive for the government: they were used to cultivate opposition without losing a lot of revenue from a lower-rate VAT. In contrast to these concessions, the government resisted any concession that would lead to eroding the tax base significantly. Tax exemption on basic items such as food was an example, and the government was especially careful to refute the demand to allow a tax exemption with a zero-rate system, which would serve to decrease the disadvantages of tax exemption and thus further erode the tax base. As a result of the reform, the income tax was also reduced by compressing twelve tax brackets to five ranging from 10 to 50 percent, increasing the minimum taxable income, and allowing generous basic and special personal deductions. The burdens of the inhabitant tax as an income tax at the local level and the corporate tax were also lowered.

As a result of a political scandal, however, public opposition was strongly organized after the VAT became effective. This scandal, the Recruit problem, had started earlier in 1988 when a newspaper covered the bribery case of a deputy mayor in a real estate company, Recruit Cosmos, but became a major political scandal in which many incumbent and opposition politicians, bureaucrats, and journalists were implicated. The Recruit Cosmos was one of the affiliates of the Recruit that solicited these people to buy securities before going public, expecting a big surge in their prices. The Recruit also contributed money to many politicians and some bureaucrats. Soliciting the purchase of securities was regarded as insider trading, but the accusation was not made by the existing securities trading law at that time. Only a few cases were eventually labeled bribery because finding a clear link between the purchase and the Recruit's rewards expected from the purchasers was difficult. The reform provided no effective measures to comprehend the income from exchange of securities or to impose a tax on capital gains. Thus it further increased the public resentment against the consumption tax.[7] The Recruit problem became closely intertwined with the tax issue when people started to pay the VAT, the so-called consumption tax (*shohizei* literally in Japanese), which had been price exclusive[8] and was thus regarded as an additional burden.

In April 1989, owing to public resentment concerning the consumption tax and the Recruit problem, the support rate for the Takeshita cabinet declined significantly to a single digit number. Takeshita resigned, Sosuke Uno formed a cabinet, and the government announced the revision of the system. In the election of the House of Councilors on July 23, however, the LDP experienced an historic defeat and won only 36 out of 126 seats. In addition to the Recruit problem and the consumption tax, Uno's personal scandal and the issue of agricultural liberalization damaged the LDP. However, the waning of public opposition to the consumption tax was also rapid. In the election of the House of Representatives on February 18, the LDP won 275 out of 512 seats and restored its support. The Socialist Party, which had attracted public support because of its consistent opposition to the consumption tax, also won seats. In the unified local elections in April, however, the surge of public support for the Socialist Party ended, and it lost many seats and positions. The Socialists had to accept the government's plan to revise the consumption tax. The revision of the consumption tax in May 1991 involved lowering the maximum annual sales for marginal tax reduction from ¥ 60 million to ¥ 50 million and making a simple tax calculation method more suitable for the different industrial sectors while lowering the maximum annual sale for an application of a simplified rule of tax calculation from ¥ 500 million to ¥ 400 million.

In 1993, the LDP's long-term predominance was interrupted.[9] In early 1994, disagreement over the consumption tax increase led to the collapse

---

[7] The MOF, however, had conceived the implementation of a capital gains tax. The public opposed the consistent numbering of taxpayers, which is essential for effective taxation on capital gains. The MOF had once proposed such a system, a green-card system, in 1981, but this was blocked by strong public opposition.

[8] Price exclusive practice was chosen because the public was concerned about the increasing burden "hidden" by this practice. In 2002, however, the Japanese government announced that it planned to introduce price inclusive practice in fiscal year 2004. If it is introduced, the VAT rate increase may be more politically feasible in Japan.

[9] Although the consumption tax was not directly related to the LDP breakup and the subsequent end of its one-party dominance in 1993, the repression of line members by leaders such as was observed during the tax reform process was an important reason for its breakup. The LDP breakup was characterized as the revolt of backbenchers who had little vested interest in the existing system. They revolted against the leaders although a conflict between the party leaders in the biggest faction was also involved (Kato 1998).

of the non-LDP coalition government. The consumption tax increase had been subsequently decided during a coalition government of the LDP, the Socialist Party, and the Harbinger (a splinter party of the LDP). As a result, 5 percent of the consumption tax became effective in April 1997.[10] At the same time, the system of marginal tax reduction for small traders was abolished. Tax exemption was no longer allowed for new corporations with capital of more than ¥ 10 million, and a simplified rule of tax calculation was to be applied to only small traders with less than ¥ 200 million. This 2 percent tax increase in 1997 was widely regarded as the reason for the worsening recession. In the 1990s, therefore, several ad hoc income tax cuts were implemented, but the tax revenue structure in Japan has not changed drastically with the consumption tax, and its total tax level continues to be low.

The Japanese government's attempt to enhance its revenue-raising capacity by shifting revenue reliance from income to consumption failed. The attempted shift, which was quite modest compared with the Western European countries, has been incomplete, and, with the current tax rate level (5 percent as of 2000), the VAT raises a modest amount of revenue. This consequence is a product of tax politics, which were symbolized by the changing reform aims. The VAT was blocked by strong opposition both in the late 1970s when revenue enhancement was a reform aim and again in the mid-1980s when the revenue reliance shift was advocated. This opposition was an explicit expression of the public's rejection of increasing the state's funding capacity by a revenue reliance shift. The public finally recognized that the revenue shortfall and budget deficits would not be solved simply by an austerity policy and accepted the new tax. But, they continue to suspect the increasing tax and show strong antipathy toward a tax rate increase. The Japanese low tax level goes well with the small welfare state.

The Tax Issue and the Welfare State

The low Japanese tax may be attributed to the fact that its welfare state has had a shorter history than other industrial democracies. The health insurance system developed early and fully, but the expansion of the pension system was delayed. The foundation of a national health insurance system was established as early as 1938 and was reformed during the postwar period to guarantee full coverage of basic medical care for the entire population. As a result, in Japan, private insurance is usually regarded as an optional

[10] For details of this process, see Kato (1997).

preparation for specific kinds of diseases rather than a necessity to cover basic medicare costs. However, the public pension system that originated with occupational pensions during the prewar period was fully extended to the total population in 1961 (the establishment of *kokumin nenkin seido*), and benefits were increased to a level comparable to other industrial democracies in the 1970s.

This timing resulted in a much shorter golden age of expansion of the welfare state than in other industrial democracies that utilized the abundant and increasing tax revenue from a long period of postwar prosperity for welfare expansion (Hiroi 1999). The welfare expansion under the LDP rule since 1955 did not take place until the 1970s, when the LDP endured declining support. Stimulated by the radical expansion of welfare provision by local autonomies controlled by the opposition parties at the national level, the LDP started in 1973 to increase pension benefits drastically and to subsidize medical payments for the aged, which was called "the first year of welfare." Unfortunately, however, the oil shock ended this high-growth period. Japan did not adopt a strong revenue-raising capability before the 1970s and since then has clung to a restraint in public expenditures in the face of chronic budget deficits caused by the revenue shortfall. In the 1980s, welfare retrenchment involved a quick reversal or qualification of the expansion in the 1970s (i.e., extending the minimum period of contributions for pension entitlements, raising the eligibility age for the entitlement, and increasing the burden on the insured for medical service in the health insurance system).

The low tax level with a heavy revenue reliance on an income tax in Japan is that of a liberal welfare state when viewed in terms of the welfare state classification presented in Chapter 1. One strong evidence that is counter to this classification has been the unexpectedly high income equality in this small-sized welfare state. This characteristic is now regarded as the one of the East Asian welfare state:

[W]hat does 'welfare' mean in different societies? For example, options available to a person with disabilities in Britain or the Untied States, where a substantial network of state support exists, may be greater than in a welfare system where the only or main provider is the family and the state plays a residual role. The latter welfare system may be cheaper, but are they producing less 'welfare' in terms of quality and quantity? (White and Goodman 1998, 18)

Here, the authors are talking about the possibility of a society that provides a high level of welfare that coexists with the withdrawal of government intervention. This view concurs with the "Japanese welfare mix," as a distinctive model of welfare capitalism in which welfare provision and promotion of equality have been closely linked with a life-long employment practice of private enterprises and company-based benefits instead of reliance on government-sponsored universal programs (Estevez-Abe 1999).

How well has this model of the welfare state survived the welfare retrenchment since the 1980s? The long-term conservative dominance by the LDP and a divided labor are frequently named as causes for retrenchment. The weak labor organization in Japan has been closely associated with ineffective social democratic representation at the national level, and the resulting conservative dominance has been the ultimate reason why the Japanese government has attempted to deregulate the market and retrench the public sector when faced with a chronic budget deficit (Shinkawa 1993). This adjustment has been supported by the government's market-centered approach to solving conflicting interests over public policies, more specifically wage and employment policy and welfare provision for employees that have been agreed upon by employers (Hiwatari 1991).[11] This approach is possible only when there is a coordination of interests between labor and capital in each enterprise and in the industrial sector instead of across-the-sectors coordination in the government.[12]

The welfare reform in the 1980s focused on making the system more consistent, for example, integrating several separate occupational pension systems into one basic pension as a minimum guarantee rather than implementing a simple system and outright retrenchment (Campbell 1992). As a result, a common basic benefit has been entitled for everyone covered by eight separate pension systems, such as the Government Managed Pension Program of Corporate Employees (GMPPCE; *Koseinenkin*), the Government Managed Pension Program of Self-Employees (GMPPSE; *Kokuminnenkin*), the Mutual Benefits Association for Public Servants (*Komuinkyosai*), and so on. However, the increasing number of aged and a decreasing birth rate further aggravated the financial difficulties across the pension and the national health insurance systems at the turn of the century. In this regard, future welfare retrenchment would be inevitable without a drastic increase in

---

[11] Hiwatari also explains that a combination of industry-centered adjustment and bureaucratic coordination in Japan facilitated party convergence in public policy making in the 1980s in comparison with the party polarization in the United Kingdom and United States (Hiwatari 1998).

[12] For a more detailed account for this "enterprise unionism," see Kume (1998).

tax.[13] The Gold Plan in the 1990s, although proposed to prepare for the aging of the society, has not brought about explicit welfare expansion. The public insurance of nursing care (of the disabled and aged), which became effective in April 2000, is a new step but is also unlikely to bring about innovative welfare expansion or to promote significantly quality service for the welfare of the aged. Moreover, the introduction of private welfare service covered by a government program may possibly cause a new kind of problem: public suspicion of collusion between the private sector and bureaucrats as exemplified by a series of scandals in the early 1990s. Public confidence in the social security program has been declining: for example, one in three people eligible for the GMPPSE did not pay contributions in 1999.[14]

The politics behind the welfare and tax policies in 2000 symbolized this situation at the turn of the century. First, during the recession, when the annual growth recovered to 0.5 percent in 1999 but with a high unemployment rate of around 5 percent, the financial situation of the pension and health insurance programs declined, as did the long-term effect of the increasing proportion of the aged population. However, many reforms were postponed. The reform of the health insurance system was postponed until 2002 (and became effective in 2003) despite rapidly looming costs of medicare for those over 70, whose share of the total national health insurance expenditure was expected to increase from one-third in 2000 to one-half in 2025.

The introduction of the Japanese version of the 401K retirement savings plans (private pensions) in the United States was also postponed after 2001.[15] Pension reform was implemented without a complete solution for financial difficulties. The GMPPCE reform would raise the eligible age for old-age pensions from 60 to 65 between 2013 and 2025,[16] gradually cut by 5 percent a proportional provision for preretirement wages, and freeze the indexation of provision for the current level of wages of the working population for the first time since 1973. This would result in pushing

---

[13] All the literature on the Japanese social security system or the welfare state concur on this point. For example, see Hori (1997), Murakami (1997), Ishiyama (1998), Hatta and Yashiro (1998), and Oshio (1998).

[14] *Asahi Shimbun*, September 24, 1999.

[15] Under the 401K plan, employers and employees deposit equal amounts of pre-tax income (adjusting for inflation annually) into investment accounts under an employee-selected plan.

[16] This will be applied for the part of the pension that is proportional to the wage before retirement. The same procedure for a basic part of the pension had already been decided to be instituted between 2001 and 2013.

social security contributions in 2025 down to 25.2 percent from 34.5 percent without the reform (the level in 2000 was 17.35 percent). However, the reform did not present an effective measure for preventing enterprises from exiting the GMPPCE system because of increasing social security contributions.[17] Nor did it provide an explicit procedure for integrating different pension systems while solving their financial relationship.[18] In addition, the government debt was expected to increase to the level of more than 90 percent of the GDP by the 2005 fiscal year as a result of a steep 20 percent increase for five years.

As a result, both tax and welfare policies were issues in the 2000 general elections. But, both the governing and opposition coalitions tried to shy away from making commitments to specific proposals. The governing coalition of the LDP, the Komei Party, and the Conservative Party refused to raise the rate of the consumption tax in the near future (i.e., before economic recovery). The Democratic Party in opposition proposed to reduce the income level liable for tax and promoted a compensation plan but failed to come up with a concrete proposal. The parties were divided into two groups – one supporting the financing of social security only by contributions and the other by taxes – but this division did not necessarily correspond to their expectations about the level of benefit provision, and thus there was no clear cleavage.[19]

---

[17] The number of corporate enterprises under the system dropped for the first time in 1998, and this trend has continued at the turn of the century. *Asahi Shimbun* estimated the proportions of participating corporate enterprises to the total and reported a drop from 69 percent at the end of the 1997 fiscal year to 67 percent at the end of the 1998 fiscal year. Exiting is illegal but is implicitly accepted by government officials because a strict enforcement of the law often causes a bankruptcy of that enterprise (*Asahi Shimbun*, April 16, 2000).

[18] The integration of the Mutual Benefit Association of Agricultural and Forestry Workers, the GMPPCE, and the Mutual Benefit Association of Private School Teachers to the private sector as well as the integration of the Mutual Benefit Associations of National and Local Public Servants to the public sector is the first step, followed by ensuring an equal level of provision. The purpose of integration is to help the systems with worse financial conditions. Unifying all of them into one system has also been considered: as already explained, the basic part of this provision was already integrated in the mid-1980s.

[19] For example, the governing coalition supported the maintenance of a social insurance principle, whereas the LDP advocated restraining the benefit level, and the Komei Party supported more generous provisions. Among the parties supporting tax finance, the Liberal Party and the Conservative Party supported a low level of provisions financed specifically by the consumption tax, whereas the Democratic Party, the Communist Party, and the Democratic Socialist Party proposed more generous provisions financed by taxes in addition to contributions.

Conseqently, the Japanese style of welfare state (i.e., one that ensures equality and welfare without a large expenditure) appears to have reached a crossroads at the turn of the century. The deepening recession threatens the system of lifelong employment as well the companies' commitment to securing benefits provision for their employees.[20] The maintenance of even the existing level of welfare provision is impossible without increasing public expenditures and tax. There has been a recurrent proposal since the 1980s to earmark part of the revenue from the VAT for welfare expenditures (*fukushimokutekizei*). But this idea is counter to the MOF's strong intention to control spending. It also runs against public antipathy toward the VAT, which prevents the tax rate from increasing. Thus, implementation of the tax is likely to face strong opposition in sharp contrast with the implementation of social security taxes in France (Chapter 2).

South Korea: The Funding Capacity of a Strong State

Postwar Korean Tax Policy and the Introduction of the VAT

South Korea has been a typical case of a successful newly industrializing country. It is also a strong state that allegedly serves industrialization and economic development (White and Wade 1985; Amsden 1989; Haggard 1990). These characterizations of Korea have not been drastically changed by democratization since 1987, although the economic crisis since 1997 has caused a reconsideration of the competitiveness of its economy. The tax system was established during the period before democratization.

Choi (1997, 240–8) distinguishes four periods in the transformation of the postwar tax system in Korea that roughly overlaps with the periodization of the six Republics during the postwar period.[21] Although the postwar tax laws were passed in the late 1940s, the major direction of the postwar Korean tax system was determined in the 1950s after the Korean War. The tax revenue structure used to finance enormous military expenditures was changed into a peacetime system, and revenue reliance shifted from direct to indirect taxes. From 1961 to 1971, there was economic development as well as the rule of a military junta and a civilian government filled by

---

[20] Estevez-Abe (1998) also shows reservation about the performance of the Japanese welfare mix in the 1990s.

[21] They are First Republic (Rhee Syng Man, 1948–60), Second Republic (Chang Myun, 1960–1), Third Republic (Park Chung Hee, 1963–72), Fourth Republic (Park Chung Hee, 1972–9), Fifth Republic (Chun Doo Hwan, 1981–8), and Sixth Republic (Roh Tae Woo, 1988–93).

the same military personnel. The eighteen-year-long rule by Park Chung Hee continued from the military coup in 1961 (from 1963 as President) to his assassination in 1979. The declaration of martial law and introduction of the Yushin Constitution were turning points. There were three major tax reforms in 1961, 1967, and 1971, involving increases in tax rates of and revenue reliance on indirect taxation, adoption of a global income tax system, and decreases in both the personal and corporate income tax. The Economic Planning Board (EPB) was established in 1961, and the Office of National Tax Administration (ONTA) was founded in 1966. The latter is independent from the Bureau of Taxation of the Ministry of Finance and assumes the responsibility of tax administration.

Between 1972 and 1978, the heavy industrial sectors developed rapidly. An almost global income tax was introduced in 1975, and the VAT was introduced in 1977. From 1979 to 1986 during structural adjustment and liberalization, there were no major tax changes, but the debate over tax reforms was activated, especially lowering personal and corporate income tax rates, consideration of tax incentives, and taxes on financial transactions. Since 1987, democratization and structural changes in the economy advanced, and the latter ushered in the economic and financial crisis in 1997. However, it is unlikely that the Korean tax system, which relies on an indirect tax on consumption with a relatively low income tax, will drastically change in the near future.

This brief overview of Korean postwar tax policy shows that the VAT was introduced at an early stage of industrialization, that is, in a period of development of heavy industry as well as immediately after the organization of the tax administration. When the European countries introduced the VAT around 1970, heavy industrialization had already occurred, and the postwar reorganization of the government had ended. Compared with Japan, the timing of the VAT's introduction was even earlier: Japan experienced the rapid development of heavy industries after the 1950s and caught up with other industrial democracies in the 1960s, but the VAT was introduced much later, in 1989. The process of introducing the VAT in Korea demonstrates that it was a result of technocratic planning and preparation, which did not meet the formidable opposition peculiar to democratic policy making.[22]

---

[22] Several studies detail the process of introducing the VAT, both in English and Korean (Choi 1990; Han 1990; Kim 1991, 287–306; Cha 1986), and were the basis for the reorganization of the process here.

The study of the VAT began in the Ministry of Finance and the Office of the Senior Presidential Secretary for Economic Affairs in 1971 (Kim 1991). To learn from experience abroad, the office invited the assistance of James C. Duignan, member of a fiscal panel at the IMF, and Carl S. Shoup from Columbia University. With the special direction of President Bok, the first proposal of the VAT was made at the end of 1971 by the Tax Deliberation Committee as a long-term measure to integrate and rationalize indirect taxes. In 1974, three officials were sent to study the VAT in the United Kingdom, West Germany (at that time), and Belgium. In addition, an official went to the headquarters of the EEC, and one was sent to the United Kingdom in 1975 and 1976. From 1975 to 1976, the government also invited two officials from the IMF – Duignan and Alan T. Tait – to study the impact of the VAT on prices and income distributions and to draft the VAT legislation.

The VAT was preferred because of its efficiency, consistency of indirect taxation, discouragement of tax evasion, and revenue-raising capability. In 1976, immediately before the introduction of the VAT, the business tax (a multistage turnover tax or cascade) raised 34 percent of the total revenue from a tax on goods and services, whereas the commodity taxes raised 66 percent. Not only was the existing general consumption tax an inferior type with six rates from 0.5 to 3.5 percent, but revenue was raised from more complex and inconsistent taxes on specific commodities and taxes with seventeen rates from 5 to 200 percent (Kim 1991). In terms of economic effect, neutrality over economic activities and the promotion of investment and exports were expected from the VAT. The increasing cost and difficulty of tax compliance and the possible effect of price increases had been considered problematic, but they were solved mainly by six years of intensive preparation with the help of economists from international economic organizations. The regressive effect on income distribution was also a concern, but the government implemented a progressive tax rate structure and reduced the tax of low-income earners in the 1970s.

The VAT was introduced in 1977 to replace the business tax and merge several existing commodity taxes. The VAT legislation passed in parliament in November 1976 despite opposition based on the early timing of its introduction,[23] its effect on price increases, and regressivity. Immediately

---

[23] There was a reason for opposition because Korea's neighbors, such as Taiwan and Japan, did not yet have the VAT. The Korean government explained that it was hard for the Japanese government to introduce the VAT because Japan had no general consumption tax, and thus

before implementation in July 1977, there was a demand that the introduction be postponed for fear that it would exceed the target of a 10 percent price increase. A compromise was made applying 10 percent of the tax rate in July instead of the original 13 percent. The VAT legislation stipulated 10 percent of the rate but allowed upward and downward fluctuations of 3 percent. Otherwise, the introduction was smooth mainly because the business community, including small- and medium-sized businesses and the public, had been well informed about the VAT (Han 1990, 131). The government did an intensive campaign with the help of the Korean Chamber of Commerce and Industry and media to increase public understanding of the VAT. Films, pamphlets, and conferences were used to explain the nature of the tax and its filing method. The government did three trial runs on filing tax returns, and almost all the potential tax-filing units participated in the last two trials. They facilitated the government tax collection, although the transformation was relatively easy because the collection of existing business taxes was already computerized.

The process of the VAT introduction in Korea involved several interesting points when compared with other industrial democracies. Korea fully enjoyed outside help, including learning from the experience of the European countries and consulting with economists from international organizations. Owing to its quasi-authoritarian nature, the government was concerned exclusively with the technical aspects of tax policy and so omitted the need to persuade the public about the new tax. In other words, the transformation was smooth, the new tax was administered well, and little expression of public opposition was expected. However, the lack of democratic policy making should not be exaggerated here. Fiscal solvency was not a reason for the Korean introduction of the VAT, and this was expected to decrease public opposition significantly even if the country had been fully democratized. In this regard, the Korean introduction of the VAT was directly opposite the Japanese situation in which the government spent energy to quell the antipathy of businesses toward the new tax and public suspicions about a tax increase.

Although the smooth introduction of the VAT in Korea was similar to cases of early introducers in Europe, its consequences were completely different. Although the total tax revenue increased by about 5 percent as a percentage of GDP from 1980 to 2000, the share of taxes on goods

the VAT proposal was to be a tax increase during a period of budget deficit in Japan. In retrospect, this turned out to be true for the Japanese case when the VAT was introduced.

and services did not increase despite the introduction of the VAT in Korea (Figure 4.1). As Choi (1997, 239) stipulates, this tendency is explicit though "[m]any people have mistakenly believed that the overall tax burden and share of indirect taxes in total tax revenue increased with the introduction of the value added tax (VAT)." The Korean case is peculiar in the sense that the VAT has been used to provide a stable revenue source while preserving both the level of total tax revenue and tax revenue structure. Of course, if Korea had not introduced the VAT and kept a complicated and inconsistent indirect tax system, it would not have been able to raise a stable revenue from it. But, it is noteworthy that Korea has used revenue from the VAT only to replace revenue from the former indirect taxes on consumption while restraining an increase in total tax revenue.

Is South Korea Destined to Be a Small Welfare State Like Japan?

South Korea has kept a relatively low tax level despite rapid economic development and the early institutionalization of a revenue machine. This is likely to lead to the limited development of a welfare state. The Korean welfare state is still young and is often compared with Japan. More specifically, it is considered a variant of a "Japan-focused" model of welfare in East Asia (Goodman and Peng 1996) that refutes the theory that the East Asian welfare states should follow the Western model. Instead, this position advocates the distinctiveness of the East Asian welfare states that share a common institutional legacy resulting from past Japanese colonization and the tradition of Confucianism in their societies. They are distinct from the Western states because of a difference in cultural background (White and Goodman 1998) instead of being an underdeveloped and incomplete form of the Western model. They have developed in close association with their nation building and survival and relied on families and communities at the expense of intense government intervention in redistribution as observed in the Western model. A slightly different focus by Kwon (1999) leads to a view that the development of the Korean welfare state has been facilitated by a weakly legitimized and quasi-authoritarian government, which desired that the implementation of social policies would serve to fortify its fragile base of legitimacy.

The development of social security programs in Korea has been much slower than in Japan and has been initiated under authoritarian rule. The first welfare program, Industrial Accident Insurance, with contributions only from employers with no subsidy from the government, was established in 1963, two years after the military coup. After the failure of a pilot program for health insurance from 1965 to 1975, a compulsory national health insurance for workers of certain sized firms began in 1977. The National Pension Program, which was supposed to be introduced but was postponed by the oil shock, was finally introduced in 1987. The development of these programs, however, has been quite limited because of financial difficulties (Kwon 1998a, 50–4; 1998b). The coverage of these programs has not been fully extended; the coverage of the Health Insurance Program is limited to employees, and the National Pension Program covered only 26.7 percent of the working population in 1994.

Whether the Korean welfare state, or, more broadly, the East Asian welfare state, will be able to achieve income equality in a way that is different from the Western model remains to be seen. But the Korean welfare state exhibits the characteristics of a limited welfare state. In this regard, it is like the Japanese state, but its development, especially combined with the attention to state funding capacity, implies a divergence between the two countries. Japan apparently lacked the opportunity to increase its state revenue-raising capacity as exemplified by the late introduction of the VAT after the experience of a chronic budget deficit. The Korean government has abundant opportunity to expand its state funding capacity. For example, it introduced the VAT at a very early stage of industrialization, that is, even earlier than the earliest introducer in Western Europe, but Korea used a strong revenue machine exclusively for the purpose of stabilizing revenue. At least, despite the potential of the state funding capacity, the expansion of the Korean welfare state will be controlled more than the current Japanese one.

The Korean case appears to embody an overall trend among newly industrializing countries, that is, the early adoption of a strong revenue machine combined with the restrained growth of a welfare state. Its neighbor, Taiwan, provides further evidence for this trend. Taiwan introduced the VAT, which is called the value-added "business tax," in 1986 when it enacted a major tax reform including the simplification of its income tax structure from fifteen brackets with a maximum rate of 60 percent to thirteen brackets with a maximum rate of 50 percent.[24] The business tax has only a 5 percent standard rate but with few exemptions. Entertainment

---

[24] The income tax structure has been further simplified since 1990 to five brackets with a maximum rate of 40 percent (Koryukyokai 1998, 61).

shops such as night clubs, bars, and coffee shops have higher rates of 15 and 25 percent, and small-sized family businesses have a lower rate of 1 percent. The business tax replaced the turnover tax, which accumulated tax amounts from one stage of transaction to another. As a result, the introduction of the VAT did not necessarily increase revenue reliance on an indirect tax on consumption. Rather, the revenue reliance on an indirect tax decreased immediately after the introduction of the VAT. The revenue reliances on direct and indirect taxation in Taiwan in 1985 before the major tax reform were 38.0 and 62.0 percent, respectively. The relative percentages changed drastically to 56.8 percent for direct taxation and 43.2 percent for indirect taxation in 1990. In the mid-1990s, these shares were almost even, for example, 51.8 percent for direct taxation and 48.2 percent for indirect taxation in 1996 (Koryukyokai 1998, p. 61). Except for the expansion of health insurance programs in the 1980s, the welfare state, including the old-age pension, is still at the beginning of development in Taiwan (Kwon 1998a, 44–50). Its tax state is a long way from providing abundant revenue despite the introduction of a strong revenue machine.

Conclusion

In this chapter, the survey of the VAT's diffusion into newly developing countries shows that it spreads more smoothly and earlier in terms of the stage of industrialization than in industrial democracies. Newly developing countries have never conceived of the income tax as a major revenue source and without it have come to rely on a general consumption tax. As a result, tax systems have developed differently. To confirm this, the two East Asian cases, Japan as an industrial democracy and South Korea as a newly developing country, are compared. This comparison shows that the timing of the VAT introduction was much earlier in Korea. More important, the government of a newly developing country is unlikely to be seduced by increasing the revenue-raising capacity of the VAT and has tended to restrain the growth of the public sector. Here, the possibility emerges that the newly industrializing countries are likely to have a completely different pattern of path dependence than the industrial countries. This difference is caused mainly by the presence or absence of a common knowledge about how to institutionalize a strong revenue-raising capacity. For example, the governments of newly developing countries already knew the VAT as an effective revenue measure at the time of its introduction and thus have tried to restrain the expansion of the size of the public sector. This is in sharp

Conclusion

contrast to existing industrial democracies, that is, either early introducers where the introduction of the VAT led to the expansion of the state funding capacity or late introducers where the revenue increase was under severe constraint from public opposition during budget deficits. In this regard, policy diffusion, like technological diffusion, causes irreversible changes, but these changes depend upon the presence or absence of knowledge about policies. Here, the path is determined not only by policy diffusion itself but also by politics that is shaped by knowledge about policies.

5

The Political Foundation of Financing the Welfare State

A COMPARATIVE VIEW

Hypotheses Examined: The Coexistence of Regressive Taxation and the Welfare State

The development of a welfare state and the resistance to welfare retrenchment are path-dependent upon the expansion of the state's funding capacity. The quantitative analysis in Chapter 1 and case studies in Chapters 2 through 4 confirm that the size of a welfare state is strongly associated with the institutionalization of a regressive tax to raise revenue more effectively. This point is illuminated by the postwar history of tax policies across industrial democracies. Immediately after World War II, comprehensive income taxes started to be diffused across countries, but the income tax base was eroded by political pressure, and progressive rates became excessively high. Gradually, a flat-rate regressive tax on a broad base of consumption has become a more important revenue source. Among regressive taxes, except social security contributions, the value-added tax, a representative form of a flat-rate tax on general consumption, has come to be used widely to raise more revenue. As reviewed in detail in Chapter 1, high-tax countries have added the revenue from enhanced regressive taxation while preserving their income tax revenue. As a result, the revenue reliance shift from progressive income tax to regressive consumption taxes reflects the expansion of a state's funding capacity. The strong revenue-raising machine that was institutionalized before the early 1970s has subsequently developed a large public sector and resisted the welfare state backlash since the 1980s. Typical countries in this category are Sweden and France, and both have a high level of total tax revenue of which the VAT is an important part. The countries that have relied heavily on an income tax tend to have a weak revenue-raising capacity. These countries, Canada, Japan,

New Zealand, and Australia, have attempted to shift revenue reliance from income to consumption to enhance revenue since the 1980s, often in the face of strong public opposition. Consequently, the countries that increased their total revenue with a regressive tax during a longer period of postwar prosperity have easily raised more revenue. In contrast, the countries that have attempted to enhance their revenue-raising capacity since the 1980s have coped with public antipathy toward an increasing level of total tax revenue during chronic budget deficits, and any significant tax increase will be less likely in the future.

As these contrasts make clear, the timing of the diffusion is important to divide one consequence from another. As discussed in detail in Chapter 1, policy diffusion may be analyzed analogous to the diffusion of technology in the market, which leads to divergent and irreversible consequences. As with technological diffusion, the intentions of the individuals who cause the diffusion do not matter in policy diffusion. The early institutionalization of revenue-raising capacity determined the relationship between the government and the public, specifically, the public's attitude toward the government, regardless of the intention of policy makers and the partisanship of the government. The comparison between Sweden and France illuminates this point. In Sweden, when the sales tax precedent for the VAT was reintroduced, policy makers were fully conscious of its revenue-raising power as well as its regressive effect on income distribution. The social democratic policy makers intended to redistribute the increased revenue and enhance the welfare provision from a strong revenue machine so that the regressivity of the taxation would be offset. The Swedish high tax level has been supported by taxes on consumption (of which the VAT is a major part) and social security contributions. This tendency has even been strengthened by the tax reform in 1991 that slashed progressive tax rates. In contrast, the French policy makers were not aware of the revenue-raising power or inevitable regressivity of the VAT, which was a French innovation. But, once it had been introduced, it helped the expansion of the public sector, and its funding power effectively resisted the pressure of welfare retrenchment in the 1980s. After the burden of regressive taxes (the VAT and social security contributions) seemed to have reached its upper limit, the French government introduced new social security taxes, which are again flat-rate taxes on income. These replace social security contributions and lower employment costs that are common problems among conservative welfare states. In other words, the extensive use of regressive taxes goes beyond the VAT and social security contributions that were introduced first.

Among the early introducers, the happy experience of the simultaneous expansion of tax revenue and public expenditure during the postwar economic prosperity has become a solid base for public support for the large tax and welfare state.

The process is path-dependent in the sense that the formation of the state funding capacity is determined by the timing of the institutionalization of a strong revenue machine that changed the tax revenue structure. At the same time, the cases employed indicate that some incidental factors may enable some countries to change the "path" that they are expected to follow. For example, the United Kingdom's introduction of the VAT in 1973 was done exclusively to join the EEC and thus was much later than that of Sweden and France and occurred almost simultaneously with the end of the high-growth period. The United Kingdom, although compared with early introducers, is a borderline case between the early and late introducers. However, the VAT revenue was eventually used to finance an income tax cut and resist welfare retrenchment in the 1980s, although its revenue-raising capacity had not been the reason for its introduction. As Weaver (1986) succinctly summarizes, the politics of a welfare state are politics of "blame avoidance." A substantial cutback of existing benefits is difficult. Thus, politicians are eager to use financial means, if they have already been available, to maintain the benefit level and resist benefit cuts. In terms of the timing of the introduction of the VAT, the United Kingdom may well be classified as a late introducer, but the VAT's consequence there, especially the use of the once-introduced revenue machine, makes the United Kingdom comparable with a clear-cut early introducer such as Sweden and France.

Among the late introducers, New Zealand is an outlier. In Japan, Canada, and Australia, the public suspected that the governments suffering from budget deficits and weak funding capacities would increase the tax burden only for fiscal solvency. Strong opposition was about to block the introduction of the VAT. In contrast, the New Zealand government assured the public about the restraint of the future total tax burden by proposing tax reform as an integral part of the deregulatory reform aimed at small government and economic liberalization. Although New Zealand's introduction was as smooth as its western European predecessors', the consequences of the introduction were different. Despite an effective revenue extraction from the VAT, New Zealand has shown no sign of increasing its total tax level above the average of eighteen OECD countries in the same way as Japan and Canada.

The divergence of the paths among industrial democracies is caused by the lack of public knowledge about the potential revenue-raising power of the general consumption tax (ultimately converted to the VAT) and the possibility of running deficits in the government's budget before the end of high growth. This has caused a particular pattern of path dependence among industrial democracies. The introduction of the VAT in South Korea as a typical case of a newly industrializing country illuminates this point. Although the Korean introduction of the VAT in 1976 was much earlier in terms of the stage of industrial development than the early introducers among industrial democracies, Korea has not significantly increased its revenue from the VAT. Rather, it has used it as a stable revenue source to maintain the unchanged level of total tax revenue. The early institutionalization of the revenue machine is unlikely to lead to the expansion of the welfare state. This implementation is consistent with the maintenance of a relatively low tax level and small public sector in Korea compared with its growing economy. The Korean case exemplifies the tendency among newly industrializing countries where abundant opportunity to institutionalize the strong funding capacity at an early stage of industrial development has not been used to expand the public sector. The experience of the industrial democracies, especially their chronic budget deficits, has been well known among the policy makers in newly industrializing countries. Thus they are more conscious of exploring this revenue source. Unless they are confident of expansion in the public sector, like the social democratic policy makers in Sweden in the 1950s and 1960s, they are less likely to institutionalize the funding capacity of the government. The existence of "public knowledge" prevents the development of their tax and welfare states from being path-dependent on the institutionalization of the revenue machine in the same way that occurred in the industrial democracies.

The cross-tabulation of levels of total tax revenues, regressive tax revenues, and social security expenditures in Table 5.1 summarizes the implications from Chapters 2 through 4 . Among industrial democracies, there is a clear coexistence of a higher proportion of total tax revenue to GDP, a larger revenue reliance on regressive taxes, and higher social security expenditures with the size of GDP. Denmark is added as a notable exception to the cases here, but this exception is derived from the facts that the country has no revenue items that correspond to social security contributions in other countries and that it finances social security expenditures by a general revenue reliant heavily on income tax. Without the Danish case, the argument elicits a general tendency among industrial democracies. There

Table 5.1. *Cross-tabulation of levels of total tax burden, regressive tax revenue, and social security expenditure among nine OECD countries*

Proportion of regressive tax revenue[a] to GDP

Low ← → High

Proportion of social security expenditures to GDP (High ↔ Low)	Proportion of regressive tax revenue to GDP — Low	Proportion of regressive tax revenue to GDP — High	Proportion of total tax burden to GDP (High ↔ Low)
High	Denmark (1967)[b]	France (1954) Sweden (1969)	High
	United Kingdom (1973) New Zealand (1986)		
Low	Australia (2000) United States (no VAT) Japan (1989)	Korea (1976)	Low

[a] Taxes on goods and services not including social security contributions.

[b] In parentheses the year of introduction of the VAT.

198

is not necessarily a direct financial relationship between revenue reliance on regressive taxes and welfare expansion. However, the politics behind the institutionalization of state funding capacity shapes a link between high regressive taxes and social security expenditures.

To conclude this section, a qualification will be added to this conclusion. A new tax policy may thwart the existing association of reliance on a flat-rate (i.e., a regressive) tax with a broad base and a large size of the welfare state. For example, theoretically, the so-called consumption taxes of the income types or personal (or progressive) consumption taxes satisfy both progressivity and effective revenue capacity (Bradford 1986, Chapter 5; Hall and Rabushka 1996; Weidenbaum 1996). Their tax base corresponds substantially to the VAT, but progressivity can be maintained because the tax base is comprehended (by a tax return) at the individual level instead of by each transaction and exchange.[1] The flat-rate tax advocated by Milton Friedman and developed by Hall and Rabushka is also a simple progressive tax applying substantial personal allowances despite a flat rate.[2] While satisfying the three tax principles – simplicity, efficiency, and equity – these taxes are capable of effectively raising tax revenue, often enough to replace the entire existing system (Hall and Rabushka 1996). However, these taxes that enable contemporary welfare states to combine the redistribution effect and effective revenue-raising in a single taxation are still far from being implemented even if we ignore many transition problems in going from an existing tax system to a new one (Bradford 1986, Chapter 14; 1996).

An Alternative Way to Development: A Path Away from the Divergence?

As already observed in Chapters 2 through 4, each country's case clarifies why high-tax countries faced less opposition to increasing already high tax levels and low-tax countries faced more opposition to augmenting a modest tax level.

It is one thing that regressive taxation works against income equality, and it is another that the revenue from it can be used for the purpose of redistribution. The resulting income equality or inequality hinges on the

---

[1] The tax base of these taxes is, in principle, a cash-flow income excluding savings and thus corresponds substantially to individual consumption. If this idea is applied to business income, the tax base is identical to that of the VAT.

[2] This belongs to the same category as the consumption taxes of the income types because of its treatment of business investment (Bradford 1986, 10).

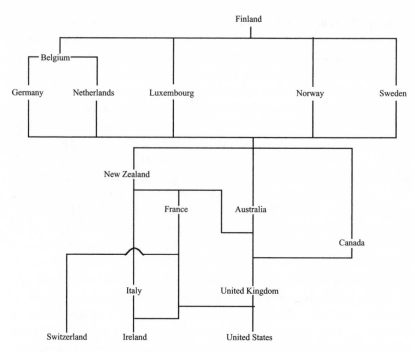

Figure 5.1. Relative inequality in terms of Lorenz comparison. *Source:* From Figure 4.4 of Atkinson, Rainwater, and Smeeding (1995) with slight modification.

extent to which the revenue from regressive taxes is used for the purpose of redistribution. If the countries that have higher tax levels, especially from regressive taxation, achieve higher income equality, the regressive taxation goes for, instead of against, the welfare state. Alternatively, if countries achieve higher income equality with a low level of total taxation (and low revenue reliance on regressive taxation), the coexistence of regressive taxation and high social security expenditures should not attract serious attention.

To compare all the industrial democracies that are cases here, I use two different studies of the recent trend of income inequality. Figure 5.1 is a slightly modified[3] Hasse diagram by Atkinson, Rainwater, and Smeeding (1995) based on a pairwise comparison in terms of the conventional Lorenz curve. If a country is located closer to the top of diagram, it achieves a lower level of inequality. A downward line means that a country at the

---

[3] Although it is modified, the vertical relationship between countries has not been changed; thus, the demonstration of the result is the same as that in the original.

top of the line has a lower level of inequality than one at the bottom, and countries with similar levels of inequality or those that cannot be compared without ambiguity are located at the same level on the diagram. In Figure 5.1, countries with a high level of total taxation and heavy regressive taxation (i.e., most of the Scandinavian countries) are located closer to the top, whereas low-tax countries with more revenue reliance on progressive income taxation are at the bottom (i.e., United States, United Kingdom, and Switzerland). New Zealand and Australia, which Castles and Mitchell (1993) classify as radical welfare states, are ranked relatively higher than expected, and France is located in the middle. These exceptions, however, do not refute the overall tendency.

The recent change in inequality in these countries confirms the argument here. Table 5.2 combines the study by Atkinson et al. (1995) using the data of the LIS (Luxembourg Income Study) (or the national statistics corresponding to it) of seventeen OECD countries and the study by Oxley et al. (1997) based on the national statistics of thirteen OECD countries.[4] The smaller Gini coefficient means more equality. In terms of the results by Atkinson et al. (1995) on the right-hand side of Table 5.2, the high-tax countries with more revenue reliance on regressive taxation generally achieve more equality. Here, the most prominent exceptions are France, which is less equal than expected, and Canada and Japan, which show outstanding levels of equality considering their low total tax levels.[5] However, as we see from the recent changes in the Gini coefficients of both countries studied by Oxley et al. on the left-hand side of Table 5.2, France improved the level of equality from the late 1970s to 1990, whereas Japan increased inequality significantly from the mid-1980s to the 1990s. The national survey by

---

[4] Both studies focus on household disposable income, that is, money income (including social insurance and welfare cash transfers) minus direct taxes and social security contributions. Both share the same inequality measures and have similar technical problems in the definition of "income" and thus are roughly comparable, although the former uses the more-consistent LIS data (Oxley et al. 1997, footnote 4). The results here exclude the impact of an indirect regressive tax such as the VAT, but the gap in the level of inequality between high- and low-tax-burden countries is significant and thus less likely to be offset by the additional effect of the indirect tax.

[5] In terms of the high equality in Japan, Kwon (1997) shows that market income in Japan (together with income in Korea) is more equal than income in the United Kingdom, but the British social policy intervention has redistributed income more effectively than in Japan (and again in Korea). Because Japan has had a weak corporatist arrangement excluding labor for so long (Pempel and Tsunekawa 1979), the apparent equal income distribution in the market is not a result of the government wage policy.

Table 5.2. *Measures of inequality in OECD countries*

	Year	Gini	Percent Change	Year	Gini
Australia	1975/76 - 1993/94	30.6	5.2		
	1975/76 - 1984	31.2	7.2		
	1984 - 1993/94	30.6	-1.9		
				1985	29.5
Belgium	1983 - 1995	29.9	2.3		
				1988	23.5
Canada	1975 - 1994	28.4	0.2		
	1975 - 1985	28.9	2.2		
	1985 - 1994	28.4	-1.1		
				1987	28.9
Denmark	1983 - 1994	21.7	-4.9		
Finland	1986 - 1995	23.1	9.1		
				1987	20.7
France	1979 - 1990	29.1	-1.7		
				1984	29.6
Germany	1984 - 1994	28.2	6.4		
				1984	25.0
Ireland				1987	33.0
Italy	1984 - 1993	34.5	12.7		
				1986	31.0
Japan	1984 - 1994	26.5	4.9		
Luxembourg				1985	23.8
Netherlands	1977 - 1994	25.3	11.8		
	1977 - 1985	23.4	3.3		
	1985 - 1994	25.3	8.2		
				1987	26.8
Norway	1986 - 1995	25.6	9.4		
				1986	23.4
Sweden	1975 - 1995	23.0	-1.0		
	1975 - 1983	21.6	-7.0		
	1983 - 1995	23.0	6.5		
				1987	22.0
Switzerland				1982	32.3
United Kingdom				1986	30.4
United States	1974 - 1995	34.4	10.0		
	1974 - 1985	34.0	8.8		
	1985 - 1995	34.4	1.1		
				1986	34.1

Source: The left part from Oxley et al. (1997) and the right from Atkinson et al. (1995).

Atkinson et al. (1995, Chapter 5) shows results consistent with this. Australia, Japan, the United Kingdom, and the United States significantly increased their inequality in terms of Gini coefficients, whereas Sweden's also increased by the same degree as these countries (and thus their gap remained the same).

Consequently, the size of the public sector, although it may not be an exclusive one, is an effective predictor for the achievement of equality in that country. A large public sector may not be a sufficient condition for the achievement of equality in the sense that high expenditure does not automatically lead to higher equality. However, as far as observing the existing welfare states is concerned, a large public sector has become a necessary condition for higher equality in the sense that it has become more difficult to ensure equality without it.

The politics of redistribution explains the diversification in the size of the public sector. Of the two different kinds of redistribution explained in Chapter 1, a direct transfer from the rich to the poor or the needy is the most efficient method of redistribution in the sense that the government can target specific social groups and concentrate a financial source on them. The opposite side of a direct transfer targeted on the poor and the needy is the universal provision of flat-rate benefits on the entire population. Obviously, universal provision is expensive and leads to a high level of tax imposition whereas targeting and means-testing can coexist with a low level. All existing industrial democracies combine the two types of provisioning but, as shown in Chapters 2 through 4, high-tax countries that rely on regressive taxes to a greater extent can afford to finance universal provision more extensively than low-tax countries.

Moene and Wallerstein (1997) formalize the logic of why a larger public sector inevitably results in more equality by contrasting universalism and targeting. In their formal model, there are distinct dynamics at play in the choice of benefit level in universalistic[6] and targeted policies. A universalistic policy produces positive benefits for everyone and then guarantees a high level of income, whereas a targeted policy tends to reduce means-tested benefits, sometimes to zero (according to Moene and Wallerstein, 1997, "a politically driven, low-benefit trap"). Because the targeted provision decreases the possibility for a majority to receive benefits, self-interested individuals wish to pay little, and, if possible, nothing at

---

[6] "Universalistic" is used in the same context with the same meaning as "universal." Both words are used interchangeably here following the usage of the word in the citation.

all for them. As a result, a targeted policy tends to push benefits down close to zero, although its original aim is to be both efficient and inexpensive in reducing inequality. Conversely, because the universal program provides certain benefits to everyone, a majority are more likely to support it, and this majority support serves to maintain or increase its cost. This plausibly explains why the implemetation of targeted programs does not reduce inequality effectively. The formal analysis is limited by several assumptions that may not apply strictly to a real situation.[7] But the asymmetric dynamics between universalism and targeting are worth serious attention.

The logic for distinguishing two equilibria is similar to the one leading to the two different self-enforcing processes of the welfare state. High-benefit provision reproduces itself because a high level of current benefits (that most likely covers most of population) increases tolerance for a further burden and constitutes a self-enforcing process of a majority support for a generous provision. Low levels of expenditure and tax result in diametrically opposed dynamics and prevent the expansion of benefits. Only the poor and needy support this, but the rich oppose it, and the middle-income earners are indifferent to it. The policy lacks majority support and fails to achieve the aim of redistribution except in special cases – for example, with a majority of politically active poor critical of the concentration of wealth among a small number of the rich or a majority of altruistic middle-income earners. The search for majority support for the welfare state has resulted in boosting the funding capacity of the government, and in turn, generous provision financed by the government makes the formation of a majority support easier.

There is empirical evidence that the public perception of the government's role is distinct across countries along the above logic. The opinion polls conducted by International Social Survey Program (ISSP) confirmed the divergent public perception in 1996 in the eight countries reviewed in the case studies here (Figure 5.2). High-tax and welfare countries such as Sweden and France have greater support for a small public sector (i.e., reducing taxes even if this results in less spending on social services) than a large public sector (i.e., spending more on social services even with high taxes). This is in clear contrast to the greater public support for a large

---

[7] For example, incomes are assumed to be stochastic, and thus welfare policies are regarded as insurance benefits: voters are self-interested and not altruistic. If voters are assumed to be somewhat altruistic, the model predicts a narrowing gap between universal and targeted benefits.

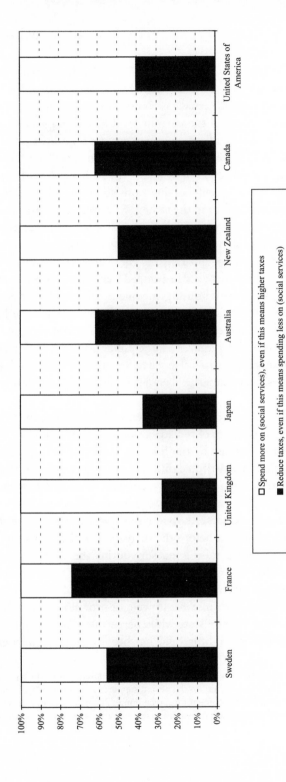

Figure 5.2. ISSP Question: If the government had a choice between reducing taxes or spending more on (social services), which do you think it should do? *Source:* International Social Survey Program 1996.

205

welfare state in the United Kingdom, Japan, New Zealand (though slightly beyond 50 percent), and the United States. The level of support for a large welfare state in Australia and Canada is comparable to that in Sweden. Has the public become critical of the current level of tax and spending (i.e., are people more critical of a large government in a high-tax and -welfare country and of a small government in a low-tax and -welfare country)?[8] Public reaction may be more complicated than such a simplistic picture. Figure 5.3 summarizes the results of questions about the government's responsibility to a specific policy in the same ISSP survey. Although the government is considered responsible in all countries for health care for the sick and a decent living standard for the elderly, that is, the basic components of welfare programs, an apparently higher percentage of respondents in Sweden and France consistently responded that the government should be responsible for job security, housing, income equality, and a decent living standard for the unemployed. In other words, the Swedes and the French assume a larger responsibility and a more active policy intervention by the government that inevitably requires a large public sector. A preference for a specific policy is more likely to influence the relative size of the public sector across countries than a superficial choice between high and low tax and welfare.

The self-enforcing interaction between tax and welfare has consolidated diametrically opposed politics of redistribution between countries. The interaction has been intensified by the financial scarcity of the government since the mid-1970s and constituted different paths between countries that are introduced at the beginning of this chapter. The early 1970s symbolized the end of high economic growth when industrial democracies began to face chronic budget deficits. As vividly illustrated in the process of the early VAT introduction (i.e., before the early 1970s), the institutionalization of an effective revenue-raising measure during the postwar economic prosperity did not trigger concern about increasing tax burdens and thus was not politicized as a tax increase. An increasing level of total tax revenue has gone hand in hand with increasing welfare provision: the public has come to accept a large welfare state while perceiving that taxation will be repaid through public expenditure and has become tolerant to high tax.

---

[8] Public support for a higher tax burden is sensitive to the economic situation expressed by, for example, the unemployment rate. In this result, support for a welfare state is higher in the countries with lower unemployment rates (Kamimura 2000). In this way, it is possible to interpret that the answers to this question are sensitive to a short-term macroeconomic situation.

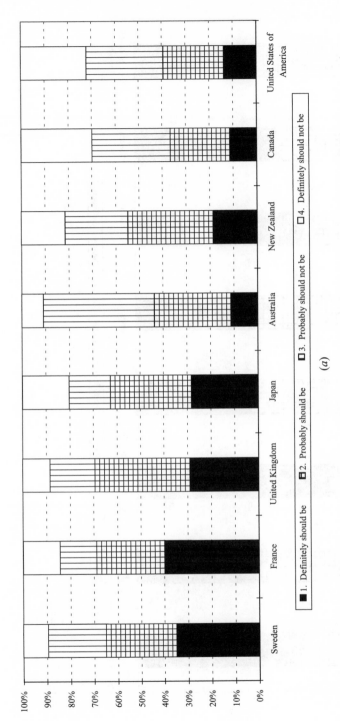

Figure 5.3. ISSP Question: On the whole, do you think it should be or should not be the government's responsibility to (a) provide a job for everyone who wants one; (b) provide health care for the sick; (c) provide a decent standard of living for the old; (d) provide a decent standard of living for the unemployed; (e) reduce income differences between the rich and poor; (f) provide decent housing for those who can't afford it. The fifth category, "Don't know," or "other," is not included here because its percentage share is negligible. *Source:* International Social Survey Program 1996.

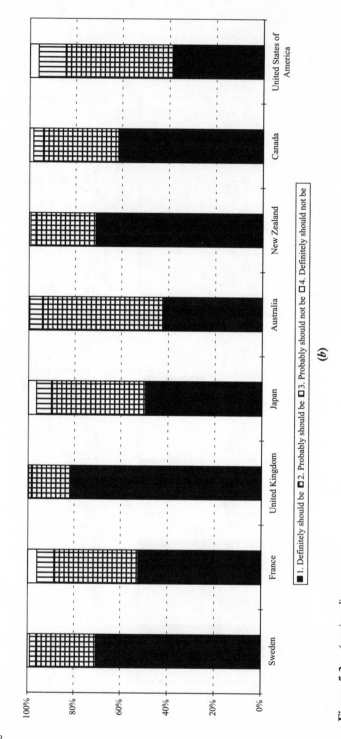

1. Definitely should be ■ 2. Probably should be ⊡ 3. Probably should not be ⊞ 4. Definitely should not be □

(b)

Figure 5.3. *(continued)*

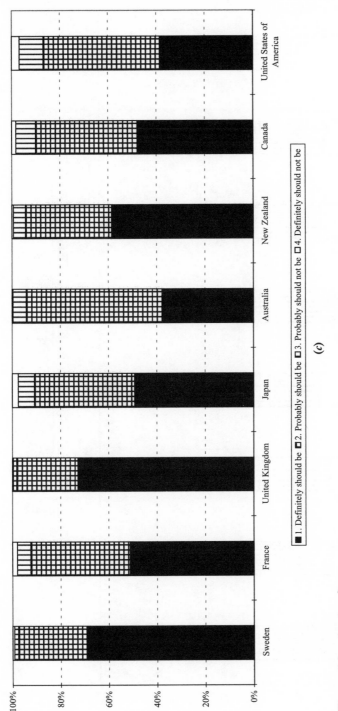

Figure 5.3. *(continued)*

209

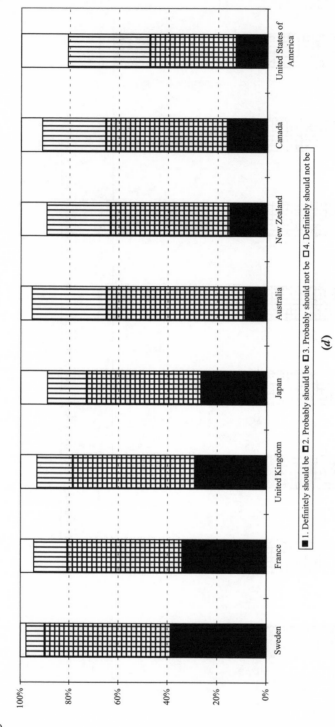

Figure 5.3. *(continued)*

210

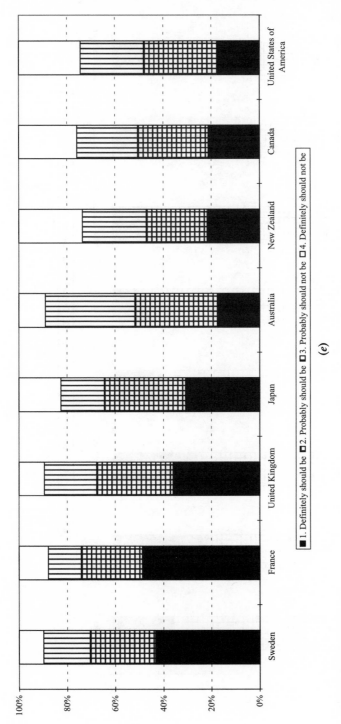

Figure 5.3. *(continued)*

211

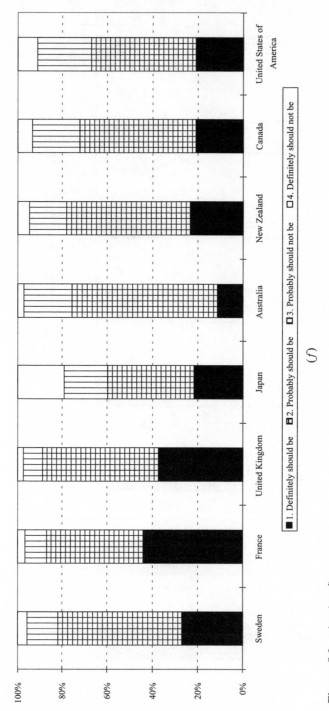

Figure 5.3. *(continued)*

The early institutionalization of that state's funding capacity not only allowed the government to expand subsequently the welfare state but has made the welfare state more resistant to welfare retrenchment during the stable growth period since the 1980s.

On the other hand, a very different process emerges in the countries that missed the opportunity to institutionalize state funding capacity during a high-growth period. During chronic budget deficits, the public tends to suspect that increasing revenue would be used only to solve those budget deficits, and the proposal to institutionalize an effective revenue measure is destined to inspire public antipathy toward heavy taxation. Without a guarantee that the increasing tax would be repaid through public expenditures or that the total tax level would not increase, the institutionalization of an effective revenue measure has been next to impossible. The VAT proposal since the 1980s exemplifies this public attitude. The subsequent implementation of the tax, even if introduced, has also been constrained by public antipathy. Here, it is noteworthy that the electorate responds to a government proposal in a distinct way. Remembering that the augmented tax level in the past has accompanied direct and indirect compensation through expenditures, the electorate is more likely to accept the maintenance of or further increase in the existing high tax level. Without such assurance based on past memory, the electorate may refuse to accept a marginal addition to a currently low tax level. The counterintuitive implication here is that the public tolerance of the tax level is higher with the currently high tax level in the existing industrial democracies, and thus the funding base of the welfare state increases in importance in the politics of the welfare state during chronic budget deficits.

The regressivity of the taxation to be used as a revenue-raising measure further strengthens distinct public responses. Spending aimed at redistribution may alleviate the regressive effect of taxation, but this will not be evident until both spending and tax increase. Although high tax revenue, even if supported by regressive taxation, may well lead to more redistribution through spending, low tax revenue is likely to result in preserving the regressive effect because of ineffective redistribution by limited spending. This point is critical in explaining cases in Chapters 2 through 4. In all cases, regressivity was the most legitimate reason for opposition to tax reform.[9] The government's ability to persuade the public that the welfare

[9] This point is clearer in the cases of late introducers of the VAT. Firms were concerned about the imposition of a tax without transferring the amount to consumers. The consumers were

spending would alleviate the regressive effects of taxation influenced the introduction of the VAT. In this way, during the period of deficit finance since the mid-1970s, the diversification of the politics of redistribution has continued[10] and the cross-national divergence has been consolidated.

Consequently, if a government has already institutionalized a strong revenue-raising power, policy makers can afford to increase spending without risking the unpopularity of tax increase nor regressivity of taxation.[11] Alternatively, to introduce a revenue-raising measure during chronic budget deficits, the government is forced to assure the public about the restraint of the tax increase and alleviation of tax regressivity, which are not compatible, as already shown. Diametrically opposed self-enforcing processes are the result of distinct behaviors that appear rational in distinct contexts.[12] In a high-tax and -welfare country, the politicians can afford to increase taxes by existing means, and the electorate accepts the high tax level expecting compensation based on the past. In a low-tax and -welfare country, the politicians are deprived of an effective revenue-raising means and face hostile opposition toward a tax increase from the public without a prospect for compensation assured by the past. As a result, a high-tax country is more likely to maintain high spending and will put up with a high tax, and a low-tax country is more likely to restrain spending and tax. The politics of the welfare state has a reciprocal relationship with the formation of state funding capacity. An important intervening factor is the public's perception of the government's role that has formed through experience both in the expansion of the public sector during the high-growth period and in the deficit-ridden finance of the government since the mid-1970s.

worried that their burden would be further increased by price increases. The reasons for their opposition were different, but the regressivity of the taxation was the strongest reason for opposition that they had in common.

[10] Alesina and Wacziarg (2000, 165) draw the same conclusion about two different dynamics in existing democracies when they start the analysis from a problem of civic trust.

[11] The bureaucrats are motivated by increasing their discretion – often expressed by the budget size under their discretion (Niskanen 1971; Blais and Dion 1991). Their job security is principally independent of a policy's unpopularity, and they may be less sensitive to it than the politicians, but in policy making, they take it into consideration, expecting politicians' response.

[12] In this regard, rationality of behavior in politics is "bounded" by subjective perception of where one is placed to take an action. For more details on the concept of bounded rationality by Herbert Simon and its utility in comparative political analysis, see Kato (1996, 573–81). Institutional analysis and the concept of bounded rationality are not only compatible but also indisputable.

This study sheds a new light on a neglected subject – the funding base of the welfare state. While appreciating the importance of other sociopolitical factors, such as government partisanship and social classes, the study demonstrates that the funding capacity of the welfare state has differed from one country to another and eventually works as a consistent constraint on welfare policies. This results from the association of reliance on regressive taxes and large welfare expenditures across countries that this study demonstrates. If a country wants to achieve equality, a politically feasible way to accomplish that goal is to maintain a large program to create a majority support from beneficiaries of universal provision. Regressive taxes more effectively increase the state funding capacity that results from flat rates and a tax base resistant to erosion. Politics preclude an efficient direct transfer from the rich to the poor and needy who lack a majority support, and prevent progressive taxation from raising large revenues by increasing loopholes and special tax measures. At the same time, however, the formation of the state funding capacity is a historical product and path-dependent upon a peculiar pattern of tax policy development. Among the existing industrial democracies, the early institutionalization of regressive taxes is a critical cause of a self-enforcing process of high tax and high welfare: both policy makers and the public accepted high taxes to finance high welfare after the expansion of state funding capacity during the high growth in the 1950s and 1960s. Institutionalization of an effective revenue-raising measure inevitably faces public opposition during low growth without the experience of a reciprocal expansion of tax and welfare. Combined with the politics of a majority support formation, the politics of the public's expectation toward the government's role has diversified the levels of both tax and welfare across countries.

In terms of this diversification, the politics of the welfare state across industrial democracies has not been very different during the slow economic growth since the 1980s from what it was during the golden age of postwar prosperity. The prospect of a welfare state in industrial democracies is largely determined by policy inertia from the past. Only the diffusion of an innovative policy may be able to change it. The newly industrializing countries are free of the constraints of the path dependence evident in industrial democracies because of the latecomers' advantage. But, in the near future, they are likely to face a difficult political choice between tolerating a certain level of inequality and putting up with a large public sector and a heavy taxation.

List of Variables Used for Statistical Analyses

ALTGOV

Definition: Frequency of alternation of governments (the number of different party governments for the last three years, including the one that existed on the last day of the third year; = 1, 2, 3, 4, 5, 6, or 7)

Period: 1960–95

Source: *European Journal of Political Research*, Vol. 24, No. 1 (July 1993)

CITAXP

Definition: Taxes on corporate income as a percentage of GDP

Period: Ireland, 1965–92 (1990; linearly interpolated)
Netherlands, Norway, Switzerland, 1965–89
New Zealand, 1965–94 (1990–2; linearly interpolated)
Sweden, United Kingdom, 1965–91
All the other countries, 1965–94

Unit: Percentage

Source: OECD, *Revenue Statistics*

CONCEN

Definition: Export concentration index

Period: All countries, 1962–92 (1963–7, 1969, 1971, 1973, 1975, 1979; linearly interpolated)

Unit: Hirschmann index normalized to make values ranking 0 to 1 (maximum concentration)

Source: UNCTAD, *Handbook of International Trade and Development Statistics*

CPI

Definition: Consumer price index, all items

Period: All countries, 1960–93

Unit:	1987 = 100
Source:	OECD, *Main Economic Indicators*

DEFICITP

Definition:	Government deficit or surplus as a percentage of GDP
Unit:	Percentage
Formula:	$(DEFICIT \div GDPNOM) \times 100$

DEFICIT

Definition:	Government deficit (−) or surplus (+)
Period:	Australia, 1960–94
	Austria, 1960–93
	Belgium, 1960–93
	Canada, 1960–91
	Denmark, 1960–95
	Finland, 1960–93
	France, 1960–94
	Germany, 1960–93
	Ireland, 1960–95 (1990–3; linearly interpolated)
	Italy, 1960–91
	Japan, 1960–93
	Netherlands, 1960–94 (1991–3; linearly interpolated)
	New Zealand, 1960–95 (1989, 1991–3; linearly interpolated)
	Norway, 1960–89
	Sweden, 1960–95 (1990–4; linearly interpolated)
	Switzerland, 1960–95
	United Kingdom, 1960–95 (1991–3; linearly interpolated)
	United States, 1960–95
Unit:	In local currency units
Source:	IMF, *International Fiscal Statistics*

GDPNOM
See *SSEXPT*

EUDUM

Definition:	A dummy variable for EEC/EC/EU member countries (= 1 for member countries, = 0 for nonmember countries)
Period:	1960–96
Note:	1960–6 (EEC members), 1967–92 (EC members), 1993–6 (EU members)

FEDDUM

Definition:	A dummy variable for the federal system (= 1 for the federal system; = 0 for the nonfederal system)
Period:	1960–96

Appendix

Source: Lijphart, *Democracies* (Table 10.2)
Note: The federal system: Australia, Austria, Canada, Germany, Switzerland, United States

GCTAXP

Definition: Taxes on general consumption as a percentage of GDP
Period: All countries, 1965–94
Unit: Percentage
Source: OECD, *Revenue Statistics*
Note: Insertion (zero for Japan, 1965–88)

GROWTH

Definition: Economic growth rate
Period: Switzerland, 1961–89
               All the other countries, 1961–93
Unit: Percentage
Formula: $\{(GDPREA[t+1] \div GDPREA[t])-1\} \times 100$

GDPREA

Definition: GDP at market prices (real)
Period: Switzerland, 1960–89
               All the other countries, 1960–93
Unit: In local currency units, 1987 constant
Source: World Bank, *Economic Indicators*

OPEN

Definition: Openness of the economy
Period: All countries, 1960–93
Unit: Percentage
Formula: $\{(EXPORTS+IMPORTS) \div GDPNOM\} \times 100$

EXPORTS

Definition: Exports of goods and NF services (nominal)
Period: All countries, 1960–93
Unit: In local currency units
Source: World Bank, *Economic Indicators*

IMPORTS

Definition: Imports of goods and NF services (nominal)
Period: All countries, 1960–93
Unit: In local currency units
Source: World Bank, *Economic Indicators*

GDPNOM
See *SSEXPT*

PARTY

Definition:	A discrete variable ($= 1, 2, 3, 4,$ or 5) for leftist party leadership in a party (coalition) government
Period:	1960–95
Source:	*European Journal of Political Research*, Vol. 24, No. 1 (July 1993)

POP65P

Definition:	Total aged population (65 years and over) as a percentage of total population
Unit:	Percentage
Formula:	$(POP65 \div TOTPOP) \times 100$

POP65

Definition:	Total population 65 years and over
Period:	Austria, Belgium, Germany, 1960–92
	Ireland, 1960–91
	All the other countries, 1960–93
Unit:	In thousands
Source:	ILO, *Labour Force Statistics*

TOTPOP

Definition	Total population
Period:	Austria, Belgium, 1960–92
	Ireland, 1960–91
	Sweden, 1960–89
	United Kingdom, 1960–90
	All the other countries, 1960–93
Unit:	In thousands
Source:	ILO, *Labour Force Statistics*

SSCONTOT

Definition:	Total social security receipts as a percentage of GDP
Unit:	Percentage
Formula:	$(SSREV \times 1,000,000 \div GDPNOM) \times 100$

SSREV

Definition:	Total social security receipts (contributions, taxes, general state revenues, other state participation, capital income)
Period:	Australia, 1960–92
	Austria, 1960–93 (1990–2; linearly interpolated)
	Belgium, 1960–91 (1987–90; linearly interpolated)
	Canada, 1960–93 (1990; linearly interpolated)
	Denmark, 1960–93
	Finland, 1960–93
	France, 1960–90 (1967; linearly interpolated)

Appendix

Germany, 1960–93 (1992; linearly interpolated)
Ireland 1960–93
Italy, 1960–93 (1990; linearly interpolated)
Japan, 1960–92
Netherlands, 1960–93
New Zealand, 1960–91
Norway, 1960–92
Sweden, 1960–93 (1990; linearly interpolated)
Switzerland, 1960–93
United Kingdom, 1960–93 (1990; linearly interpolated)
United States, 1960–91 (1990; linearly interpolated)

Unit: In millions of local currency units
Source: ILO, *The Cost of Social Security*

GDPNOM
See *SSEXPT*

SS_expt

Definition: Total social security benefit expenditures as a percentage of GDP
Unit: Percentage
Formula: $(\text{SSEXP} \times 1{,}000{,}000 \div \text{GDPNOM}) \times 100$

SSEXP

Definition: Total social security benefit expenditures (benefits plus administrative expenses and transfers to other schemes)
Period: Australia, 1960–92
Austria, 1960–93 (1990–92; linearly interpolated)
Belgium, 1960–91 (1987–90; linearly interpolated)
Canada, 1960–93 (1990; linearly interpolated)
Denmark, 1960–93
Finland, 1960–93
France, 1960–90 (1967; linearly interpolated)
Germany, 1960–93 (1991, 1992; linearly interpolated)
Ireland, 1960–1993
Italy, 1960–93 (1990; linearly interpolated)
Japan, 1960–92
Netherlands, 1960–93
New Zealand, 1960–91
Norway, 1960–92
Sweden, 1960–93 (1990; linearly interpolated)
Switzerland, 1960–93
United Kingdom, 1960–93 (1990; linearly interpolated)
United States, 1960–91 (1990; linearly interpolated)

Unit: In millions of local currency units
Source: ILO, *The Cost of Social Security*

GDPNOM

Definition:	GDP at market prices (nominal)
Period:	New Zealand, 1990–2; linearly interpolated
	Switzerland, 1960–89
	All the other countries, 1960–93
Unit:	In local currency units
Source:	World Bank, *Economic Indicators*

UNEMPL

Definition:	Unemployment rate
Period:	Ireland, 1960–92 (1990; linearly interpolated)
	Netherlands, Norway, Switzerland, 1960–89
	New Zealand, 1960–94 (1990–2; linearly interpolated)
	Sweden, United Kingdom, 1960–95 (1992–4; linearly interpolated)
	United States, 1960–95
	All the other countries, 1960–94
Unit:	Percentage
Source:	OECD, *Economic Outlook*

Bibliography

Aaron, H. J., ed. 1981. *The Value Added Tax: Lesson from Europe.* Washington, D.C.: Brookings Institution.

———. 1982. *VAT: Experiences of Some European Countries.* Deventer, Netherlands: Kluwer Law and Taxation Publishers.

Abbott, A., and S. Deviney. 1992. The Welfare-State as Transnational Event: Evidence from Sequences of Policy Adoption. *Social Science History* 16 (2): 245–74.

Abelson, Peter. 1998. *The Tax Reform Debate: The Economics of the Options.* St Leonards, Australia: Allen and Unwin.

Åberg, Rune. 1989. Distributive Mechanism of the Welfare State. *European Sociological Review* 5 (2): 167–82.

Agell, Jonas, Peter Englund, and Jan Södersten. 1996. Tax Reform of the Century – The Swedish Experiment. *National Tax Journal* 49 (4): 643–64.

———, eds. 1998. *Incentives and Redistribution in the Welfare State: The Swedish Reform.* London: Macmillan.

Alesina, Alberto, and Roberto Perotti. 1997. The Welfare State and Competitiveness. *American Economic Review* 87 (5): 921–39.

Alesina, Alberto, and Romain Wacziarg. 1998. Openness, Country Size, and Government. *Journal of Public Economics* 69 (3): 305–21.

———. 2000. The Economics of Civic Trust. In *Disaffected Democracies: What's Troubling the Trilateral Countries?* edited by Susan J. Pharr and Robert D. Putnam. Princeton, N.J.: Princeton University Press.

Amenta, E. 1993. The state-of-the-art in welfare-state research on social spending efforts in capitalist democracies since 1960. *American Journal of Sociology* 9 (3): 750–63.

American Bar Association Tax System Task Force. 1997. A Comprehensive Analysis of Current Consumption Tax Proposals: A Report of ABA Section of Taxation.

Amsden, Alice H. 1989. *Asia's Next Giant: South Korea and Late Industrialization.* New York: Oxford University Press.

Andersson, Krister, and Leif Mutén. 1994. The Tax System of Sweden. *Tax Notes International* (October 10, 1994): 1147–63.

Arnold, B. J. 1990. The process of tax policy formulation in Australia, Canada and New Zealand. *Australian Tax Forum* 7 (4).

Arthur, W. Brian. 1989. Competing technologies, increasing returns, and lock-in by historical events. *The Economic Journal* 99: 116–31.

———. 1994. Positive feedbacks in the economy. Chapter 1 in *Increasing Returns and Path Dependence in the Economy*, 1–12. Ann Arbor: University of Michigan Press.

Ashford, Douglas E. 1986. The British and French Social Security Systems: Welfare States by Intent and by Default. In *Nationalizing Social Security in Europe and America*, edited by E. W. Kelley and D. E. Ashford. Greenwich, Conn.: JAI Press.

Atkinson, Anthony B. 1993. On Targeting Social Security: Theory and Western Experience with Family Benefits: Discussion Paper. The Welfare State Programme, Suntory-Toyota International Centre for Economics and Related Disciplines. London School of Economics.

———. 1999. *The Economic Consequences of Rolling Back the Welfare State*. Cambridge: MIT Press.

Atkinson, Anthony B., Lee Rainwater, and Timothy M. Smeeding. 1995. *Income Distribution in OECD Countries: Evidence from Luxembourg Income Study. OECD Social Policy Studies No. 18*. Paris: OECD.

Aylott, Nicholas. 1999. *Swedish Social Democracy and European Integration: The People's Home on the Market*. Aldershot, U.K.: Ashgate.

Baldwin, Peter. 1990. *The politics of solidarity*. New York: Cambridge University Press.

Balladur, Jean-Pierre, and Antoine Coutière. 1981. France. In *The Value Added Tax: Lesson from Europe*, edited by H. J. Aaron. Washington, D.C.: Brookings Institute.

Balloch, Susan. 1998. New Partnerships for Social Services. In *Social Issues and Party Politics*, edited by Helen Jones and Susanne Macgregor. Bodmin, U.K.: MPG Books.

Barr, Nicholas, and Fiona Coulter. 1990. Social Security: Solution or Problem? In *The State of Welfare*, edited by John Hills, 274–337. Oxford: Oxford University Press.

Bates, Robert H., and Da-Hsiang Donald Lien. 1985. A Note on Taxation, Development and Representative Government. *Politics and Society* 14 (1): 53–70.

Birnbaum, Jeffrey H., and Alan S. Murray. 1988. *Showdown at Gucci Gulch: Lawmakers, Lobbyists, and the Unlikely Triumph of Tax Reform*. New York: Vintage Books.

Blais, A., and S. Dion, eds. 1991. *The Budget Maximizing Bureaucrats: Appraisal and Evidence*. Pittsburgh: University of Pittsburgh Press.

Blotnicki, Laurence, and Christophe Heckly. 1994. The tax system of France. *Tax Notes International* (November 7, 1994): 1477–95.

Blundell, Richard, and Paul Johnson. 1999. Pensions and Retirement in the United Kingdom. In *Social Security and Retirement Around the World*, edited by Jonathan Gruber and David A. Wise, 403–36. Chicago: The University of Chicago Press.

Bibliography

Boix, Charles. 1998. *Political Parties, Growth and Equality: Conservative and Social Democratic Strategies in the World Economy*. Cambridge: Cambridge University Press.

Bonoli, Giuliano. 1997. Classifying Welfare States: A Two-Dimension Approach. *Journal of Social Policy* 26 (3): 351–72.

———. 2000. *The Politics of Pension Reform*. Cambridge: Cambridge University Press.

———. 2001. Political Institutions, Veto Points and the Process of Welfare State Adaptation. In *The New Politics of the Welfare State*, edited by Paul Pierson, 238–64. New York: Oxford Univesity Press.

Bonoli, Giuliano, and Bruno Palier. 1998. Changing the Politics of Social Programmes: Innovative Change in British and French Welfare Reforms. *Journal of European Social Policy* 8 (4): 317–30.

Borowski, Allan, Sol Encel, and Elizabeth Ozanne. 1997. Introduction. In *Aging and Social Policy in Australia*, edited by A. Borowski, Sol Encel, and Elizabeth Ozanne. Cambridge: Cambridge University Press.

Boskin, Michael, ed. 1996. *Frontiers of Tax Reform*. Stanford, Cal.: Hoover Institution.

Boskin, Michael J., and Charles E. McLure. 1990. *World Tax Reform: Case Studies of Developed and Developing Countries*. San Francisco: International Center for Economic Growth and Institute for Contemporary Studies; ICS Press; Lanham.

Boston, Jonathan. 1992. The Treasury: Its Role, Philosophy, and Influence. In *New Zealand Politics in Perspective*, edited by H. Gold. Auckland, N.Z.: Longman Paul.

Boston, Jonathan, John Martin, June Pallot, and Pat Walsh. 1996. *Public Management: The New Zealand Model*. Auckland, N.Z.: Oxford University Press.

Bradford, David F. 1986. *Untangling the Income Tax*. Cambridge, Mass.: Harvard University Press.

———. 1996. Taxes: Some Fundamental Transition Issues. In *Frontiers of Tax Reform*, edited by M. Boskin. Stanford, Cal.: Hoover Institution.

Bradley, David, Evelyne Huber, Stephanie Moller, François Nielsen, and John Stephens. 2001. Distribution and Redistribution in Post-Industrial Democracies. Paper presented at the Annual Meeting of American Political Science Association, San Francisco, August 30–September 2, 2001.

Brecher, Stephen M., Donald W. Moore, Michael M. Hoyle, and Peter G. B. Trasker. 1982. *The Economic Impact of the Introduction of VAT*. Morristown, N.J.: Research Foundation of the Financial Executives Institute.

Brooks, Neil. 1992. *The Canadian Goods and Services Tax: History, Policy, and Politics, Research Study/Australian Tax Research Foundation, Public Sector Management Institute, No. 16*. Sydney: Australian Tax Research Foundation.

Caillé, Alain, and Jean-Pierre Le Goff, eds. 1996. *Le tournant de decembre: Le grand malentendu vers un nouveau contrat social?* Paris: Editions La Decouverte.

Cameron, David. 1978. The Expansion of the Public Economy: A Comparative Analysis. *American Political Science Review* 72: 1243–61.

Campbell, John Creighton. 1992. *How Policies Change: The Japanese Government and the Aging Society*. Princeton, N.J.: Princeton University Press.

Cass, Bettina. 1998. The Social Policy Context. In *Contesting the Australian Way: States, Markets and Civil Society*, edited by Paul Smyth and Bettina Cass. Cambridge: Cambridge University Press.

Castles, Francis G. 1985. *The Working Class and Welfare: Reflections on the Political Development of the Welfare State in Australia and New Zealand, 1890–1980*. Wellington; Boston: Allen & Unwin.

———. 1993. *Families of Nations: Patterns of Public Policy in Western Democracies*. Aldershot, Hants, England; Brookfield, Vt.: Dartmouth Publishing Company.

———. 1994. On Religion and Public Policy: Does Catholicism Make a Difference? *European Journal of Political Research* 25: 19–40.

———. 1996. Needs-Based Strategies of Social Protection in Australia and New Zealand. In *Welfare States in Transition: National Adaptations in Global Economies*, edited by G. Esping-Andersen. London: Sage Publications.

———. 1998. *Comparative Public Policy: Patterns of Post-war Transformation*. London: Edward Elgar.

Castles, Francis G., Rolf Gerritsen, and Jack Vowels. 1996. Introduction: Setting the Scene from Economic and Political Change. In *The Great Experiment: Labour Parties and Public Policy Transformation in Australia and New Zealand*, edited by F. G. Castles, R. Gerritsen, and J. Vowels. Auckland, N.Z.: Auckland University Press.

Castles, Francis G., and Peter Mair. 1984. Left-Right Political Scales: Some 'Expert' Judgments. *European Journal of Political Research* (12): 73–88.

Castles, Francis G., and Deborah Mitchell. 1992. Identifying Welfare State Regimes: The Links Between Politics, Instruments and Outcomes. *Governance* 5 (1): 1–26.

———. 1993. Worlds of welfare and families of nations. In *Families of Nations: Patterns of Public Policy in Western Democracies*, edited by G. C. Francis. Brookfield, Vt.: Dartmouth Publishing Company.

Castles, Francis G., and Ian F. Shirley. 1996. Labour and Social Policy: Gravediggers or Refurbishers of the Welfare State. In *The Great Experiment: Labour Parties and Public Policy Transformation in Australia and New Zealand*, edited by F. G. Castles, R. Gerritsen, and J. Vowels. Auckland, N.Z.: Auckland University Press.

Cha, Byung-Kwon. 1986. Kaebal yeondeŭi seje kaehyeokkwa pukakachieŭi toipkyeongwi, *Seoul Daehakkyo Kyeongje Nonjip* XXV: 2.

Chapman, Richard A. 1997. *The Treasury in Public Policy-Making*. London: Routledge.

Cheibub, José Antonio. 1998. Political Regimes and the Extractive Capacity of Governments: Taxation in Democracies and Dictatorships. *World Politics* 50 (3): 349–76.

Choi, Kwan. 1990. Value-Added Taxation: Experiences and Lessons of Korea. In *Taxation in Developing Countries*, edited by Richard M. Bird and Oliver Oldman. Baltimore: Johns Hopkins University Press.

———. 1997. Tax Policy and Tax Reform in Korea. In *Tax Reform in Developing Countries*, edited by Wayne Thirsk. Washington, D.C.: The World Bank.

Bibliography

Clarke, Harold D., Marianne C. Stewart, and Paul Whiteley. 1998. New Models for New Labour: The Political Economy of Labour Party Support, January 1992–April 1997. *American Political Science Review* 92 (3): 559–76.

Clayton, Richard, and Jonas Pontusson. 1998. Welfare State Retrenchment Revisited: Entitlement Cuts, Public Sector Restructuring, and Inegalitarian Trends in Advanced Capital Societies. *World Politics* 51 (1): 67–98.

Cnossen, Sijbren. 1991. Design of the Value Added Tax: Lessons from Experience. In *Tax Policy in Developing Countries*, edited by Javad Khalilzadeh-Shirazi and Anwar Shah. Washington, D.C.: World Bank.

Collier, D. 1991. New Perspectives on the Comparative Method. In *Comparative Political Dynamics: Global Research Perspectives*, edited by D. A. Rustow and K. P. Erickson. New York: HarperCollins Publishers.

Collier, David, and Richard Messick. 1975. Prerequisites Versus Diffusion: Testing Alternative Explanations of Social Security Adoption. *American Political Science Review* 69: 1299–1315.

Conlan, Timothy J., Margaret T. Wrightson, and David R. Beam. 1990. *Taxing Choices: The Politics of Tax Reform*. Washington, D.C.: Congressional Quarterly.

Cook, F. L., and E. J. Barrett, eds. 1992. *Support for the American Welfare State: The Views of Congress and the Public*. New York: Columbia University Press.

Cousins, Christine. 1999. *Society, Work and Welfare in Europe*. New York: Macmillan.

Cox, Robert H. 1992. Can the Welfare State Grow in Leaps and Bounds?: Non-incremental policymaking in the Netherlands. *Governance* 5 (1): 68–87.

Crane, John A. 1994. *Directions for Social Welfare in Canada: The Public's View*. Vancouver: School of Social Works, University of British Columbia.

Crepaz, Markus M. L. 1998. Inclusion Versus Exclusion: Political Institutions and Welfare Expenditures. *Comparative Politics* 31 (1): 61–80.

Davidson, Alexander. 1989. Two Models of Welfare: The Origins and Development of the Welfare State in Sweden and New Zealand, 1888–1988, Ph.D. diss., Uppsala University, Stockholm.

Deakin, Nicholas, and Richard Parry. 2000. *The Treasury and Social Policy: The Contest for Control of Welfare Strategy*. London: Macmillan.

Denver, David, Justin Fisher, Philip Cowley, and Charles Pattie, eds. 1997. *British Elections and Parties Review, Vol. 8: The 1997 General Election*. London: Frank Cass.

Dickson, Ian. 1989. Taxation. In *Rogernomics: Reshaping New Zealand's Economy*, edited by S. Walker. Auckland, N.Z.: GP Books.

Dilnot, Andrew W., and J. A. Kay. 1990. Tax Reform in the United Kingdom: The Recent Experience. In *World Tax Reform: Case Studies of Developed and Developing Countries*, edited by M. J. Boskin and C. E. McLure. San Francisco: International Center for Economic Growth and Institute for Contemporary Studies; ICS Press; Lanham.

Dilnot, A. W., J. A. Kay, and C. N. Morris. 1984. *The Reform of Social Security*. Oxford: Clarendon Press; New York: Oxford University Press.

Dilnot, Andrew, and Graham Stark. 1989. The Poverty Trap, Tax Cuts, and the Reform of Social Security. In *The Economics of Social Security*, edited by A. W. Dilnot and I. Walker. New York: Oxford University Press.

Disney, Richard, and Steven Webb. 1990. Why Social Security Expenditure in the 1980s Has Risen Faster Than Expected: The Role of Unemployment. *Fiscal Studies* 11 (1): 1–20.

Douglas, Roger, and Louise Callen. 1987. *Toward Prosperity*. Auckland, N.Z.: D. Bateman.

Driver, Stephen, and Luke Martell. 1998. *New Labour: Politics after Thatcherism*. Cambridge, U.K.: Polity Press.

Dubergé, J. 1984. Résistance comparée à l'impôt et aux cotisations de couverture sociale. *Revue Française de Frances Publiques* (5).

Dunleavy, Patrick. 1989. The United Kingdom: Paradoxes of an Underground Statism. In *The Comparative History of Public Policy*, edited by F. G. Castles. New York: Oxford University Press.

Easton, B. H. 1989. *The Making of Rogernomics*. Auckland, N.Z.: University of Auckland Press.

Eckstein, H. 1975. Case Studies and Theory in Political Science. In *Handbook of Political Science*, edited by F. Greenstein and N. W. P. Reading, Mass.: Addison Wesley.

Edlund, Jonas. 1999. Progressive Taxation Farewell? Attitudes to Income Redistribution and Taxation in Sweden, Great Britain and the United States. In *The End of the Welfare State?: Responses to State Retrenchment*, edited by S. Svallfors and P. Taylor-Gooby, 106–34. London: Routledge.

Eitrheim, Pål, and Stein Kuhnle. 2000. Nordic Welfare States in the 1990s: Instiutional Stability, Signs of Divergence. In *Survival of the European Welfare State*, edited by Stein Kuhnle, 39–57. London: Routledge.

Ellis, James W. 1998. Voting for Markets or Marketing for Votes? : The Politics of Neoliberal Economic Reform, Ph.D. diss., Harvard University, Boston.

Elvander, Nils. 1972. *Svensk skattepolitik 1945–1970: En studie i partiers och organisationers funktioner [Rabén & Sjögren samhallsvetenskapliga bibliotek]*. Stockholm: Rabén & Sjögren.

———. 1994. Självbelåten välfärdnationalism styr nej-sidan. In *Svenska Dagbladet* November 6th.

Esping-Andersen, Gøsta. 1985. *Politics Against Market: The Social Democratic Road to Power*. Princeton, N.J.: Princeton University Press.

———. 1990. *The Three Worlds of Welfare Capitalism*. Princeton, N.J.: Princeton University Press.

———. 1999. *Social Foundations of Postindustrial Economics*. New York: Oxford University Press.

Estevez-Abe, Margarita. 1998. Challenges to the Japanese Model of Capitalism and Its Welfare State: Becoming More like the US? Paper presented at the Annual Meeting of the American Political Science Association, Boston, August 27–30.

———. 1999. Welfare and Capitalism in Postwar Japan, Ph.D. diss., Harvard University, Boston.

Evans, Edward. A. 1988. Australia. In *World Tax Reform: A Progress Report*, edited by J. A. Pechman. Washington, D.C.: Brookings Institution.

Bibliography

Evans, Lewis, Arthur Grimes, Bryce Wilkinson, and David Teece. 1996. Economic Reform in New Zealand 1984–95: The Pursuit of Efficiency. *Journal of Economic Literature* 34 (4), 1856–902.

Evans, Martin. 1996. Fairer or Fowler? The Effects of the 1986 Social Security Act on Family Income. In *New Inequalities: The Changing Distribution of Income and Wealth in the United Kingdom*, edited by J. Hills. Cambridge: Cambridge University Press.

Fawcett, Helen. 2000. Understanding British Exceptionalism: The Importance of the Policy Legacies of the 1960s in Explaining Welfare State Reform under the Thatcher and Blair Administrations. Paper presented to the 96th Annual Meeting of the American Political Science Association, Washington, D.C., August 31–September 3, 2000.

Ferejohn, John. 1998. A Tale of Two Congresses: Social Policy in the Clinton Years. In *The Social Divide: Political Parties and the Future of Activist Government*, edited by M. Weir. Washington, D.C.: Brookings Institution.

Freeman, Richard. 1995. The Large Welfare State as a System. *American Economic Review* 85 (2): 16–21.

Freeman, R. B., R. Topel, and B. Swedenborg, eds. 1997. *The Welfare State in transition, (NBER Conference Report)*. Chicago: University of Chicago Press.

Frith, Royce. 1991. *Hoods on the Hill: How Mulroney and His Gang Rammed the GST Past Parliament and Down Our Throats, #1 in Hooligans*. Toronto: Coach House Press.

Frizzell, Alan, Jon H. Pammett, and Anthony Westell. 1994. *The Canadian General Election of 1993*. Ottawa: Carleton University Press.

Galbraith, John Kenneth. 1958. *The Affluent Society*, 1st ed. Boston: Houghton Mifflin Company.

––––––. 1969. *The Affluent Society*, 2nd ed., revised. Boston: Houghton Mifflin Company.

Gamble, Andrew, and T. Wright, eds. 1999. *The New Social Democracy*. London: Blackwell.

Ganghof, Steffen. 2000. Corporate Tax Competition, Budget Constraints, and the New Trade-offs in Domestic Tax Policy. Paper presented at the Annual Meeting of the American Political Science Association, Washington, D.C., August 31–September 3, 2000.

Garrett, Geoffrey. 1998. *Partisan Politics in the Global Economy*. Cambridge: Cambridge University Press.

––––––. 1999. Global Markets and National Politics: Collision Course or Virtuous Circle? In *Exploration and Contestation in the Study of World Politics*, edited by P. Katzenstein, R. O. Keohane, and S. D. Krasner. Cambridge, Mass.: MIT Press.

Geddes, Andrew, and J. Tonge, eds. 1997. *Labour's Landslide: The British General Election 1997*. Manchester, U.K.: Manchester University Press.

Geddes, B. 1992. The Use of Case Studies in Path Dependent Arguments. Paper presented at the Annual Meeting of American Political Science Association, Chicago, August 27–30.

Gest, Guy. 1997. General Description: France. In *Comparative Income Taxation: A Structural Analysis*, edited by H. J. Ault. Hague: Kluwer Law International.

Giles, Christopher, and Paul Johnson. 1994. Tax Reform in the UK and Changes in the Progressivity of the Tax System, 1985–95. *Fiscal Studies* 15 (3): 64–86.

Glennerster, Howard. 1990. Social Policy Since the Second World War. In *The State of Welfare: The Welfare State in Britain since 1974*, edited by John Hills, 11–27. Oxford: Oxford University Press.

Goldfinch, Shaun. 1997. Treasury and Public Policy Formation. In *The Political Economy of New Zealand*, edited by B. Roper and C. Rudd. Auckland, N.Z.: Oxford University Press.

Goldstein, Judith, and Robert O. Keohane, eds. 1993. *Idea and Foreign Policy: Belief, Institutions, and Political Change*. Ithaca, N.Y.: Cornell University Press.

Goodman, Alissa, Paul Johnson, and Steven Webb. 1997. *Inequality in the UK*. Oxford: Oxford University Press.

Goodman, Roger, and Ito Peng. 1996. The East Asian Welfare States: Peripatetic Learning, Adaptive Changes, and Nation-Building. In *Welfare States in Transition: National Adaptations in Global Economies*, edited by Gøsta Esping-Andersen. London: Sage Publications.

Goodman, Roger, Gordon White, and Huck-ju Kwon. 1998. *The East Asian Welfare Model: Welfare Orientalism and the State*. London: Routledge.

Gravelle, Jane G. 1992. Equity Effects of the Tax Reform Act of 1986. In *The Journal of Economic Perspectives* 6 (1): 27–44.

Greenstein, Robert. 1991. Universal and Targeted Approaches to Relieving Poverty: An Alternative View. In *The Urban Underclass*, edited by J. Christopher and P. Paul. Washington, D.C.: Brookings Institution.

Groenewegen, P. D. 1988. Tax-Reform in Australia and New-Zealand. *Environment and Planning C-Government and Policy* 6 (1): 93–114.

Groux, Guy, and René Mouriaux. 1996. The Dilemma of Unions without Members. In *The Mitterrand Era: Policy Alternatives and Political Mobilization in France*, edited by A. Daley. London: Macmillan.

Guest, D. 1985. *The Emergence of Social Security in Canada*. Vancouver: University of British Columbia Press.

Gustafsson, Bjørn, Rolf Aaberge, Ådne Cappelen, Peder J. Pedersen, Nina Smith, and Hannu Uusitalo. 1999. The Distribution of Income in the Nordic Countries: Changes and Causes. In *Nordic Social Policy: Changing Welfare States*, edited by M. Kautto, M. Heikkilä, B. Hvinden, S. Marklund, and N. Ploug. London: Routledge.

Hacker, Jacob S. 2001. Learning from Defeat? Political Analysis and the Failure of Health Care Reform in the United States. *British Journal of Political Science* 31 (1): 61–94.

Hadenius, Axel. 1986. *A Crisis of the Welfare State?: Opinions about Taxes and Public Expenditure in Sweden*. Stockholm, Sweden: Almqvist & Wiksell International.

Hage, Jerald, Edward T. Gargan, and Robert Hanneman. 1989. *State Responsiveness and State Activism*. London: Unwin Hyman.

Haggard, Stephen. 1990. *Pathways from the Periphery: The Politics of Growth in the Newly Industrializing Countries*. Ithaca, N.Y.: Cornell University Press.

Hall, Peter, ed. 1989. *The Political Power of Economic Ideas: Keynesianism Across Nations*. Princeton, N.J.: Princeton University Press.

Hall, Robert E., and Alvin Rabushka. 1996. The Flat Tax: A Simple, Progressive Consumption Tax. In *Frontiers of Tax Reform*, edited by M. Boskin. Stanford, Cal.: Hoover Institution.

Hamilton, R. W., and J. Whalley, eds. 1989. Efficiency and Distributional Effect of the Tax Reform Package. In *The Economic Impacts of Tax Reform, Canadian Tax Paper* No. 84, edited by J. Mintz and J. Whalley. Toronto: Canadian Tax Foundation.

Han, Seung Soo. 1990. The VAT in the Republic of Korea. In *Value Added Taxation in Developing Countries, A World Bank Symposium*, edited by Malcolm Gillis, Carl S. Shoup, and Gerardo P. Sicat. Washington, D.C.: World Bank.

Hansen, Bent. 1958. *The Economic Theory of Fiscal Policy*, translated by P. E. Burke. London: Allen & Unwin.

Hansen, Erik Jørgen, Stein Ringen, Hannu Uusitalo, and Robert Erikson. 1993. *Welfare Trends in the Scandinavian Countries*. Armonk, N.Y.: M. E. Sharpe.

Hansson, Ingmar, and Charles Stuart. 1990. Sweden: Tax Reform in a High-Tax Environment. In *World Tax Reform: Case Studies of Developed and Developing Countries*, edited by Michael J. Boskin and Charles E. McLure, Jr. San Francisco: ICS Press; Lanham.

Hatta, Tatsuo, and Nohiro Yashiro. 1998. *Shakai Hoken Kaikaku*. Tokyo: Nihonkeizai Shimbunsha.

Hay, Colin. 1999. *The Political Economy of New Labour: Labouring under False Pretences?* Manchester: Manchester University Press.

Heß, Jurgen C. 1981. The Social Policy of the Attlee Government. In *The Emergence of the Welfare State in Britain and Germany, 1850–1950*, edited by W. Mock and W. J. Mommsen. London: Croom Halm on behalf of the German Historical Institute.

Hicks, Alexander. 1999. *Social Democracy and Welfare Capitalism. A Century of Income Security Politics*, Ithaca, N.Y.: Cornell University Press.

Hicks, Alexander, and Joya Misra. 1993. Political Resources and the Growth of the Welfare State in Affluent Capitalist Democracies, 1960–82. *American Journal of Sociology* 99 (3): 750–63.

Hicks, Alexander, Joya Misra, and Tang Nah Ng. 1995. The Programmatic Emergence of the Social-Security State. *American Sociological Review* 60 (3): 329–49.

Hicks, Alexander, Duane H. Swank, and Martin Ambuhl. 1989. Welfare Expansion Revisited: Policy Routines and Their Mediation by Party, Class and Crisis, 1957–1982. *European Journal of Political Research* 17 (4): 401–30.

Hill, Michael. 1999. Rolling Back the (Welfare) State: The Major Governments and Social Security Reform. In *The Major Premiership. Politics and Policies under John Major, 1990–97*, edited by P. Dorey. London: Macmillan.

Hills, John, ed. 1996. *New Inequalities: The Changing Distribution of Income and Wealth in the United Kingdom*. Cambridge: Cambridge University Press.

Hills, John, and Beverley Mullings. 1990. Housing: A Decent Home for All at a Price Within Their Means? In *The State of Welfare*, edited by John Hills, 135–205. Oxford: Oxford University Press.

Hirst, Paul. 1999. Globalisation and Social Democracy. In *The New Social Democracy*, edited by A. Gamble and T. Wright. London: Blackwell.

Hiroi, Yoshinori. 1999. *Nihon no Shakai Hoshō*. Tokyo: Iwanami Shoten.

Hiwatari, Nobuhiro. 1991. *Sengo Nihon no Shijō to Seiji*. Tokyo: University of Tokyo Press.

———. 1998. Adjustment to Stagflation and Neoliberal Reforms in Japan, the United Kingdom and the United States. *Comparative Political Studies* 30 (5): 602–32.

Hood, C. Christopher. 1985. British Tax Structure Development as Administrative Adaptation. *Policy Sciences* 18: 3–31.

Hori, Katsuhiro. 1997. *Nenkinseido no Saikōchiku*. Tokyo: Tōyōkeizai Shimpōsha.

Howard, Christopher. 1997. *The Hidden Welfare State: Tax Expenditures and Social Policy in the United States*. Princeton, N.J.: Princeton University Press.

Hsaio, Cheng. 1986. *Analysis of Panel Data*. New York: Cambridge University Press.

Huber, Evelyne. 1996. Options for Social Policy in Latin America: Neoliberal Versus Social Democratic Models. In *Welfare States in Transition: National Adaptations in Global Economies*, edited by G. Esping-Andersen. London: Sage Publications.

Huber, Evelyne, Charles Ragin, and John D. Stephens. 1993. Social Democracy, Christian Democracy, Constitutional Structure, and the Welfare State. *American Journal of Sociology* 99 (3): 711–49.

Huber, Evelyne, and John D. Stephens. 1998. Internationalization and the Social Democratic Model-Crisis and Future Prospects. *Comparative Political Studies* 31 (3): 353–97.

———. 2001. *Development and Crisis of the Welfare State: Parties and Policies in Global Markets*. Chicago: University of Chicago Press.

Huber, John D. 1996. *Rationalizing Parliament: Legislative Institutions and Party Politics in France*. New York: Cambridge University Press.

———. 1999. "Parliamentary Rules and Party Behavior During Minority Government in France." In *Policy, Office, or Votes?* edited by Wolfgang C. Müller and Kaare Strøm. New York: Cambridge University Press.

Immergut, Ellen. 2000. "Constitutional Politics." The Joint JPSA/ECPR workshop, "Politics of Crisis," Konstanz, July 19–22, 2000.

International Social Survey Program [Computer file]. 1996. International Social Survey Program: Role of Government III. Cologne, Germany: Zentralarchiv fuer Empirische Sozialforschung [producer], 1999. Cologne, Germany: Zentralarchiv fuer Empirische Sozialforschung/Ann Arbor, Mich.: Inter-university Consortium for Political and Social Research [distributors], 1999.

Ishiyama, Yoshihide. 1998. *Chōkōreikashakai no Keizaigaku*. Tokyo: Nihon Hyōronsha.

Iversen, Torben. 1999. *Contested Economic Institutions: The Politics of Macroeconomics and Wage Bargaining in Advanced Democracies*. Cambridge: Cambridge University Press.

Bibliography

Iversen, Torben, and Thomas R. Cusack. 2000. The Causes of Welfare State Expansion: Deindustrialization or Globalization? *World Politics* 52 (3): 313–49.

Iversen, Torben, Jonas Pontusson, and David Soskice, eds. 2000. *Unions, Employers, and Central Banks: Macroeconomic Coordination and Institutional Change in Social Market Economies*. Cambridge: Cambridge University Press.

Iversen, Torben, and Anne Wren. 1998. Equality, Employment, and Budgetary Restraint: The Trilemma of the Service Economy. *World Politics* 50 (4): 507–46.

Jacobs, Lawrence R., and Robert Y. Shapiro. 1998. Myths and Misunderstandings about Public Opinion Toward Social Security. In *Framing the Social Security Debate: Values, Politics and Economics*, edited by R. D. Arnold, M. J. Graetz, and A. H. Munnell. Washington, D.C.: National Academy of Social Insurance.

Jallade, Jean-Pierre. 1988. *The Crisis of Redistribution in European Welfare States*. Stoke-on-Trent: Trentham.

James, Estelle. 1996. Social Security Around the World. In *Social Security: What Role for the Future?* edited by P. A. Diamond and D. C. Lindeman. Washington, D.C.: Brookings Institute.

Jenkins, Stephen P. 1996. Recent Trends in the UK Income Distribution: What Happened and Why? *Oxford Review of Economic Policy* 12 (1): 29–46.

Jesson, Bruce. 1989. *Fragments of Labour: The Story Behind the Labour Government*. Auckland, N.Z.: Penguin Books.

Johnstone, Dorothy. 1975. *A Tax Shall Be Charged, Civil Service Studies, No. 1*. London: H.M. Stationery Office.

Jones, Michael. 1997. *Reforming New Zealand Welfare*. St Leonards, Australia: The Center for Independent Studies Limited.

Jowell, Roger, ed. 1996. *British Social Attitudes: The 13th Report*. London: Social and Community Planning Research.

Junankar, P. N., and C. A. Kapuscinski. 1997. *Was Working Nation Working?* Canberra: Australian National University.

Kamimura, Yasuhiro. 2000. Fukushi Kokka ha Ima Nao Shiji Sareteiruka. In *Shakai-chōsa no Kōkai Dēta*, edited by Hiroki Sato, Hiroshi Ishida, and Kenichi Ikeda. Tokyo: University of Tokyo Press.

Kato, Junko. 1994. *The Problem of Bureaucratic Rationality: Tax Politics in Japan*. Princeton, N.J.: Princeton University Press.

————. 1996. Institutions and Rationality in Politics: Three Varieties of Neo-Institutionalisms. *British Journal of Political Science* 26 (4): 553–82.

————. 1997. Tax Policy in Japan After the Demise of Conservative Dominance. In *Japanese Politics Today*, edited by P. Jain and T. Inoguchi. South Melbourne: Macmillan Education Australia PTY LTD.

———— 1998. When the Party Breaks Up: Exit and Voice Among Japanese Legislators. *American Political Science Review* 92 (4): 857–70.

Katzenstein, Peter. 1985. *Small States in World Market*. Ithaca, N.Y.: Cornell University Press.

Keith, E. Gordon. 1966. Introduction and Summary. In *Foreign Tax Policies and Economic Growth: A Conference Report of the National Bureau of Economic Research*. New York: National Bureau of Economic Research.

Kelly, E. W., and D. E. Ashford, eds. 1986. *Nationalizing Social Security in Europe and America*. Greenwich, Conn.: JAI Press.

Kesselman, Mark. 1996. Does the French Labor Movement Have a Future? In *Chirac's Challenge: Liberalization, Europeanization and Malaise in France*, edited by J. T. S. Keeler and M. A. Schain. London: Macmillan.

Kim, Jeong-Ryeom. 1991. Han'guk Kyeongje jeongchaek 30nyensa: Kim, Jeong-Ryeom hoikorok. Seoul: Joong Ang Ilbosa.

Klausen, Jytte. 1998. *War and Welfare: Europe and the United States, 1945 to the Present*. London: Macmillan.

Kohler, Peter A., Hans Friedrich Zacher, and Martin Partington. 1982. *The Evolution of Social Insurance, 1881–1981: Studies of Germany, France, Great Britain, Austria, and Switzerland*. New York: St. Martin's Press on behalf of the Max-Planck-Institut fur Ausländisches und Internationales Sozialrecht.

Koopman-Boyden, Peggy G. 1990. Social Policy: Has There Been One? In *The Fourth Labour Government: Politics and Policy in New Zealand*, edited by M. Holland and J. Boston. Auckland, N.Z.; New York: Oxford University Press.

Korpi, Walter. 1980. Social Policy Strategies and Distributional Conflict in Capitalist Democracies. *West European Politics* 3 (3): 296–316.

Korpi, Walter, and Joakim Palme. 1998. The Paradox of Redistribution and Strategies of Equality: Welfare State Institutions, Inequality, and Poverty in the Western Countries. *American Sociological Review* 63 (5): 661–87.

Kōryūkyokai. 1998. *Taiwan no Keizaijijō*. Tokyo: Zaidanhōjin Kōryūkyōkai.

Krever, Richard, ed. 1997. *Tax Conversations: A Guide to the Key Issues in the Tax Reform Debate*. London: Kluwer Law International.

Kuhnle, Stein. 2000. The Scandinavian Welfare State in the 1990s: Challenged but Viable. In *Recasting European Welfare States*, edited by Maurizio Ferrera and Martin Rhodes. London: Frank Cass.

Kume, Ikuo. 1998. *Disparaged Success: Labor Politics in Postwar Japan*. Ithaca, N.Y.: Cornell University Press.

Kwon, Huck-Ju. 1997. Beyond European Welfare Regimes: Comparative Perspectives on East Asian Welfare Systems. *Journal of Social Policy* 26 (4): 467–84.

———. 1998a. Democracy and Politics of Social Welfare: A Comparative Analysis of Welfare Systems in East Asia. In *The East Asian Welfare Model: Welfare Orientalism and the State*, edited by Roger Goodman, Gordon White, and Huck-ju Kwon. London: Routledge.

———. 1998b. The South Korean National Pension Programme: Fulfilling Its Promise? In *The East Asian Welfare Model: Welfare Orientalism and the State*, edited by Roger Goodman, Gordon White, and Huck-ju Kwon. London: Routledge.

———. 1999. *The Welfare State in Korea: The Politics of Legitimation*. London: Macmillan Press.

Lamaignère, Pierre. 1996. La loi de financement de la Sécurité sociale: Un débat morose pour une étrange politique sociale. *Droit Social* December (12): 1058–60.

Bibliography

Lawson, Nigel. 1992. *The View from No. 11: Memoirs of a Tory Radical*. London: Bantam.

Le Grand, Julian. 1990. The State of Welfare. In *The State of Welfare: The Welfare State in Britain Since 1974*, edited by J. Hills. Oxford: Oxford University Press.

Le Grand, Julian, and Robert E. Goodwin. eds. 1987. *Not Only the Poor*. London: Allen & Unwin.

Leibfried, Stephan, and Paul Pierson. 1995. Semisovereign Welfare State: Social Policy in Multitiered Europe. In *European Social Policy: Between Fragmentation and Integration*, edited by S. Leibfried and P. Pierson. Washington, D.C.: Brookings Institution.

Levi, Margaret. 1988. *Of Rule and Revenue*. Berkeley: The Univesity of California Press.

Liebowitz, S. J., and S. E. Margolis. 1995. Path Dependence, Lock-In and History. *The Journal of Law, Economics and Organization* 11 (1): 205–26.

Lienard, Jean-Louis, Kenneth C. Messere, and Jeffrey Owens. 1987. France. In *Comparative Tax Systems: Europe, Canada, and Japan*, edited by Joseph A. Pechman. Arlington, Va.: Tax Analysts.

Ljungh, Claes. 1988. Sweden. In *World Tax Reform: A Progress Report*, edited by Joseph A. Pechman, 187–210. Washington, D.C.: Brookings Institution.

Lowe, Rodney. 1994. A Prophet Dishonoured in His Own Country? The Rejection of Beveridge in Britain, 1945–70. In *Beveridge and Social Security: An International Retrospective*, edited by J. Hills, J. Ditch, and H. Glennerster. New York: Oxford University Press.

Lynes, Tony. 1997. The British Case. In *Enterprise and the Welfare State*, edited by Martin Rein and Eskil Wadensjö. Northampton, U.K.: Edward Elgar.

Mabbett, Deborah. 1995. *Trade, Employment, and Welfare: A Comparative Study of Trade and Labour Market Policies in Sweden and New Zealand, 1880–1980*. Oxford: Clarendon Press.

Mabuchi, Masaru, 1994. *Ōkurashō Tōsei no Seiji Keizaigaku*. Tokyo: Chūōkōron-shinsha.

MacGregor, Susanne. 1998. Taxing and Spending the People's Money. In *Social Issues and Party Politics*, edited by Helen Jones and Susanne Macgregor. Bodmin, U.K.: MPG Books.

Mackie, Thomas T., and Richard Rose. 1982. *The International Almanac of Electoral History*, 2nd ed. London: Macmillan.

———. 1991. *The International Almanac of Electoral History*, fully revised 3rd ed. London: Macmillan.

Maillard, Didier. 1993. Tax Policies in the 1980s and the 1990s: The Case of France. In *Confederation of European Economic Associations Conference Volume*, edited by S. Knoester. New York: Macmillan.

Massey, Patrick. 1995. *New Zealand: Market Liberalization in a Developed Economy*. London: Macmillan.

McGilly, Frank. 1997. *Canadian Governments and Social Policy Issues: Fiscal Urgency, Federal Tensions and Social Change*. International Institute of Administrative Sciences (IIAS) Working Group on Social Security.

Melz, Peter. 1997. General Description: Sweden. In *Comparative Income Taxation: A Structural Anlysis*, edited by H. J. Ault. Hague: Kruwer Law International.

Merrien, François-Xavier, and Giuliano Bonoli. 1999. Implementing Major Welfare State Reforms: A Comparison of France and Switzerland – A New-Institutionalist Aproach. In *The End of the Welfare State?: Responses to State Retrenchment*, edited by S. Svallfors and P. Taylor-Gooby, 128–45. London: Routledge.

Messere, Ken. 1993. *Tax Policy in OECD Countries: Choices and Conflicts*. Amsterdam: IFBD Publications BV.

———, ed. 1998. *The Tax System in Industrialized Countries*. New York: Oxford University Press.

Milner, Susan. 2000. Trade Unions: A New Civil Agenda? In *Structures of Power in Modern France*, edited by Gino G. Raymond, 37–62. London: Macmillan.

Mishra, Ramesh. 1990. *The Welfare State in Capitalist Society: Policies of Retrenchment and Maintenance in Europe, North America and Australia*. Toronto: Harvester Wheatsheaf.

Miyamoto, Taro. 1999. *Fukushi Kokka to Iu Senryaku: Sweden Moderu no Seiji Keizai Gaku*. Kyoto: Horitsu Bunkasha.

Moene, Karl Ove, and Michael Wallerstein. 1997. *Political Support for Targeted Versus Universalistic Welfare Policies*. Institute for Policy Research Working Paper WP-97-2, Northwestern University.

Müller, Wolfgang C., and Kaare Strøm, eds. 1999. *Policy, Office, or Votes?: How Political Parties in Western Europe Make Hard Decisions*. New York: Cambridge University Press.

Murakami, Kiyoshi. 1997. *Nenkinseido no Kiki*. Tokyo: Toyokeizai Shimposha.

Musgrave, Peggy B. 1997. Consumption Tax Proposals in the International Setting. In *Tax Conversations: A Guide to the Key Issues in the Tax Reform Debate*, edited by R. Krever. London: Kluwer Law International.

Mutén, Leif. 1988. Comment. In *World Tax Reform: A Progress Report*, edited by J. A. Pechman. Washington, D.C.: Brookings Institution.

Mutén, Leif, and Karl Faxén. 1966. Sweden. In *Foreign Tax Policies and Economic Growth: A Conference Report of the National Bureau of Economic Research and Brookings Institute*. New York: National Bureau of Economic Research.

Myles, John. 1996. When Markets Fail: Social Welfare in Canada and the United States. In *Welfare States in Transition: National Adaptations in Global Economies*, edited by G. Esping-Andersen. London: Sage Publications.

Myrdal, Alva Reimer, et al. 1969. *Jämlikhet: Första rapport från SAP-LO:s arbetsgrupp för jämlikhetsfrågor*. Stockholm : Prisma.

Nabseth, Lars. 1966. Sweden – Comment. In *Foreign Tax Policies and Economic Growth: A Conference Report of the National Bureau of Economic Research and Brookings Institute*. New York: National Bureau of Economic Research.

Niskanen, W. A., Jr. 1971. *Bureaucracy and Representative Government*. Chicago: Aldine.

Nizet, Jean-Yves. 1991. *Fiscalité, economie et politique: l'impôt en France, 1945–1990*. Paris: Libr. générale de droit et de jurisprudence.

Noble, Charles. 1997. *Welfare As We Knew It: A Political History of the American Welfare State*. Oxford: Oxford University Press.

Norman, Erik, and Charles E. McLure, Jr. 1997. Tax Policy in Sweden. In *The Welfare State in Transition*, edited by R. B. Freeman, R. Topel, and B. Swedenborg. Chicago: University of Chicago Press.

Norr, Martin. 1961. The Retail Sales Tax in Sweden. *National Tax Journal* 14 (2): 174–81.

Norr, Martin, Frank J. Duffy, and Harry Sterner. 1959. *Taxation in Sweden*. World Tax Series. Harvard Law School, International Tax Program. Chicago: Commerce Clearing House.

Norr, Martin, and Nils G. Hornhammar. 1970. The Value added Tax in Sweden. *Columbia Law Review* 70 (3): 379–422.

Norr, Martin, and Pierre Kerlan. 1966. *Taxation in France*. Harvard Law School, International Tax Program. Chicago: Commerce Clearing House.

North, Douglas. 1990. *Institutions, Institutional Change and Economic Performance*. Cambridge: Cambridge University Press.

Oliver, W. Hugh. 1989. The Labour Caucus and Economic Policy Formation, 1981–1984. In *The Making of Rogernomics*, edited by Brian Easton. Auckland, N.Z.: University of Auckland Press.

Orchard, Lionel. 1998. Public Sector Reform and the Australian Way. In *Contesting the Australian Way: States, Markets and Civil Society*, edited by Paul Smyth and Bettina Cass. Cambridge: Cambridge Unviersity Press.

Organisation for Economic Co-operation and Development. 1993. *Taxation in OECD Countries*. Paris: OECD.

———.1996. *Tax Expenditures: Recent Experiences*. Paris: OECD.

———. 1997a. *Consumption Tax Trends*. Paris: OECD.

———. 1997b. *Revenue Statistics of OECD Member Countries, 1965–1996*. Paris: OECD.

———. 1998a. Maintaining Prosperity in an Aging Society. Paris: OECD.

———. 1998b. *Harmful Tax Competition*. Paris: OECD.

———. 1998c. *Value Added Taxes in Central and Eastern European Countries: A Comparative Survey and Evaluation*. Paris: OECD.

———. 1999. *Consumption Tax Trends*. Paris: OECD.

———. 2000. *Revenue Statistics of OECD Member Countries, 1965–1999*. Paris: OECD.

———. 2001a. *Revenue statistics of OECD member countries, 1965–2000*. Paris: OECD.

———. 2001b. *OECD Tax Policy Studies No. 6. Tax and the Economy: A Comparative Assessment of OECD Countries*. Paris: OECD.

———. 2001c. *Consumption Tax Trends: VAT/GST, Excise and Environmental Taxes*. Paris: OECD.

Oshio, Takashi. 1998. *Nenkin Mineika heno Kōsō*. Tokyo: Nihonkeizai Shimbunsha.

Owens, Jeffrey. 1997. Emerging Issues in Tax Reform: The Perspective of an International Bureaucrat. *Tax Notes International* (December 22, 1997): 2035–75.

Oxley, Howard, Jean-Marc Burniaux, Thai-Thanh Dang, and Marco Mira D'Ercole. 1997. Income Distribution and Poverty in 13 OECD Countries. *OECD Economic Review* 29: 55–92.

Palier, Bruno. 2000. 'Defrosting' the French Welfare System. *West European Politics* 23 (2): 113–36.

———. 2001a. Reshaping the Social Policy Making Framework: France from the 1980s to 2000. In *Welfare State Under Pressure*, edited by Peter Taylor-Gooby, London: Sage Publications.

———. 2001b. Beyond Retrenchment: Four Problems in Current Welfare State Research and One Suggestion How to Overcome them. In *What Future for Social Security? Debates and Reforms in National and Cross-National Perspective*, edited by Jochen Clasen, 93–105. Bristol: Policy Press.

Palme, Mårten, and Ingemar Svensson. 1999. Social Security, Occupational Pensions, and Retirement in Sweden. In *Social Security and Retirement Around the World*, edited by Jonathan Gruber and David A. Wise, 355–402. Chicago: The University of Chicago Press.

Palmer, Geoffrey. 1987. *Unbridled Power: An Interpretation of New Zealand's Constitution and Government*, 2nd ed. Auckland, N.Z.: Endeavour Press.

Pampel, Fred, and John B. Williamson. 1988. Welfare Spending in Advanced Industrial Democracies, 1950–1980. *American Journal of Sociology* 93 (6): 1424–56.

Parry, Richard. 2000. Exploring the Sustainable Limits of Public Expenditure in the British Welfare State. In *The End of the Welfare State?: Responses to State Retrenchment*, edited by S. Svallfors and P. Taylor-Gooby, 88–105. London: Routledge.

Peacock, Alan T., Jack Wiseman, and Jindrich Veverka. 1967. *The Growth of Public Expenditure in the United Kingdom*, revised 2nd ed. London: Allen & Unwin.

Pechman, J. A. 1988. *World Tax Reform: A Progress Report*. Washington, D.C.: Brookings Institution.

Pempel, T. J., and K. Tsunekawa. 1979. Corporatism Without Labor. In *Trends Toward Corporatist Intermediation*, edited by P. C. Schmitter and G. Lehmbruch. Beverly Hills, Cal.: Sage Publications.

Peters, B. Guy. 1991. *The Politics of Taxation: A Comparative Perspective. Comparative Politics*. Cambridge, Mass.: Basil Blackwell.

Pierre-Brossolette, S. 1988. Impôts, Ce Qui Va Monter, Ce Qui Baisser. *Le Point* 27 (March): 55–9.

Pierson, Christopher. 1991. *Beyond the Welfare State?: The New Political Economy of Welfare*. Cambridge, U.K.: Polity Press.

Pierson, Paul. 1994. *Dismantling the Welfare State?: Reagan, Thatcher, and the Politics of Retrenchment*. Cambridge: Cambridge University Press.

———. 1996. The New Politics of the Welfare-State. *World Politics* 48 (2): 143–79.

———. 1998. The Deficit and the Politics of Domestic Reform. In *The Social Divide: Political Parties and the Future of Activist Government*, edited by M. Weir. Washington, D.C.: Brookings Institution.

———. 2000. Increasing Returns, Path Dependence, and the Study of Politics. *American Political Science Review* 94 (2): 251–67.

Bibliography

———, ed. 2001. *The New Politics of the Welfare State*. New York: Oxford University Press.

Pollack, Sheldon D. 1996. *The Failure of U.S. Tax Policy: Revenue and Politics*. University Park: The Pennsylvania State University Press.

Pontusson, Jonas. 1992. *The Limits of Social Democracy: Investment Politics in Sweden*. Ithaca, N.Y.: Cornell University Press.

Prest, A. R. 1980. *Value Added Taxation: The Experience of the United Kingdom. AEI Studies; 298*. Washington, D.C.: American Enterprise Institute for Public Policy Research.

Przeworski, Adam. 1985. *Capitalism and Social Democracy*. New York: Cambridge University Press.

Radcliffe, James, and Malcolm McVicar. 1997. From Welfare State to Welfare Management: Changes in the United Kingdom Social Security System. In *Transformations in Social Security Systems*, edited by International Institute of Administrative Sciences Working Group on Social Security System. Amsterdam: IOS Press.

Ragin, C. C. 1987. *The Comparative Method: Moving Beyond Qualitative and Quantitative Strategies*. Berkeley: University of California Press.

———. 1994. Introduction to Qualitative Comparative Analysis. In *The Comparative Political Economy of the Welfare State*, edited by T. J. A. M. Hicks. Cambridge: Cambridge Unviersity Press.

Rehn, Gösta. 1952. The Problem of Stability: An Analysis and Some Policy Proposals. In *Wages Policy Under Full Employment*, written by Erik Lundberg, Rudolf Meidner, Gösta Rehn, and Krister Wickman, edited and translated by Ralph Turvey. London: William Hodge and Company.

Rentoul, John. 1999. Tony Blair 1994–. In *Leading Labour: From Keir Hardie to Tony Blair*, edited by Kevin Jefferys, 208–28. London: I. B. Tauris.

Robinson, Ann, and C. T. Sandford. 1983. *Tax Policy-making in the United Kingdom: A Study of Rationality, Ideology and Politics*. London: Heinemann Educational Books.

Rodrik, Dani. 1996. Why Do More Open Countries Have Bigger Governments? NBER Working Paper # 5537, April.

———. 1997. *Has Globalization Gone Too Far?* Washington, D.C.: Institute for International Economics.

Roper, Brian. 1997. The Changing Class Structure. In *Political Economy of New Zealand*, edited by B. Roper and C. Rudd. Auckland, N.Z.: Oxford University Press.

Rose, Richard, and Terrance Karran. 1986. *Taxation by Political Inertia*. London: Macmillan.

Rose-Ackerman, Susan. 1999. *Corruption and Government: Causes, Consequences, and Reform*. Cambridge: Cambridge University Press.

Rosenberry, Sara A. 1982. Social Insurance, Distributive Criteria and the Welfare Backlash: A Comparative Analysis. *British Journal of Political Science* 12 (4): 421–47.

Rothstein, Bo. 1998. *Just Institutions Matter*. New York: Cambridge University Press.

Rudd, Chris. 1990. Politics and Markets: The Role of the State in the New Zealand Economy. In *The Fourth Labour Government: Politics and Public Policy in New Zealand*, edited by M. Holland and J. Boston. Auckland, N.Z.; New York: Oxford University Press.

———. 1997a. The Welfare State. In *New Zealand Politics in Transition*, edited by Raymond Miller, 245–67. Auckland, N.Z.: Oxford University Press.

———. 1997b. The Welfare State. In *The Political Economy of New Zealand*, edited by Chris Rudd and Brian Roper, 237–255. Auckland, N.Z.: Oxford University Press.

Ruggie, John G. 1983. International Regimes, Transactions and Change: Embedded Liberalism in the Postwar Economic Order. In *International Regimes*, edited by D. K. Stephen. Ithaca, N.Y.: Cornell University Press.

Salsbäck, Johan. 1993. The Tax Reform Process in Sweden. In *Tax Reform in the Nordic Countries: 1973–1993 Jubilee Publication*, edited by N. S. Forskningsradet. Uppsala: Instus Forlag AB.

Sandford, Cedric Thomas. 1988. Tax-Reform in the United-Kingdom and Ireland. *Environment and Planning C – Government and Policy* 6 (1): 53–70.

———. 1993a. *Successful Tax Reform: Lessons from an Analysis of Tax Reform in Six Countries*. Bath, U.K.: Fiscal Publications.

———. ed. 1993b. *Key Issues in Tax Reform*. Bath, U.K.: Fiscal Publications.

Särlvik, Bo. 1967. Party Politics and Electoral Opinion Formation: A Study in Issues in Swedish Politics 1956–1960. *Scandinavian Political Studies* 2: 167–202.

Scarbrough, Elinor. 2000. West European Welfare States: The Old Politics of Retrenchment. *European Journal of Political Research* 38: 225–59.

Scharpf, Fritz Wilhelm. 2000. Welfare and Work in the Open Economy: Constraints, Challenges and Vulnerabilities. Paper presented at the 2000 Annual Meeting of the American Political Science Association, Washington, D.C. August 31–September 3, 2000.

Scheu, Frederick Joseph. 1943. *British Labor and the Beveridge Plan*. New York: Island Press.

Schneider, Saundra K. 1982. The Sequential Development of Social Programs in Eighteen Welfare States. *Comparative Social Research* 5: 195–200.

Schwartz, Harman. 1998. Social Democracy Going Down or Down Under: Institutions, Internationalized Capital, and Indebted States. *Comparative Politics* 30 (3): 253–72.

Scott, Claudia D. 1987. The 1985 Tax Reform Package. In *The Fourth Labour Government: Radical Politics in New Zealand*, edited by J. Boston and M. Holland. Auckland, N.Z./New York: Oxford University Press.

Scott, Claudia, and Howard Davis. 1985. *The Gist of GST: A Briefing on the Goods and Services Tax*. Wellington, Australia: Victoria University Press for Institute of Policy Studies.

Sen, Amartya. 1995. The Political Economy of Targeting. In *Public Spending and the Poor: Theory and Evidence*, edited by D. van de Walle and K. Nead. Baltimore: Johns Hopkins University Press.

Bibliography

Sharp, Andrew. 1994. *Leap into the Dark: The Changing Role of the State in New Zealand Since 1984*. Auckland, N.Z.: Auckland University Press.

Shaughnessy, Scott. 1994. The Cotisation Sociale Généralisée: An Idea Whose Time Had Come. *Modern and Contemporary France* 2 (4): 405–19.

Shinkawa, Toshimitsu. 1993. *Nihongata Fukusi no Seijikeizaigaku*. Tokyo: San'ichi Shobo.

Shome, Parthasarathi. 1995. *Tax Policy Handbook*. Washington, D.C.: Tax Policy Division, Fiscal Affairs Department, International Monetary Fund.

Shonfield, Andrew. 1965. *Modern Capitalism: The Changing Balance Between Public and Private Power*. Oxford: Oxford University Press.

Shoup, Carl S. 1990. Choosing Among Types of VATs. In *Value Added Taxation in Developing Countries, A World Bank symposium*. edited by Malcolm Gillis, Carl S. Shoup, and Gerardo P. Sicat. Washington, D.C.: World Bank.

Silverstone, Brian, Alan Bollard, and Ralph Latimore. 1996. Introduction. In *A Study of Economic Reform*, edited by B. Silverstone, A. Bollard, and R. Latimore. Amsterdam: Elsevier.

Skocpol, Theda. 1991. Targeting Within Universalism: Political Viable Policies to Combat Poverty in the United States. In *The Urban Underclass*, edited by J. Christopher and P. Paul. Washington, D.C.: Brookings Institution.

———. 1992. *Protecting Soldiers and Mothers: The Political Origins of Social Policy in the United States*. Cambridge, Mass.: Belknap Press of Harvard University Press.

Slemrod, Joel, and Jon Bakija. 1996. *Taxing Ourselves: A Citizen's Guide to the Great Debate over Tax Reform*. Cambridge, Mass.: MIT Press.

Smith, Daniel. 1998. *Tax Crusaders and the Politics of Direct Democracy*. New York: Routledge.

Smith, Stephen. 1997. The Definitive Regime for VAT: An Assessment of the European Commission's Proposals. In *Commentary*. London: Institute for Fiscal Studies.

Sørensen, Peter Birch. 1994. From the Global Income Tax to the Dual Income Tax: Recent Tax Reforms in the Nordic Countries. *International Tax and Public Finance* 1 (1): 57–79.

Stanley, Robert. 1993. *Dimensions of Law in the Service of Order: Origins of the Federal Income Tax, 1861–1913*. New York: Oxford University Press.

Steinmo, Sven. 1988. Social Democracy vs. Socialism: Goal Adaptation in Social Democratic Sweden. *Politics and Society* 16: 403–45.

———. 1993. *Taxation and Democracy*. New Haven, Conn.: Yale University Press.

———. 1997a. The New Political Economy of Taxation: International Pressures and Domestic Policy Choices. Filed with the author.

———. 1997b. Why Tax Reform? Understanding Tax Reform in its Political and Economic Context. Filed with the author.

Steinmo, Sven, and Duane Swank. 1999. The New Political Economy of Taxation. Paper read at the Annual Meeting of the American Political Science Association, Atlanta, September 1–5, 1999.

Steinmo, Sven, and Caroline J. Tolbert. 1998. Do Institutions Really Matter? – Taxation in Industrialized Democracies. *Comparative Political Studies* 31 (2): 165–87.

Steinmo, Sven, and Jon Watts. 1995. It's the Institutions, Stupid! Why Comprehensive National Health Insurance Always Fails in America. *Journal of Health Politics, Policy and Law* 20 (2): 329–72.

Stephens, John D. 1996. The Scandinavian Welfare States: Achievements, Crisis, and Prospects. In *Welfare States in Transition: National Adaptations in Global Economies*, edited by G. Esping-Andersen. London: Sage Publications.

Stephens, John D., Evelyne Huber, and Leonard Ray. 1999. The Welfare State in Hard Times. In *Continuity and Change in Contemporary Capitalism*, edited by H. Kitschelt, P. Lange, G. Marks and J. D. Stephens. New York: Cambridge University Press.

Stephens, Robert. 1993. Radical Tax Reform in New Zealand. *Fiscal Studies* 14 (3): 45–63.

———. 1997. The Interaction and Coordination of Taxation and Expenditure Programs. In *Tax Conversations: A Guide to the Key Issues in the Tax Reform Debate*, edited by R. Krever. London: Kluwer Law International.

Steuerle, G. Eugene. 1992. *The Tax Decade: How Taxes Came to Dominate the Public Agenda*. Washington, D.C.: Urban Institute Press.

Strahan, Randall. 1988. Agenda Change and Committee Politics in the Postreform House. *Legislative Studies Quarterly* 13 (2): 177–97.

Suarez, James M. 1999. The Federal Budget Process in the United States. In *Budget Deficits and Debt: A Global Perspective*, edited by S. Shojai. Westport, Conn.: Praeger.

Suleiman, Ezra N. 1974. *Politics, Power, and Bureaucracy in France: The Administrative Elite*. Princeton, N.J.: Princeton University Press.

Svallfors, Stefan. 1995. The End of Class Politics? Structural Cleavages and Attitudes to Swedish Welfare Policies. *Acta Sociologica* 38: 53–74.

———. 1997a. *Political Trust and Attitudes Towards Redistribution: A Comparison of Sweden and Norway*. Manuscript filed with the author.

———. 1997b. Worlds of Welfare and Attitudes to Redistribution: A Comparison of Eight Western Nations. *European Sociological Review* 13 (3): 283–304.

———. 1999. The Middle Class and Welfare State Retrenchment: Attitude to Swedish Welfare State Policies. In *The End of the Welfare State?: Responses to State Retrenchment*, edited by Stefan Svallfors and Peter Taylor-Gooby. London: Routledge.

Svallfors, Stefan, and Peter Taylor-Gooby. 1999. *The End of the Welfare State?: Responses to State Retrenchment*. London: Routledge.

Svensson, Torsten. 1994. *Socialdemocratins Dominans*. Stockholm: Almqvist & Wicksell International.

Swank, Duane. 2000. Social Democratic Welfare States in Global Economy: Scandinavia in Comparative Perspective. In *Globalization, Europeanization, and the End of Scandinavian Social Democracy?*, edited by Robert Geyer, Christine Ingebritsen, and Jonathon W. Moses, 85–138. London: Macmillan.

———. 2002. Global Capital, Political Institutions, and Policy Change in Developed Welfare States. New York: Cambridge University Press.

Tanzi, Vito. 1990. Quantitative Characteristics of the Tax Systems of Developing Countries. In *Taxation in Developing Countries*, edited by Richard M. Bird and Oliver Oldman. Baltimore: Johns Hopkins University Press.

———. 1991. *Public Finance in Developing Countries*. Aldershot; Brookfield, Vt.: E. Elgar Publishers.

———. 1992. Structural Factors and Tax Revenue in Developing Countries: A Decade of Evidence. In *Open Economies: Structural Adjustment and Agriculture*, edited by Ian Goldin and L. Alan Winters. New York: Cambridge University Press.

———. 1995. *Taxation in an Integrating World, Integrating National Economies*. Washington, D.C.: Brookings Institution.

———. 1996. *Globalization, Tax Competition and the Future of Tax Systems*. IMF Working Paper: WP/96/141.

Tanzi, Vito, and Ludger Schuknecht. 1995. The Growth of Government and the Reform of the State in Industrial Countries. In *IMF Working Paper*. Washington, D.C.: International Monetary Fund.

Teixeira, Alan, Claudia Scott, and Martin Devlin. 1986. *Inside GST: The Development of the Goods and Services Tax*. Wellington: Victoria University Press for Institute of Policy Studies.

Thain, Colin, and Maurice Wright. 1995. *The Treasury and Whitehall: The Planning and Control of Public Expenditure, 1976–1993*. Oxford: Oxford University Press.

Thelen, Kathleen. 1999. Historical Institutionalism in Comparative Politics. *Annual Review of Political Science* 2: 369–404.

———. 2003. How Institutions Evolve. In *Comparative Historical Analysis in the Social Sciences*, edited by James Mahoney and Dietrich Rueschemeyer, 208–40. New York: Cambridge University Press.

Thelen, Kathleen, and Sven Steinmo. 1992. Historical Institutionalism in Comparative Politics. In *Structuring Politics*, edited by Sven Steinmo, Kathleen Thelen, and Frank Longstreth, 1–32. New York: Cambridge University Press.

Therborn, Goran. 1989. "Pillarization" and "Popular Movements": Two Variants of Welfare State Capitalism: The Netherlands and Sweden. In *The Comparative History of Public Policy*, edited by F. G. Castles. New York: Oxford University Press.

Thirsk, Wayne R. 1991. *Lessons from Tax Reform: An Overview*. Policy, Research, and External Affairs Working Papers; WPS 576. Washington, D.C.: Country Economics Dept.

———, ed. 1997. *Tax Reform in Developing Countries*. Washington, D.C.: The World Bank.

Toder, Eric, and Susan Himes. 1992. Tax Reform in New Zealand. *Tax Notes International* (August 17, 1992).

Vaisanten, I. 1992. Conflict and Consensus in Social Policy Development: A Comparative-Study of Social Insurance in 18 OECD Countries 1930–1985. *European Journal of Political Research* 22 (3): 307–27.

van Kersbergen, Kees. 1995. *Social Capitalism: A Study of Christian Democracy and the Welfare State*. London: Routledge.

Virmani, A. 1988. Tax-Reform in Developing Countries: Issues, Policies, and Information Gaps. *Public Finance – Finances Publiques* 43 (1): 19–38.

Vowles, Jack Aimer Peter. 1993. *Voters' Vengeance: The 1990 Election in New Zealand and the Fate of the Fourth Labour Government*. Auckland, N.Z.: Auckland University Press.

Wadensjö, Eskil. 1997. The Welfare Mix in Pension Provisions in Sweden. In *Enterprise and the Welfare State*, edited by Martin Rein and Eskil Wadensjö. Northampton, U.K.: Edward Elgar.

Walker, Simon. 1989. *Rogernomics: Reshaping New Zealand's Economy*. Auckland, N.Z.: GP Books.

Weaver, R. Kent. 1986. "The Politics of Blame Avoidance." *Journal of Public Policy* 6 (4): 371–98.

Webber, Carolyn, and Aaron B. Wildavsky. 1986. *A History of Taxation and Expenditure in the Western World*. New York: Simon and Schuster.

Weidenbaum, Murray. 1996. The Nunn-Domenici USA Tax: Analysis and Comparison. In *Frontiers of Tax Reform*, edited by M. Boskin. Stanford, Cal.: Hoover Institution.

Wells, Graeme. 1996. Fiscal Policy. In *A Study of Economic Reform*, edited by B. Silverstone, A. Bollard, and R. Latimore. Amsterdam: Elsevier.

Whalley, John. 1990. Recent Tax Reform in Canada: Policy Responses to Global and Domestic Pressures. In *World Tax Reform: Case Studies of Developed and Developing Countries*, edited by M. J. Boskin and C. E. McLure. San Francisco: ICS Press.

White, Gordon, and Roger Goodman. 1998. Welfare Orientalism and the Search for and East Asian Welfare Model. In *The East Asian Welfare Model: Welfare Orientalism and the State*, edited by Roger Goodman, Gordon White and Huck-ju Kwon. London: Routledge.

White, Gordon, and Robert Wade, eds. 1985. *Developmental States in East Asia, Institute of Developmental Studies Research Report 16*. Brighton: Institute of Developmental Studies.

Whiteford, Peter. 1998. Is Australia Particularly Unequal? Traditional and New Views. In *Contesting the Australian Way: States, Markets and Civil Society*, edited by Paul Smyth and Bettina Cass. Cambridge: Cambridge Unviersity Press.

Wilensky, Harold L. 1976. *The New Corporatism, Centralization, and the Welfare State*. Sage Professional Papers in Contemporary Political Sociology Ser. No. 06-020. London; Beverly Hills, Cal.: Sage Publications.

Zelizer, Julian E. 1998. *Taxing America: Wilbur D. Mills, Congress and the State, 1945–1975*. New York: Cambridge University Press.

Index

Index

Index

Japan
  administrative reform, 173, 174
  aging of society, 178, 184
  budget deficits, 33, 172, 173, 182,
    183
  coalition government, 185
  commodity taxes, 170
  conservative dominance in, 183
  Conservative Party, 185
  consumption tax increase, 180–1
  corporate taxes, 174–5, 177
  deficit bonds, 172, 173, 174
  Democratic Party, 185
  Diet, 173
  expenditure cuts, 174
  fiscal reconstruction, 173–4
  funding capacity, 170
  Gold Plan, 184
  Government Managed Pension Program
    of Corporate Employees (GMPPCE),
    183, 184–5
  Government Managed Pension Program
    of Self-Employees (GMPPSE), 183,
    184
  Government Tax System Research
    Council, 176
  Harbinger, 181
  health insurance system, 181–2, 184
  House of Councilors, 176, 180
  House of Representatives, 176, 180
  income equality, 33, 182, 201–3
  income taxes, 158, 175, 176, 177–8, 179
  inhabitant tax, 179
  Keidanren, 175
  Komei Party, 185
  labor organization, 183
  Liberal Democratic Party, 33, 170, 171–2,
    173, 176, 180–1, 182, 183, 185
  lifelong employment in, 186
  market-centered approach, 183
  Ministry of Finance, 171–2, 173, 174,
    175–6, 177, 178, 186
  nursing care insurance, 184
  occupational pensions, 182
  oil shocks, and welfare state, 182
  pensions system, 181–2, 184–5
  price-exclusiveness of VAT, 71, 180
  private welfare service, 184
  public attitude to social security system,
    184
    public attitude to VAT, 170–1, 178,
      179–80, 181, 186
    public sector, 174
    recession in, 33, 181, 184
    Recruit Cosmos, 179–80
    revenue reliance on income tax, 170, 182
    revenue-reliance shift from income to
      consumption taxes, 181
    scandals in, 179–80, 184
    Shoup Mission, 172, 175
    simplification of income tax, 177–8
    as small tax/welfare state, 170
    Socialist Party, 173, 180, 181
    social security contributions, 184–5
    tax exemptions, 177, 178–9, 181
    tax experts in, 178
    tax inequities, 178
    tax level, 170, 181
    tax politics, 181
    tax rates, 33
    tax reforms, 175, 177, 178, 181
    tax revenue structure, 170, 181
    unemployment rate, 184
    VAT, and listed prices, 71
    VAT and income tax cut, 158
    VAT in, 32, 33, 117, 178–81, 189, 191,
      192, 196
    VAT proposals, 33, 171–3, 175–8
    visibility of VAT, 71
    welfare state in, 170, 181–6
job security, public support for government
  responsibility, 206
Jospin, Lionel, 103
Juppé, Alain, 97–8, 101, 102–3, 103, 108

Keating, Paul, 142, 143, 144

labor
  in Australia, 133–4, 148, 155
  in Europe, 109
  in France, 102, 106, 109
  globalization, and welfare protection for,
    39
  in Japan, 183
  in New Zealand, 134, 147
  strength of, 6
  in Sweden, 58, 63
labor mobility, and personal income taxes,
  36
la Martinière, Dominique de, 98

Index

Index

Index

Index

Continued from page iii